Praise for *Political Troglodytes and Economic Lunatics*

'This is the story of the last great shift in Australian politics, a tale of plutocrats and reactionaries who defied the times to drag Australia to the right.'
—DAVID MARR

'A lucid and compelling account of the men and advocacy groups that drove Australia to the right.'
—JUDY BRETT

'If you hope to understand the rightward drift of our recent politics, Dominic Kelly's calm and clear, fascinating and fair-minded account of the work of Australia's three hard right amigos – Hugh Morgan, John Stone and Ray Evans – is the place to start.'
—ROBERT MANNE

'This is a controversial subject about polarising figures, but Kelly's approach is fair and honest. An important contribution to the literature on modern conservatism and neoliberalism.'
—ANDREW HARTMAN, PROFESSOR OF HISTORY, ILLINOIS STATE UNIVERSITY

'*Political Troglodytes and Economic Lunatics* contributes to a deeper understanding of the Right in Australia, which has been relatively neglected.'
—DAVID McKNIGHT, AUTHOR OF *Populism Now* AND *Beyond Right and Left*

Political Troglodytes and Economic Lunatics

The Hard Right in Australia

Dominic Kelly

LA TROBE
UNIVERSITY PRESS

IN CONJUNCTION WITH BLACK INC.

Published by La Trobe University Press in conjunction with Black Inc.
Level 1, 221 Drummond Street
Carlton VIC 3053, Australia
enquiries@blackincbooks.com
www.blackincbooks.com
www.latrobeuniversitypress.com.au

La Trobe University plays an integral role in Australia's public intellectual life, and is
recognised globally for its research excellence and commitment to ideas and debate.
La Trobe University Press publishes books of high intellectual quality, aimed at general
readers. Titles range across the humanities and sciences, and are written by distinguished
and innovative scholars. La Trobe University Press books are produced in conjunction
with Black Inc., an independent Australian publishing house. The members of the LTUP
Editorial Board are Vice-Chancellor's Fellows Emeritus Professor Robert Manne and
Dr Elizabeth Finkel, and Morry Schwartz and Chris Feik of Black Inc.

9781760641092 (paperback)
9781743820766 (ebook)

A catalogue record for this
book is available from the
National Library of Australia

Cover design by Jen Clark
Text design and typesetting by Akiko Chan
Printed in Australia by McPherson's Printing Group.

For Sarah

CONTENTS

ABBREVIATIONS

ABC	Australian Broadcasting Corporation
ACF	Australian Conservation Foundation
ACM	Australians for Constitutional Monarchy
ACTU	Australian Council of Trade Unions
AEF	Australian Environment Foundation
AIGN	Australian Industry Greenhouse Network
AIPP	Australian Institute for Public Policy
ALP	Australian Labor Party
AMIC	Australian Mining Industry Council
ATA	Australian Taxpayers' Alliance
ATR	Americans for Tax Reform
ATSIC	Aboriginal and Torres Strait Islander Commission
BCA	Business Council of Australia
CAI	Confederation of Australian Industry
CEI	Competitive Enterprise Institute
CIA	Central Intelligence Agency
CIS	Centre for Independent Studies
CNI	Council for the National Interest
CPRS	Carbon Pollution Reduction Scheme
CSIRO	Commonwealth Scientific and Industrial Research Organisation
DLP	Democratic Labor Party
ETS	Emissions Trading Scheme
IPA	Institute of Public Affairs
IPCC	Intergovernmental Panel on Climate Change
MUA	Maritime Union of Australia
NFF	National Farmers' Federation

NRA   National Rifle Association of America
SEC   State Electricity Commission of Victoria
UAP   United Australia Party
UNESCO   United Nations Educational, Scientific and Cultural
            Organization
UNFCCC   United Nations Framework Convention on Climate
            Change
UWA   University of Western Australia
WMC   Western Mining Corporation
WWF   Waterside Workers' Federation

INTRODUCTION

5 December 2016. The Australian Minister for Environment and Energy, Josh Frydenberg, suggests that the government will consider implementing an emissions intensity scheme – effectively a carbon price for power companies – as a way to reduce carbon pollution. The next day, after a furious response from the conservative wing of the Liberal Party, Frydenberg backs down. Prime Minister Malcolm Turnbull denies that the scheme was ever under consideration.

27 October 2017. The Turnbull government announces its rejection of the Uluru Statement from the Heart, which called for the establishment of a First Nations "Voice to Parliament," enshrined in the Constitution. The prime minister says that such a proposal is inconsistent with Australian notions of equal civil rights, and infuriates Indigenous people by misleadingly referring to a potential "third chamber of parliament."

1 January 2018. Turnbull, who was chairman of the Australian Republican Movement in the 1990s, is asked about the prospects of Australia becoming a republic in the near future. The once passionate republican is notably cautious, warning that "the Australian people have shown themselves to be very conservative when it comes to constitutional change. There is no point pretending that there is an appetite for change when there isn't one at the moment."[1] But he nevertheless floats the idea of a plebiscite or postal survey to begin the process, should Queen Elizabeth die during his prime ministership. Faced with an insurgency from the Liberal Party right, Turnbull is forced to walk back his remarks within twenty-four hours.

25 January 2018. The Fair Work Commission, applying the legislation set out in the *Fair Work Act 2009*, orders New South Wales rail workers

1

to abandon their indefinite overtime ban and planned twenty-four-hour strike on the grounds that both actions "threaten to endanger the welfare of part of the population" and "cause significant damage to the economy of Sydney."[2] In other words, an institution created by the Rudd Labor government uses Labor-backed legislation to effectively rule what many view to be legitimate industrial action unlawful. In response, the Australian Council of Trade Unions secretary, Sally McManus, declares that "the basic right to strike in Australia is very nearly dead."[3]

24 August 2018. Having spent the majority of his prime-ministership appeasing the hard right of the Liberal–National Coalition, Malcolm Turnbull is torn down by his own party. Conservatives hope to install Minister for Home Affairs Peter Dutton as prime minister, but they are thwarted by the marginally more moderate treasurer, Scott Morrison.

27 August 2018. Morrison chooses Angus Taylor, a prominent climate change sceptic and anti-renewable energy campaigner, as his energy minister. Morrison says Taylor will be "the minister for getting energy prices down," while resources minister Matt Canavan calls for "a new era of energy and resources abundance."[4] Morrison's chief of staff is John Kunkel, who was the deputy CEO of the Minerals Council of Australia for six years and a senior political lobbyist for mining giant Rio Tinto for two.

On the same day Morrison horrifies Indigenous leaders by appointing Tony Abbott as "special envoy for Indigenous affairs," seemingly a consolation prize for being left out of the ministry. "Many of us don't have any confidence in Tony Abbott's return to save us," says Jackie Huggins, co-chair of the National Congress of Australia's First Peoples. "We reflect on his history of supporting harmful and paternalistic policies relating to our people. One of his accomplishments has been to rob our people of a right to self-determination."[5]

*

As these fragments from contemporary Australian politics all illustrate in different ways, Australians live in an age in which hardline conservative views on a range of issues set the terms of public policy, sometimes in direct opposition to the desires of the public at large. Why is this so? The answers to this question are many and multifaceted, but this book illuminates one of them: the powerfully influential role of a small group of committed political activists and the remarkably effective organisations they created.

From New Right to hard right

Beginning in the mid-1980s, a new organisational form was born in Australian politics: the single-issue advocacy group of the right. The H.R. Nicholls Society (which was formed in 1986 and concerned with industrial relations), the Samuel Griffith Society (1992, constitutional issues), the Bennelong Society (2000, Indigenous affairs) and the Lavoisier Group (2000, climate change) were each established by Western Mining Corporation executives Hugh Morgan and Ray Evans, with the assistance of various other figures associated with the political right. These four organisations did much more than argue for specific policy reforms – they set out to change the way Australians thought.

These organisations emerged out of the "New Right," a movement that emphasised the doctrines of economic liberalism and social conservatism. The abundance of terms used to describe the New Right can seem confusing and even contradictory, but whether it was "liberalism," "libertarianism," "dry economics," "radical conservatism," "economic rationalism" or "neoliberalism," at its core the movement was about free market economics. As Andrew Norton has chronicled, "the New Right" was the most commonly used term for the movement in Australia in the 1980s. Then gradually, as the New Right no longer seemed new, "economic rationalism" took over as the preferred term in the 1990s. That term also died out, and in the 2000s "neoliberalism" became, and remains, the dominant term.[6]

Taken together, the four advocacy groups formed by Hugh Morgan and Ray Evans are about much more than free market economics. They specialise in four significant domestic policy areas, providing both micro and macro insights into the politics of the past three decades. The H.R.

Nicholls Society engages in the ever-present battles between capital and labour, and the broader economic debates in which industrial relations is a central component. The Samuel Griffith Society concerns itself with legal and constitutional issues, raising questions about the status and nature of Australian political institutions. The Bennelong Society focuses on cultural and racial issues, and the legacy of what some refer to as Australia's original sin: the dispossession of Indigenous peoples. The Lavoisier Group engages in environmental politics and disputes the view of the majority of scientists that climate change is a serious and alarming threat to humanity. The preoccupations of this quartet of advocacy groups can tell us much about the nature of the Australian right, as well as Australian political culture more broadly.

The political and ideological positions of the groups can be defined as "hard right." They exist somewhere on the spectrum between the mainstream right of the Liberal and National parties, and the far or extreme right, in recent times most successfully represented by Pauline Hanson's One Nation party, but also encompassing a number of racist and anti-immigration groups and political parties that have blossomed in the online age. In putting a respectable face on some deeply reactionary positions, the single-issue advocacy groups have managed to drag the Coalition further from the mainstream and into the realm of the hard right.

The groups have often been treated in conspiratorial terms. Their shared post-office boxes and overlapping memberships gave rise to rumours that they formed a secret cabal, pulling the strings of government and industry from smoky boardrooms.[7] This exaggerated characterisation is partly an effect of the lack of sustained examination of the groups. In this book I reject that characterisation. Right-wing activists in fact made no secret of their vision for Australia: most of their political advocacy was done brazenly, out in the open. Their vast archives of conference papers, government submissions and articles are freely available on their respective websites for anyone to peruse.

Outsized influence

Two commentators from opposite ends of the political spectrum suggest that these groups and their allies have played an enormous role in shaping the Australia we live in today. Here is Mark Davis, a left-leaning scholar at the University of Melbourne, in his 2008 book *The Land of Plenty*:

> Whatever we are now, the New Right made us. Without F.A. Hayek or Milton Friedman or Hugh Morgan or John Stone or Bert Kelly or Keith Joseph or George Wallace or P.P. McGuinness, or Ray Evans and the activists of the H.R. Nicholls Society and the Crossroads Group, or the IPA or the CIS, or the writers of *Quadrant*, Australia wouldn't be what it is today.[8]

And here is conservative elder statesman Peter Coleman, former Liberal MP and editor of *Quadrant*, and father-in-law of Peter Costello, writing in *The Weekend Australian* in 2009:

> There would probably have been no privatisation, deregulation or tax reform if it had been left to politicians. It was the think tanks ranging from the Centre for Independent Studies and the Institute of Public Affairs to the Institute for Private Enterprise and the Sydney Institute, or pressure groups such as the H.R. Nicholls Society, magazines such as *Quadrant* and publishers such as Connor Court that laid the foundation for the reforms in industrial relations, financial regulation, taxation and indigenous policy. What would have been the state of the debate on global warming and the ETS without the think tanks and a few independent journalists?[9]

Are they correct? Largely, yes. Despite their limited size and public profile, the four groups examined in this book have been remarkably successful in achieving their goals. The H.R. Nicholls Society set out to radically transform the culture of industrial relations in Australia, especially its trade union-friendly system of conciliation and arbitration. Though they have faced setbacks and disappointments along the way, its members believe that the pendulum has swung back towards employers in a significant way since the 1980s. The Samuel Griffith Society has less to be pleased about, given that its founding purpose was to promote federalism, and the centralisation of power in Canberra has continued apace since 1992. It can, however, point to the failed republic referendum in 1999 as a major victory.

The Bennelong Society can also point to substantial achievements. It rejected the doctrine of Aboriginal self-determination, which had become dominant since the 1970s, and argued for a return to the assimilation policies of the mid-twentieth-century, usually re-branded as "integration". The Society could not have asked for a more receptive prime minister in John Howard, and many of his policies were closely aligned with their views. Likewise, the Lavoisier Group found willing allies in the corridors of political power. The group set out to prevent – or, failing that, delay – any significant action on climate change, and it has been alarmingly successful in this mission.

It was Prime Minister Bob Hawke who in 1986 described the H.R. Nicholls Society as "political troglodytes and economic lunatics." Despite their alleged lunacy, this book shows how these groups have been able to influence the direction of government policies, playing a forceful role in a general shift to the right since the 1980s. In detailing their histories in this book, I want to make the important distinction that these four groups differed from other institutions of the Australian right in that they zealously dedicated themselves to a single policy area, rather than spread their limited resources across several issues. By chronicling their intriguing tactics and machinations, *Political Troglodytes and Economic Lunatics* makes a claim for the powerfully determinative role of single-issue advocacy groups of the right in Australian politics. I explore the similarities and differences between these four groups themselves, and I argue that, although they all draw on elements of the Australian conservative tradition, their ideological position can more accurately be described as a form of reactionary conservatism.

The players

As part of the research for this book I sought interviews with some of the key protagonists of these groups, as well as other figures whose connection to them was less direct. Some were willing to speak to me, while others were reticent. The two key players I was most eager to interview were Ray Evans and Hugh Morgan. Evans was sceptical upon receiving my initial request, but after explaining my interest in the groups as an organisational form and their influence on Australian politics, he was happy to talk to me. Unfortunately, I had no such success with Hugh Morgan.

After a genial and revealing conversation with Evans at his home in Melbourne's west, in which we discussed all four advocacy groups at length, I enquired about my prospects of doing the same with Morgan. Evans predicted that Morgan would be very reluctant to talk to me due to his having been bitten badly in the past. Evans agreed to speak to Morgan and explain that our interview had been fine, but this seemingly did nothing to persuade him to talk to me. Attempts to contact him through other avenues proved fruitless.

John Stone, prominent in the early years of H.R. Nicholls and by far the most important figure in the Samuel Griffith Society, was similarly reluctant to meet face to face. However, he agreed to answer questions via email, and his vivid memories of his political activities in the groups proved especially valuable. Further detail about the Samuel Griffith Society was provided in a phone interview with founding member Greg Craven, now vice-chancellor of Australian Catholic University. I also interviewed Stone's long-time friend and colleague Des Moore in his South Yarra home. Moore is a veteran right-wing activist who runs his own think tank, the Institute for Private Enterprise, and has been involved in all four single-issue advocacy groups.

The most important figure in the Bennelong Society was former Liberal minister Peter Howson, who died in February 2009. Former Labor politician Gary Johns became central to the organisation in its later years, and he agreed to meet me for an interview at his waterfront home in Brisbane. Johns also put me in contact with two other Bennelong Society associates in Brisbane: former Liberal Indigenous affairs minister John Herron and conservative Indigenous activist Wesley Aird. All three were forthcoming about their roles in the Bennelong Society and their perception of its political impact.

I also sought interviews with prominent conservatives who were not closely connected with the four groups, but whose experience and knowledge of the world of right-wing institutions is extensive. Unfortunately, John Roskam of the Institute of Public Affairs (IPA), Greg Lindsay of the Centre for Independent Studies (CIS) and Gerard Henderson of the Sydney Institute all declined to speak to me. However, Andrew Norton, presently at the Grattan Institute but formerly with the CIS, did agree to an interview. Though a past member of the H.R. Nicholls Society who also attended Samuel Griffith Society conferences, Norton was able to offer a more detached and critical view of the groups.

1

IDEAS AND INSTITUTIONS OF THE AUSTRALIAN RIGHT

FOR A LONG TIME IN AUSTRALIA, as political historian Judith Brett writes, "to be called a conservative has more often been an accusation than a self-description."[1] Australians who would have been natural supporters of the Conservative Party if they were British were reluctant to adopt the term. Robert Menzies explicitly rejected the label "conservative" when he led the formation of the Liberal Party in 1944–1945. "We took the name 'Liberal' because we were determined to be a progressive party," he explained in his memoirs, "willing to make experiments, in no sense reactionary but believing in the individual, his rights, and his enterprise, and rejecting the Socialist panacea."[2]

Although conservatives are generally resistant to unnecessary change, they tend not to oppose change at all costs. This is important, and it is a convention traceable to the birth of conservatism as a concrete political idea, which stretches back to the eighteenth-century Irish political philosopher Edmund Burke. A member of the British parliament from 1765 to 1794, Burke was a resolute defender of social, political and religious institutions that developed organically, for they, he asserted, contain inherent forms of wisdom that remain beneficial for current and future generations. On this basis, conservatives are hostile to any political project that aims to overthrow established institutions in the pursuit of abstract ideals, whatever their supposed good intentions. However, even Burke explicitly acknowledged that "a state without the means of some change is without the means of its conservation."[3] Philosophers and political theorists have been debating and refining his ideas ever since, yet Burke's core principles remain at the heart of modern conservatism.

The contemporary Australian right is made up of a variety of institutions that have coalesced around a few core ideas and values. This chapter will outline the most important ideas and institutions that paved the way for the rise of the New Right and, more specifically, the single-issue advocacy groups that are the subject of the book. First we need to look abroad, because although Australia is geographically isolated from the western world, its political traditions have always drawn inspiration from its great and powerful friends the United States and the United Kingdom.

Post-war conservative movements in the United States and United Kingdom

The post-war period in American politics saw the rise of a new conservative movement, whose ideas would gradually come to dominate the Republican Party and spread throughout the western world. An important milestone for this new conservatism was the 1953 publication of Russell Kirk's *The Conservative Mind*, a comprehensive history of Anglo-American conservatism that identified six canons of conservative thought: belief in divine intent; affection for traditional life; acceptance of society's natural orders and classes; conviction that private property and freedom are inseparable; belief that humans are governed more by emotion than reason; and wariness of enforced change and innovation.[4] In identifying and espousing the concept of a unified American conservative tradition that had evolved since Edmund Burke's seminal *Reflections on the Revolution in France* (1790), Kirk's book "dramatically catalyzed the emergence of the conservative intellectual movement."[5]

One of those inspired was the young Yale graduate William F. Buckley Jr, who founded the magazine *National Review* in 1955 and would go on to become America's preeminent conservative intellectual. *National Review* and other anti-communist, "neo-conservative" publications such as *Commentary* magazine, under the editorship of Norman Podhoretz, and

Irving Kristol and Daniel Bell's journal *The Public Interest,* became essential reading for American conservatives in the following decades.[6] American neo-conservatism grew out of a small group of predominantly Jewish New York intellectuals who had abandoned the leftist radicalism of their youth. Instead they became virulently anti-communist, and relentlessly critical of the failings of American liberalism. This phenomenon was largely a backlash against the liberal-dominated post-war era, which culminated in the mass social movements of the 1960s. Neo-conservatives feared that increasing permissiveness was leading to social fragmentation and breakdown. In a famous line, Kristol described a neo-conservative as "a liberal who has been mugged by reality."[7]

In 1964 hardline conservative Barry Goldwater won the Republican presidential nomination against the party's establishment candidate, Nelson Rockefeller. Though he went on to lose the election to Democrat Lyndon Johnson in a landslide, Goldwater's nomination signalled the arrival of movement conservatism in mainstream politics, an arrival that was confirmed by Ronald Reagan's election as governor of California two years later.

In addition to the publications mentioned above, the new conservative movement institutionalised itself through the establishment of a new kind of think tank. These organisations, prominent examples of which include the American Enterprise Institute for Public Policy Research (founded in 1943), the Heritage Foundation (1973) and the Cato Institute (1977), were to become materially and ideologically central to the cause of movement conservatism. Abandoning the non-partisan principles of the first wave of think tanks, which had emerged in the early twentieth century, this new form was "more engaged in selling predetermined ideology to politicians and the public than undertaking scholarly research."[8] Also new was the concerted effort to engage with the wider public. While the more established think tanks were concentrating their efforts on maintaining relationships with the political elite in Washington, the new guard, while of course continuing to cultivate contacts in Washington, attempted to communicate directly with ordinary people via newspapers, radio and television.

The guiding economic ideology of many of these conservative think tanks was what came to be known as neoliberalism. Neoliberalism has been defined by David Harvey as "a theory of political-economic practices that proposes that human well-being can best be advanced by liberating individual entrepreneurial freedoms and skills within an institutional framework characterized by strong private property rights, free markets, and free trade."[9] The so-called "Austrian School" economists such as Friedrich Hayek and Ludwig von Mises had been developing these ideas for some decades. In 1947 they founded the Mont Pelerin Society, a key institution in the history of neoliberalism, which Hayek envisioned as "something halfway between a scholarly association and a political society."[10] The Society formalised their position as the most prominent intellectual critics of the economic theories of John Maynard Keynes, which promoted full employment and stable currencies by regulating demand, and dominated western economic policy from the 1940s to the 1970s. In the United States, the leading intellectual proponent of neoliberalism was the University of Chicago economist Milton Friedman.

A significant neoliberal landmark was the Heritage Foundation's twenty-volume, 3000-page *Mandate for Leadership: Policy Management in a Conservative Administration*. Produced for the incoming Reagan administration in 1980, this unprecedented publication was the work of more than 300 people across twenty project teams.[11] President-elect Reagan was appreciative, and fourteen Heritage Foundation staff were appointed to his transition team. An eleven hundred–page abridged version of *Mandate for Leadership* was published for the general trade in 1981, and the book made *The Washington Post* bestseller list.[12] A second edition, *Mandate for Leadership II: Continuing the Conservative Revolution*, was produced upon Reagan's re-election in 1984, and the series continues to this day, albeit in a less comprehensive form.

Heritage Foundation president Edwin Feulner visited Australia in 1985 and gave a lecture in which he explained the importance of think tanks in the Anglosphere:

> Ideas like Supply Side economics, privatisation, enterprise zones, and the flat tax are produced by individuals first – the academic scribblers, as Keynes would call them. Milton Friedman and Stuart Butler in the United States and Madsen Pirie in the United Kingdom, for example, explain, and expand the ideas. They are the first-hand dealers in ideas. But, it takes an institution to

help popularise and propagandise an idea – to market an idea. Think tanks are the second-hand dealers of ideas. Organisations like the Institute of Economic Affairs or the Adam Smith Institute in London, my own Heritage Foundation in the United States and the Centre of Policy Studies and the Centre for Independent Studies here in Australia host conferences, lectures and seminars and publish policy reports, books and monographs to popularise an idea. Through "outreach" programmes an institution can promote an idea on a continuing basis and cause change. But this takes time.[13]

Here Feulner provided the clearest expression of the vital role of think tanks in propagating ideas. No matter how persuasive their ideas, individuals can only do so much. For the nascent Australian single-issue advocacy groups, this amounted to a fundamental principle.

As Feulner indicated in his Australian speech, neoliberalism was also having a huge impact in the United Kingdom. The most important think tanks in the British movement were the Institute of Economic Affairs (founded in 1955); the Centre for Policy Studies (1974), which Margaret Thatcher helped to found while an Opposition frontbencher; and the Adam Smith Institute (1977).

The founder of the Institute of Economic Affairs, Sir Antony Fisher, was an especially important figure in the worldwide neoliberal movement. Fisher was a successful farmer who, after reading Hayek's *The Road to Serfdom* (1944), a canonical text in the early history of neoliberalism, sought the author's advice about how he could help influence the political process. Hayek told him that becoming a politician was a waste of time, and that he would be better off "forming a scholarly research organisation to supply intellectuals in universities, schools, journalism and broadcasting with authoritative studies of the economic theory of markets and its application to practical affairs."[14] Fisher went on to help found a number of think tanks in the United Kingdom, the United States and Canada, as well as, in 1981, the Atlas Economic Research Foundation. The Atlas Network (as it is now called) was designed as a way of institutionalising the process of helping to create and support free market organisations. Its most recent institute directory lists 494 partners in ninety-four countries.[15]

Although the United States and the United Kingdom are the countries that Australia tends to emulate the most, the intellectual and institutional transformations described above were of course not confined to the Anglosphere. As Harvey argues, "there has everywhere been an emphatic turn towards neoliberalism in political-economic practices and thinking since the 1970s."[16] American and British think tanks played a pivotal role in neoliberalism's eventual triumph as the dominant economic orthodoxy of the late twentieth century, and this had much to do with the strategic distribution of ideas via the think-tank model. The Adam Smith Institute's Madsen Pirie once said of his organisation: "We propose things which people regard as being on the edge of lunacy. The next thing you know, they're on the edge of policy."[17] Richard Cockett, whose work *Thinking the Unthinkable: Think-Tanks and the Economic Counter-Revolution* charts the British neoliberal movement from its 1930s origins through until its eventual triumph with Margaret Thatcher's 1979 election victory and her subsequent dominance of British politics in the 1980s, largely supports this assertion, arguing that free market think tanks "did as much intellectually to convert a generation of 'opinion-formers' and politicians to a new set of ideas as the Fabians had done with a former generation at the turn of the century."[18]

Liberalism, conservatism and the Liberal Party of Australia

In Australia, the complicated mix of liberal and conservative political philosophies on the non-Labor side of politics stretches back to the merging of the Protectionist and Free Trade parties to create the Fusion Party in 1909. Various alliances were attempted in the decades that followed before non-Labor once again fell apart during World War II.

In 1939 Robert Menzies had become prime minister as leader of the United Australia Party (UAP), but over the course of the next two years he struggled to contain increasing dissension within the UAP–Country Party coalition, leading to his resignation in August 1941. Country Party leader Arthur Fadden formed a new coalition government, but it lasted less than six weeks. Two independent MPs switched their support to Labor, and

John Curtin was installed as prime minister in October. After Labor crushed the UAP–Country Party coalition at the next federal election in 1943, the Liberal Party was formed. In 1949 the new party won government in coalition with the Country Party, and has survived as the strongest national conservative party ever since.

Although Menzies disagreed with Labor on the desirable balance between private enterprise and government intervention in the economy, he accepted the fundamental assumptions of what political journalist Paul Kelly has labelled the post-Federation "Australian Settlement." In Kelly's analysis, the core policies that underpinned the Australian Settlement were: white Australia, industry protection through tariffs, a pervasive system of industrial conciliation and arbitration, state paternalism, and a foreign policy dependent on imperial benevolence.[19] On the question of the state, Menzies "explicitly rejected *laissez-faire* notions of the state's role in favour of a commitment to full employment and an expanded provision of welfare."[20] He embraced the post-war Keynesian economic consensus, including the expansion of the welfare state, having accepted that "Liberal ideology had to be reworked to accommodate the greater expectations of the role of government which were taking shape during the war."[21] From 1949 to 1966 Menzies presided over a period of unprecedented prosperity, and Australian voters rewarded the Liberal–Country Party coalition with nine successive election victories.

By the end of the 1970s, however, the long post-war boom had ended and new ideas were being proposed about how to manage economies like Australia's. Amid the turmoil of Gough Whitlam's Labor government (1972–1975), and as his Liberal successor Malcolm Fraser proved a disappointment to his own colleagues, the political and economic ideas of what became known as the New Right began to take hold more potently among members of the Liberal Party. With the encouragement of his adviser David Kemp, Fraser himself was initially enthusiastic towards these new ideas and their proponents. He even hosted Friedrich Hayek, Milton Friedman and Norman Podhoretz at the Lodge. But, according to Kemp, the former Liberal leader "consistently opposed what he saw as ideological tendencies in liberalism, believing that policy was always a matter of balancing values in the light of the best appreciation of all the circumstances."[22] An internal review of the party and its beliefs following Fraser's defeat in 1983 demonstrated an official embrace of the New Right's critique of the Fraser government: "it had failed because it lacked the courage to implement economic libertarianism."[23]

John Howard, who first entered parliament in 1974, was a central figure in the transformation of the Liberal Party in this period. Howard was both an economic liberal and a social conservative, and saw no contradiction in this hybrid political philosophy, maintaining that the Liberal Party "has always been the custodian of both the conservative and classical liberal traditions in the Australian polity."[24] As Robert Manne has written, Howard became prime minister in the aftermath of "two peaceful social revolutions" that reshaped Australian life from the 1970s onwards. The first was cultural, and it involved the abandonment of chauvinistic and racist policies in favour of ethnic diversity. The second was economic, and it involved the embrace of free markets in response to the end of the long post-war boom. "Taken together," writes Manne, "these revolutions threatened to wash away a great deal of what many Australians had, unselfconsciously, come to regard as an almost natural and even permanent way of life."[25]

As prime minister for over a decade, from 1996 to 2007, Howard's approach came to make political sense, as his support for traditional social values provided reassurance to people suffering from the disruptions of neoliberal economic policies. He sympathised with those who were unsettled by cultural and economic change, but he was an enthusiastic supporter of neoliberal economics; he chose therefore to emphasise his social conservatism in his appeals to voters. Critics saw this fusion of economic liberalism and social conservatism as inherently contradictory, but it was indisputably successful for Howard and has come to define modern Australian conservatism. Of course, Howard did not act alone; the transformation of non-Labor politics in Australia was helped along by other organisations and individuals. Of particular note were the Institute of Public Affairs, *Quadrant* magazine and the Centre for Independent Studies, which played key roles in developing a new conservative political consensus that would come to dominate the Australian political landscape.

The Institute of Public Affairs

The Institute of Public Affairs is Australia's oldest conservative think tank. Founded in Melbourne by a group of prominent businessmen in the wake of the UAP–Country Party coalition's 1943 election defeat, it was concerned that Australia was heading down a path towards centralised planning and socialism once World War II was won. The IPA's early emphasis was on free trade, promoting private enterprise and minimising industrial disputes. It accepted the basic Keynesian consensus on the federal government's necessary role in economic planning, but was suspicious of Labor's socialist sympathies, whether real or perceived. James Walter has argued that the founders were all "concerned to mobilize opinion through the IPA to counter the threat to business autonomy that ALP reconstruction plans were seen to represent."[26] So although the IPA was not yet a vehicle for free market ideology, it was concerned that the ALP favoured increasing government control and centralisation, a concern shown to have some foundation when Prime Minister Ben Chifley attempted to nationalise the banks in 1947.

The IPA's current description of itself reflects both its historical and contemporary aims and preoccupations:

> The IPA is an independent, non-profit public policy think tank, dedicated to preserving and strengthening the foundations of economic and political freedom. Since 1943, the IPA has been at the forefront of the political and policy debate, defining the contemporary political landscape. The IPA is funded by individual memberships and subscriptions, as well as philanthropic and corporate donors. The IPA supports the free market of ideas, the free flow of capital, a limited and efficient government, evidence-based public policy, the rule of law, and representative democracy. Throughout human history, these ideas have proven themselves to be the most dynamic, liberating and exciting. Our researchers apply these ideas to the public policy questions which matter today. The IPA's specific research areas include climate change, red tape reduction, economics, criminal justice, legal rights, freedom of speech, innovation and entrepreneurship, workplace relations and energy and resources.[27]

Though neoliberal economic principles remain at the core of the IPA's identity, a wider array of political and cultural battles have come to the forefront in recent decades.

The first council of the IPA included representatives from Coles, BHP and National Australia Bank, as well as Keith Murdoch, then the recently appointed chairman of the Herald and Weekly Times. Despite these associations with prominent businessmen and politicians, the IPA has always adamantly maintained that its research is independent and subject to no outside influence. Inaugural chairman George Coles defined its mission at the first annual meeting in 1944, stating that "the IPA did not wish to be directly involved in politics, but it wanted to help create a modern political faith, which would be constructive and progressive and which would receive a large measure of public support."[28]

The founder and main driving force of the IPA was Charles Kemp, who was its director from 1943 to 1976. According to Paul Kelly, Kemp was "a major influence at the inception of the Liberal Party and probably the principal intellectual architect of the original Menzies platform."[29] Menzies himself described the IPA's 1944 policy statement *Looking Forward* as "the finest statement of basic political and economic problems made in Australia for many years."[30]

After the initial enthusiasm of the early decades, the IPA entered a period of decline in the 1960s, coinciding with Menzies' retirement and the eventual election of a Labor government in 1972. The end of the post-war boom and the subsequent political and economic crises of the 1970s demanded fresh policy thinking, and many on the right were disenchanted with conservative politics as usual. They rejected the Keynesian consensus and found new answers in the laissez-faire ideas of Friedrich Hayek and Milton Friedman, economists who were gaining in academic respectability after being awarded Nobel Prizes in 1974 and 1976 respectively. Friedman came to Australia on a lecture tour in 1975, a visit described by the IPA as "like a breath of fresh air."[31] Hayek followed in 1976, and was invited by the IPA to address its annual meeting. The IPA's report of his address could not have been more gushing: "No one among the 200 people who attended the IPA Annual Meeting on October 20th will readily forget the standing ovation which greeted Professor Hayek at the conclusion of his Address. This was the spontaneous response of an audience, the members of which sensed themselves to be in the presence of a truly great mind."[32] Intellectual currents on the right were changing. A new generation of radical neoliberals was inspired by these visits, and Charles Kemp's retirement in 1976 provided an opportunity for the IPA to take a new direction. This was the beginning of a renaissance for the organisation, and a period of burgeoning political and ideological influence, especially on the increasingly hardline conservative wing of the Liberal Party.

In 1978 the brash young mining executive Hugh Morgan was appointed to the IPA Council. Morgan, as we shall see, was to become a crucial figure in this political and intellectual movement. From the outset of his appointment, he was heavily invested in the encouragement of corporate donations as well as providing funding out of his own pocket; for Morgan, this was the beginning of a long career of organisational and financial support for right-wing institutions that continues to this day. In 1979 Roger Neave, a moderate successor to Kemp, was pushed out of his position, and the takeover was completed three years later when Kemp's son, Rod – significantly more radical than his father – was appointed director. According to political scientist Damien Cahill, the IPA quickly transformed "from being a broad supporter of the postwar consensus to a critic of that model and an advocate of the radical liberalisation of the Australian economy."[33]

An important way in which the IPA was rejuvenated was through its quarterly publication, the *IPA Review*. Charles Kemp had edited the magazine in a rather staid fashion from 1947 until his retirement, and though his son David described the *IPA Review* as "the single most influential private source of liberal economic analysis over the years, both within the Liberal Party and beyond,"[34] by the 1980s the publication was ripe for an overhaul. In a 1982 message to readers Rod Kemp outlined his plan to build circulation by providing "articles which are succinct enough to meet the needs of the busy reader and which are comprehensible to the non-specialist."[35] The magazine became a glossy, full-colour publication designed to catch the eye of casual readers. More importantly, the writing became more strident and polemical, in a transparent attempt to ruffle the feathers of the political establishment.

Throughout the 1980s members of the IPA became increasingly disillusioned with the timidity of the Liberal Party. One journalist described the IPA as having "thrown up its hands in disgust at the inability of the Liberals to cope with ideas."[36] With a few notable exceptions among what were known as the "dries" (such as Bert Kelly, John Hyde, Jim Carlton and John Howard), Liberals were unwilling to argue publicly for neoliberal ideas. Hence, the IPA and other New Right organisations became critics of the party, while the ALP, under Bob Hawke and Paul Keating, went about opening up the Australian economy, something that the Liberals had failed to do while in power from 1975 to 1983.

During this period of Labor dominance, the *IPA Review* became something of a clearing house for the airing of New Right ideas in the public arena. In fact, one can track the ideas of all four of the single-issue advocacy groups examined in this book developing in the pages of the *Review* both during the lead-up to and following their establishment. The period from 1985 to 1987, for example, saw John Stone and others focusing on the industrial relations situation and the problems with trade unions; they also began publicising the work of the H.R. Nicholls Society. From the mid-1980s through until 1993 there were numerous articles on threats to the Constitution and Australia's British institutions, the proposed republic and the Mabo debate, all of which became the central preoccupations of the Samuel Griffith Society. More than a decade before the Bennelong Society was established, the *IPA Review* began publishing Hugh Morgan, Ron Brunton and others on the Indigenous "guilt industry", the Aboriginal and Torres Strait Islander Commission (ATSIC) and reconciliation. The publication was also an early proponent of climate denialism in Australia, with the *IPA Review*'s first article questioning the science of climate change appearing in 1989.

Having left his position as chief of staff to Liberal leader John Howard in 1986, Gerard Henderson took over the moribund NSW branch of the IPA the following year. Before long he was clashing with other members of the IPA over their support for Queensland Premier Joh Bjelke-Petersen's campaign to enter federal politics, which he saw as quixotic and damaging to the wider conservative cause. Henderson left the IPA in 1989 and founded his own organisation, the Sydney Institute. Less of a think tank than a current affairs forum, the Sydney Institute hosts weekly events in which guests are invited to speak on a chosen subject. The speeches are then published in its quarterly journal, *The Sydney Papers*. "People say it is like a conversation," Henderson told the *Sydney Morning Herald* in 2003.[37] Because it refrains from overt political advocacy, the Sydney Institute is better described as a "talk tank" – a forum for ideas to be shared and discussed rather than an institutional vehicle for swaying politicians to a particular point of view.

When Rod Kemp resigned as director of the IPA in 1989 after winning Liberal preselection for the Senate, Des Moore was appointed acting director. An important figure within the New Right, Moore has been involved in just about every organisation that could be associated with the term. In 1958, while studying at the London School of Economics, he introduced himself to John Stone, who was serving as a Treasury representative in Australia House. Stone recommended Moore for a job in Treasury, where he remained for the next twenty-eight years. He became a deputy secretary in 1981, but in 1984 he lost a close ally when Stone resigned as secretary. Disenchanted with the economic policy direction of the Labor government and looking for new ways to get his ideas into the public arena, in 1986 Moore spent four months in Washington DC working for two prominent conservative think tanks: the American Enterprise Institute and the Heritage Foundation. Upon his return to Australia in 1987, Moore resigned from the Treasury and took up a position with the IPA.[38] He remained there until 1996, when disagreement with the recently appointed director Mike Nahan led to his resignation.[39] Moore then established his own think tank, the Institute for Private Enterprise, which he operates from his home to this day. He has been involved in all four single-issue advocacy groups that are the focus of the following chapters.

In March 1991 the IPA amalgamated with the Perth-based Australian Institute for Public Policy (AIPP), and John Hyde became its executive director. A former Liberal MP, Hyde had founded the AIPP after he lost his Western Australian seat at the 1983 federal election. In Canberra, he was described as "the driest of all dries."[40] Another organisation that benefited from the largesse of Hugh Morgan, the AIPP's most significant contribution to public debate was *Mandate to Govern: A Handbook for the Next Australian Government*, published in the lead-up to the 1987 federal election. Inspired by the Heritage Foundation's *Mandate for Leadership*, the publication contained contributions from key New Right figures, including Ray Evans, John Stone, David and Rod Kemp, Greg Lindsay and

Michael Porter. Though it was claimed that *Mandate to Govern* was "not directed at either major party but at an unknown Government,"[41] its authors could hardly have been surprised when the re-elected Labor government paid it little attention.

Undeterred, the IPA followed the same formula at the state level. In 1990, with Victoria in recession and the state Labor government edging towards defeat, it partnered with the Tasman Institute and thirteen business organisations to form Project Victoria. The group aimed to rescue the Victorian economy by drastically reducing public spending, and in 1991 published *Victoria: An Agenda for Change* by Des Moore and Michael Porter, which it hoped would set the policy direction of the next Coalition government in Victoria. In the state's premier, Jeff Kennett, and its treasurer, Alan Stockdale, they found a most receptive audience. Financial journalist Alan Kohler later described Porter and Moore as "the unsung Marx and Engels of the Victorian revolution (with Kennett and Stockdale playing Lenin and Trotsky)," and *An Agenda For Change* as "the most successful right-wing policy manifesto ever seen in Australia."[42] When another scandal-plagued state Labor government was ousted in Western Australia in 1993 by Richard Court's Liberals, the IPA published another such manifesto, *Reform and Recovery: An Agenda for the New Western Australian Government*. One of its authors was Mike Nahan, who was director of the IPA from 1995 to 2005, before entering the WA parliament in 2008. Nahan was the state's treasurer from 2014 to 2017, and became Opposition leader after the Liberal Party's election defeat in March 2017.

The IPA has often been criticised for not revealing its sources of funding. In 2003, in the wake of the organisation winning a Howard government contract to research the political activities of non-government organisations such as charities, aid and welfare groups, Nahan promised funding disclosures in the following year's annual report. But when John Roskam took over as executive director in 2005 he reneged on the promise, blaming the immature Australian electorate. "It's not for us to reveal our supporters," he said. "Whether we like it or not, the Australian democracy is not so sophisticated that companies can reveal they support free market think tanks, because as soon as they do they will be attacked."[43] The issue was raised again in 2011 when the Gillard government introduced plain packaging of all cigarettes sold in Australia. The IPA had been a notable opponent of the plan, but was – and remains – unwilling to declare whether it receives financial backing from tobacco companies.

The IPA under Roskam's leadership has been characterised by a shift away from traditional conservatism towards more libertarian approaches to issues such as illicit drugs, gambling and same-sex marriage, and an absolutist position on freedom of speech. In a 1991 study, Ian Marsh concluded that organisations such as the IPA are "deliberately elite focused,"[44] unlike populist issues-based movements and mass parties. However, this is no longer true of the IPA under Roskam, with staff in recent years becoming increasingly visible to the general public, making regular appearances on ABC current affairs programs on television and radio, as well as writing regular columns in major daily newspapers and websites. The IPA's 2016 annual report boasted of 1378 mentions of its research in print and online media, and more than 600 staff appearances on television and radio.[45] Its increasingly youthful staff have also used social media very effectively to reach new audiences. This is not the work of an organisation that wants to fly under the radar of public debate.

"There's always been this kind of strange relationship to it," said Nahan of the relationship between the IPA and the Liberal Party in 1996.[46] The association between the party and the think tank has been close, if informal. A number of important figures in conservative politics have been prominent in both organisations, including the Kemp brothers, Hyde and Nahan. John Roskam has had multiple failed attempts at winning Liberal preselection, while younger IPA staff James Paterson and Tim Wilson entered parliament as Liberals in 2016. However, when members of the IPA believe that the Liberal Party is betraying free market, liberal principles, they have no reticence in saying so. For this reason it would not be fair to describe the contemporary IPA as a party think tank, a description which was more accurate in its early years.

Quadrant magazine

Like the IPA, *Quadrant* magazine is an "old guard" conservative institution that has been transformed in recent decades by the rise of the New Right and the end of the Cold War. Founded in 1956, *Quadrant* was an initiative of the Australian Committee for Cultural Freedom (later renamed the Australian Association for Cultural Freedom), which was the Australian arm of the Congress for Cultural Freedom, an international anti-communist advocacy group founded in 1950. *Quadrant*'s main original goal was to counteract the intellectual appeal of communism. It has maintained a small but devoted following, with its circulation never rising above five to six thousand copies.

Quadrant made its opposition to the left explicit from the beginning. Inaugural editor James McAuley wrote in his first editorial that the magazine would "try to be liberal and progressive, without falling into the delusion that to be liberal and progressive means to rehearse with childish obstinacy the rituals of a sentimental and neurotic leftism."[47] A more recent self-description (written in 2008) emphasises *Quadrant*'s editorial stance as being staunchly opposed to the left:

> While fashionable thought in much of the Australian media, universities and the arts remains influenced by left-wing moral authoritarianism, *Quadrant* has persistently questioned this orthodoxy. For the past decade, it has been at the forefront of the so-called culture wars. It has:
> - exposed the shoddiness and political bias of much academic historical and anthropological writing
> - deplored the politicisation of the arts
> - analysed the decay of our public universities from political correctness and managerialism
> - debated the place of religion in our society, especially the importance of the Judeo-Christian heritage of Western civilization
> - turned a sceptical eye on a range of intellectual fads and fashions including postmodernism, cultural relativism, multiculturalism and radical environmentalism.[48]

In particular the magazine was seen as a counter to the left-leaning *Meanjin*, which *Quadrant* founder Richard Krygier believed was pro-communist.[49] During the Cold War *Quadrant* was home to the writings of some of the most prominent Australian intellectuals, many of them émigrés from the communist regimes of Eastern Europe. Although it has always been seen as a conservative publication, David Kemp has argued that during the 1950s and 1960s it was "more interested in the conflict between Communism, Catholicism and liberalism in the Labor Party than with the domestic policy issues concerning the dominant coalition parties."[50]

In 1966 a *New York Times* investigation confirmed long-held suspicions that the Congress for Cultural Freedom had been secretly funded by the Central Intelligence Agency (CIA) since its inception. As more details gradually came to light over the course of the next year, the revelations caused considerable controversy. The left was universally damning in its criticism, but the reaction among *Quadrant* writers was mixed. Notorious anti-communist Frank Knopfelmacher saw no problem with it and wanted to publicly congratulate the CIA, while journalist and public intellectual Donald Horne was embarrassed and wanted to distance the magazine from the controversy.[51] Whatever one's view of the appropriateness of the funding, it appears that few, if any, *Quadrant* staff knew about it, and even if they had, it would hardly have altered the editorial direction of the magazine.

With the emergence of the New Right in the 1970s and 1980s, *Quadrant* was beginning to be seen by some as too focused on the Cold War and as out of step with the new intellectual fashion of neoliberal economics. A 1984 *Bulletin* article, for example, described the *Quadrant* set as not fitting in with a "younger and more libertarian network."[52] But *Quadrant* did start opening its pages to neoliberal arguments at this time, becoming a frequent forum for the voices of key members of the think tanks discussed in this chapter. Probably the most famous piece was Gerard Henderson's 'The Industrial Relations Club' in 1983, which denounced most of the participants in Australia's industrial relations system, and became an important opening salvo for the impending battle in that arena.

After a period of upheaval in the late 1980s, Robert Manne became editor of *Quadrant* on the day that the Berlin Wall came down, in November 1989. This was the beginning of what might be called a battle for *Quadrant*'s soul. As neoliberal economics continued to take hold on the right, Manne encouraged an economic debate within *Quadrant*'s pages. On one side were conservative protectionists such as Manne himself, his La Trobe University colleague and sociologist John Carroll, and IPA founder Charles Kemp; on the other were radical proponents of free trade, such as Hugh Morgan, Ray Evans and John Stone. Things came to a head in June 1992 when ongoing tensions between Manne and his opponents led the editor to offer his resignation. "If I had been a passionate supporter of economic rationalism, there would have been no problem," he explained.[53] Evans claimed that the final straw was Manne's decision to co-edit with Carroll a book on the failure of neoliberal economics called *Shutdown*. "I've never denied that this is an important debate and that *Quadrant* should be involved," Evans said. "My problem was always that the editor of *Quadrant* should not become identified with the protectionists. *Shutdown* was part of a pattern of behaviour with which I had a great many difficulties."[54] But Manne's resignation was never formally accepted, and he was soon back at the editor's desk with the support of the chair of the editorial board, Dame Leonie Kramer. The failure to oust Manne saw Evans resign from the board. "By all measurements, Manne is of the Left," he lamented to *The Bulletin*.[55]

Manne also stirred up controversy in *Quadrant* with his approach to Indigenous issues. Beginning with the publication in 1993 of his friend Raimond Gaita's two-part essay on the Mabo judgement, Manne challenged his fellow conservatives to grapple with the dispossession of Australia's original inhabitants, and the continued disadvantage and prejudice they faced. By 1997, with the publication of the *Bringing Them Home* report on Aboriginal child removal, the question of genocide was being openly debated in the magazine. This alarmed many in the *Quadrant* circle, who saw it as little more than left-wing political correctness, and eventually relations became so strained that Manne resigned as editor in November 1997, this time for good. "Because of my attitude to the dispossession I am certain that the old guard were relieved when I resigned," he later recalled.[56] Manne's replacement was P.P. "Paddy" McGuinness, a gruff, black-clad former anarchist who wrote for and edited the *Australian Financial Review* throughout the 1970s and '80s, and later wrote acerbic right-wing columns for *The Australian*, *The Sydney Morning Herald* and

The Age. Upon taking the *Quadrant* job McGuinness promised to "throw off the mawkish sentimentality which has become prevalent on a number of policy issues, most importantly on Aboriginal issues."[57]

Looking back on fifty years of *Quadrant* in 2006, Martin Krygier – son of the magazine's founder Richard Krygier – was struck by the eclecticism, the distinction, the cosmopolitanism, and the moral-political commitments of its contributors and their writings. He saw *Quadrant* as essential to the project of exposing what was in the 1950s and '60s a very parochial country to a wider world of ideas. But Krygier was also disheartened by the trajectory of the magazine since the elevation of McGuinness to the editorship in 1998. He bemoaned *Quadrant*'s petty obsessions with those it despises, chiefly journalists (especially from the ABC and the Canberra press gallery), university humanities departments and lawyers (especially those with a focus on human rights). Krygier's characterisation of an editorial on the pernicious role of lawyers could easily sum up his view of much of the magazine under McGuinness's editorship: "a mix of obvious ignorance and purported omniscience, pummelling simplifications and omnipresent derision."[58]

Naturally, Krygier's perspective was not universally shared. Speaking as a special guest at the magazine's fiftieth anniversary dinner in 2006, John Howard claimed that "*Quadrant* has been Australia's home to all that is worth preserving in the Western cultural tradition."[59] Conservative journalist Greg Sheridan has been more equivocal, as both critic and admirer. Disgusted with a "fatuous and data-free piece" by Wolfgang Kasper arguing for restricting immigration from the Islamic world, in December 2001 Sheridan lamented that *Quadrant* was "now a sad parody of the great journal of ideas it once was";[60] but by 2008 he was again full of praise for "the most cosmopolitan and sophisticated small magazine in Australian history."[61] When McGuinness stood down as editor in 2007, regular contributor Frank Devine claimed that "McGuinness's decade, with Les Murray as literary editor, is considered by many to be *Quadrant*'s most brilliant period."[62]

McGuinness's replacement as editor, the historian Keith Windschuttle, was equally uncompromising in confronting the left, especially with regard to Indigenous affairs. Like McGuinness, Windschuttle had been a leftist in his youth, but had turned sharply to the right in the 1990s as a critic of postmodernism in university arts faculties. "In the '70s I was a

Marxist, in the '80s I was a social democrat and in the '90s I'm a conservative: it's called growing up," he explained.[63] But it was Windschuttle's
accusations that Australian historians had fabricated accounts of violence
against Indigenous people that put him at the forefront of a divisive
national debate. For him, such historical work was transparently political
and part of the left's challenge to the legitimacy of the Australian state:
"The issue has been a big one because it has been the issue of the moral
foundation of the colony of Australia [sic]. Are we a legitimate society or
not? The people who argue that we need to do something about the
Aboriginals argue that this won't be a legitimate society until we have reconciliation. I don't believe that."[64] Under Windschuttle, *Quadrant*'s focus
on what would become known in Australia as the "history wars" continued, while the magazine also turned to another major battleground in the
culture wars: that over climate change.

An old guard, anti-communist magazine, *Quadrant*'s founding *raison
d'être* disappeared in 1989. Unlike its British, French and German equiva-
lents (*Encounter, Preuves* and *Der Monat* respectively), *Quadrant* continued
to publish despite the end of the Cold War and the collapse of the Soviet
Union. While there was a considerable battle for control of the magazine
in the 1990s, its direction as a deeply partisan publication focused on the
ongoing culture wars and with enemies on the left, now appears to be consolidated. As we will see in the following chapters, *Quadrant* was a pivotal
outlet for the activists of the H.R. Nicholls Society, Samuel Griffith Society,
Bennelong Society and Lavoisier Group to promote their ideas to a broader
conservative audience.

The Centre for Independent Studies

The Centre for Independent Studies was founded in 1976 in the back-
yard shed of twenty-six-year-old high-school mathematics teacher Greg
Lindsay, who remained its executive director until 2018. It has often been
referred to as Australia's leading think tank, though its fortunes have
waxed and waned over its four decades. In its own words, the CIS "seeks

to create a better Australian society through ideas, research and advocacy that support individual liberty and responsibility, free enterprise, the rule of law and limited, democratic government."[65] Elaborating on these key principles, Lindsay has argued that "the CIS receives support simply because enough Australians agree with us that a prosperous economy must be market-based within a sensible regulatory environment; that individual liberty is a critical component of a forward-looking open society; that a strong and stable society needs strong and stable families and a wide range of autonomous voluntary institutions; that civil society is the nursery of moral integrity; and that good government recognises and respects such things."[66]

Before deciding that his future lay in the world of think tanks, Lindsay was active in advertising guru John Singleton's libertarian Workers' Party. In April 1976 he wrote to Lauchlan Chipman, professor of philosophy at the University of Wollongong, outlining his plans for a new think tank and seeking his advice. Chipman agreed to become the chairman of the fledgling organisation's research committee, and delivered a lecture at the first CIS seminar in October 1976. It wasn't until April 1978 that the CIS first came to public attention, following a conference it held on government economic intervention at Macquarie University. Paddy McGuinness wrote a column about the conference in the *Australian Financial Review* titled 'Where Friedman is a pinko,' and provided the organisation's address and telephone number.[67] Lindsay was inundated with messages of support.[68]

In 1979 Hugh Morgan managed to convince nine companies to each pledge $25,000 to the CIS cause ($5000 per year over five years).[69] Thereafter the CIS rose quickly to claim a prominent place within Australian economic debates. Lindsay successfully sought the patronage of Friedrich Hayek, the globally renowned intellectual father of neoliberalism, and was accepted as a member of the exclusive Mont Pelerin Society in 1982. Lindsay hosted the Mont Pelerin Society's Pacific Regional Meeting in Sydney in 1985, and in what was undoubtedly a career highlight, was elected to a two-year term as the Society's president in 2006. A 2004 *Bulletin* article somewhat hyperbolically referred to Lindsay as "perhaps the most influential man in Australia."[70] In 2010 the CIS was the only Australian organisation to make James McGann's list of the top fifty worldwide think tanks.[71] Its director was nothing if not ambitious.

Since 1985 the CIS has published the quarterly magazine *Policy*. Though not as closely associated with the four single-issue advocacy groups as the *IPA Review*, Hugh Morgan, Ray Evans, John Stone and Greg Craven have all been published in *Policy*. In the 1990s, as neoliberal economics came to dominate thinking on both sides of politics, the CIS branched out into social issues. "The war is over in other areas," said Ian Marsh. "They've done their job on privatisation, deregulation and competition policy and now they're moving to the other major fronts of public policy: social issues."[72] These new battlefronts included the environment, family and divorce, education, welfare and poverty. Unlike the IPA, which began to take a more libertarian approach to social issues around this time, the CIS remained socially conservative. It is a defender of traditional heterosexual marriage and has produced reports claiming to prove that sole-parent families are damaging to children. Despite this, Lindsay maintains that the CIS has "always been about the support of a free society, not just free markets."[73]

Unsurprisingly, the CIS's combination of economic liberalism and social conservatism found particular favour during the Howard years. As Wilson da Silva observed in 2002, "its arguments for restoring marriage and family traditions, for parental choice in schooling, private health care, baby bonuses, and for limiting multiculturalism; and against sole parent families and welfare dependency – all find echoes in Howard government policies."[74] The CIS became the pre-eminent right-wing think tank at this time, as the IPA slid from public view under Mike Nahan's leadership. This was reflected in the budgets of the two organisations: in 1990 the CIS had a budget of less than $1 million, compared with $1.5 million for the IPA. By 2006 the CIS's had increased to $2.5 million, while the IPA's had dropped to $1.1 million.[75] However, the IPA has since regained ground, due in large part to its younger, more media-savvy staff, and by 2012 the IPA's budget had rocketed up to $4 million, while the CIS's remained stagnant at $2.7 million.[76]

While more than willing to discuss ideas with politicians, Lindsay has always been insistent that the CIS remain politically independent. And, despite the organisation's natural affinity with the conservative side of politics, it has also cultivated relationships with Labor figures. Former NSW premier Bob Carr hailed the CIS as "a jewel in Sydney's crown."[77] Mark

Latham, who led the Labor Party to defeat at the 2004 federal election, was a regular attendee at CIS functions and a contributor to its publications before falling out with Lindsay in 2002.[78] Andrew Norton, who was employed at the CIS for much of the 1990s and 2000s, thought that "Labor might even be ahead in terms of the people who have spoken at CIS functions."[79] This willingness to engage with those who were ostensibly its ideological opponents allowed the CIS to broaden its influence. "No think tank is as quoted by so many, so often and in so wide a range of forums as the CIS," wrote da Silva. "None is so well funded, nor as capable of bringing together such a powerful coterie of men and women from both sides of politics."[80]

Like the IPA, the CIS has also often been criticised for its lack of financial transparency. Marcus Smith and Peter Marden had the CIS firmly in mind when they argued: "Despite claims to being champions of cherished liberal institutions and the free market of ideas, conservative think tanks continue to flout basic principles of accountability and transparency upon which the health of a vibrant democratic politics must inevitably rest."[81] Lindsay has responded to such criticisms by arguing that its funding is "a matter between the individuals or the organisations that give to us, and us, and it's a private thing, it's nobody else's business."[82] He also argues that because no single corporation or individual accounts for more than a small percentage of funding none would be able to influence the organisation even if it tried.

Arriving just as the New Right was emerging as a significant political movement in Australia, the CIS has always been unashamed in its outspokenness, and its advocacy of what it believes in – beliefs that have been steeped mainly in the ideas of Friedrich Hayek and other neoliberal economic thinkers. It reached the peak of its powers during the Howard years, as its values coincided neatly with those of the government. Since then, the CIS has struggled to maintain its influence, as its rather dry approach of hosting seminars and preparing policy papers was eclipsed by the IPA's media competence.

The Centre of Policy Studies/ Tasman Institute

The Centre of Policy Studies (not to be confused with the UK-based Centre for Policy Studies mentioned earlier) was established by Michael Porter at Monash University in 1979. Unlike the IPA and CIS, and somewhat ironically given its focus on free market economics, the Centre of Policy Studies was reliant on a combination of government funding and private grants. The Fraser government awarded it one of ten Research Centre of Excellence grants in 1982, which brought in $2.6 million over the next six years.[83]

The Centre's most prominent work was the National Priorities Project, a major study of potential government expenditure cuts, which was commissioned and funded to the tune of $500,000 by an alliance of business groups.[84] Combining scholarly research with policy advocacy, it was this sort of work that led many Labor figures to treat the organisation with suspicion. While there was very little the ALP could do about the private think tanks that routinely attacked them, the fact that the Centre of Policy Studies was attached to a university and was receiving significant government funding made it into a political target.

In October 1986, just as the New Right was at the centre of political controversy because of its involvement in a number of fiercely fought industrial battles, Ken Coghill, parliamentary secretary to the Cabinet in John Cain's Victorian Labor government, launched a series of freedom of information requests so that he could make a "scientifically based assessment" of the Centre's activities and documents.[85] Coghill believed that the National Priorities Project was a New Right conspiracy and was determined to put an end to it. However, the requests were viewed widely as an outrageous attack on academic freedom, and Porter threatened to resign or even face prison rather than hand over some of the requested information. Most egregiously for Porter, requests were made for records of correspondence with other organisations and individuals, including Hugh Morgan, John Stone, Greg Lindsay and John Hyde. "It is absolutely intolerable, an outrage," Porter fumed. "It is the most authoritarian, totalitarian act ever perpetrated on an academic institution in Australia."[86] The controversy drew the intervention of the premier, and Coghill was forced to withdraw his request.

The Centre of Policy Studies was defunded by the Hawke government in February 1987, much to the chagrin of its supporters, who claimed that the decision was blatantly political. As the Centre floundered without government support, Porter devoted himself to setting up a private university, to be called Tasman University. He was backed by a number of prominent businessmen, including Hugh Morgan.[87] Though Porter had hoped to open the university in 1990, in late 1989 he was still struggling to raise the capital, and turned to Monash University for help. Having failed to reach agreement with Monash about the terms of a partnership, and unable to fund itself independently, Porter was finally compelled to shelve the project in January 1990.[88]

Porter's response to this failure was to establish the Tasman Institute. His goal was "to go forward from being a 'think tank' to becoming a 'do tank'."[89] The Tasman Institute would not merely produce papers and publications but try to make neoliberal economic reform a reality. This attitude was embodied in Project Victoria, the Tasman Institute's joint undertaking with the IPA in 1991, discussed earlier in this chapter, which drove the economic policy agenda of the Kennett government. Alan Stockdale, Victorian Treasurer from 1992 to 1999, later wrote that he "had considerable contact with the Tasman Institute while the Coalition was in opposition," and that it had helped to develop his ideas about the privatisation of state assets.[90] But it wasn't long before tensions emerged between Porter and his Project Victoria collaborator, the IPA's Des Moore. When Moore called for twenty-five thousand Victorian public service jobs to be cut, Porter attempted to distance himself and the Tasman Institute from the controversial remarks. Porter was also displeased with Moore's statement that the Tasman Institute "do consultancies which are under instructions from clients to produce a certain result," insisting that his organisation retained editorial control. "It is disappointing that misunderstanding on the independence of think tanks should be propagated from a person within the IPA," he wrote, "with its excellent recent record for resisting privileged interests."[91]

The early 1990s saw the Tasman Institute branching out beyond economics, advancing right-wing positions on the environment and

Aboriginal land rights almost identical to those of the IPA. As the decade progressed, it was also drawn towards consultancy work, which became a major source of revenue. The Tasman Institute provided strategic advice on privatisation and deregulation to a variety of government, non-government and private organisations and corporations both in Australia and abroad. The think tank division disappeared altogether in 2002 when the Tasman Institute merged with ACIL Consulting to form ACIL Tasman, and it became solely devoted to consulting.[92] (ACIL Consulting was founded by rural economist David Trebeck, who advised the Howard government during the 1998 waterfront dispute, discussed in more depth in Chapter 3.)

Beginning as an academic think tank with a clearly defined policy agenda, the Centre of Policy Studies was an unusual organisation in the Australian institutional context. Its difficult relationship with government demonstrated the dangers of trying to advocate for certain policy positions while receiving public funding. Once Porter switched to the privately funded Tasman Institute, he became freer to pursue his policy goals. Tasman's greatest impact came when it combined with the IPA to provide a neoliberal blueprint for the Kennett government in Victoria, before eventually transforming into a lucrative consulting business.

Other New Right organisations

The 1980s also saw the formation of a number of smaller New Right organisations. There is considerable overlap between these organisations and those already discussed in this chapter, although each has its own unique characteristics. As Greg Sheridan observed in 1986, many New Right activists were more than willing to be active in multiple organisations; however, Sheridan was dismissive of the idea that this indicated some kind of conspiracy was afoot. "When activist organisations begin they like to have a few distinguished people to act as patrons or to serve on their boards in order to give the new organisation credibility, especially with potential financial contributors," he pointed out. "Very often the only involvement these persons have with the organisations in question is their willingness to allow their names to be used."[93] Sheridan's point is valid, and yet it is still important to be aware of the people associated with the political and intellectual milieu of the New Right, in order to better understand it as a whole. Briefly outlined below are six groups that might be seen as having minor roles in the broader picture, but remain relevant to the story this book tells.

Crossroads Group

The Crossroads Group was founded in response to the 1980 publication of *Australia at the Crossroads: Our Choices to the Year 2000*. John Hyde described the book, commissioned by oil giant Shell, as the "inspiration of the dry movement in federal parliament after the 1980 election" and a blueprint for the radical liberal ideas that came to dominate the right as the 1980s unfolded.[94] In December 1980 Hyde and Jim Carlton invited around forty like-minded conservatives to the inaugural Crossroads Conference, which was held in Sydney in February 1981. Attendees included Hugh Morgan, Bert Kelly, Greg Lindsay, David and Rod Kemp, Michael Porter, Gerard Henderson, Andrew Hay, David Trebeck and Maurice Newman. John Stone did not attend but joined the group later on. The Crossroads Group met twice yearly until its disbanding in 1986. As Paul Kelly observed, this group would become "the nucleus of the 'free market' counter-establishment of the 1980s" that took control of the Australian right over the course of the decade.[95]

Society of Modest Members

Hyde and Carlton were also instrumental in the formation of the Society of Modest Members, a parliamentary grouping that first met in 1981. The group's patron was Bert Kelly, the federal Liberal member for the rural South Australian seat of Wakefield from 1958 to 1977. Kelly was an adamant opponent of industry protection, especially in the form of tariffs on imports, an unpopular position across the political spectrum at the time. (According to historian W.K. Hancock in his 1930 classic *Australia*, "protection in Australia has been more than a policy: it has been a faith and dogma."[96]) Following his demotion from John Gorton's ministry in November 1969, Kelly began writing a weekly "Modest Member" column in the *Australian Financial Review* (later renamed the "Modest Farmer").

He would go on to write almost 900 of these columns between 1969 and 1987, including during periods at *The Bulletin* and *The Australian*.[97] Kelly's columns were considered essential reading for the political class, even for many on the opposite side of the chamber, and gradually other politicians came to agree with his position that tariffs were harmful to the Australian economy. Following Kelly's death, Gough Whitlam told a CIS function that "no private member has had as much influence in changing a major policy of the major parties."[98]

Though a dry economic outlook was undoubtedly the dominant theme of the Society of Modest Members, its initial membership accounted for a wide range of views, even including Malcolm Fraser and Andrew Peacock. But this ideological diversity did not last long, as members "became increasingly discontented with the slowness of movement towards liberalization" during Fraser's prime ministership.[99] In a hyperbolic rewriting of history, one member, former National Party MP Peter McGauran, claimed in 1986 that the group was the initiative of Coalition MPs "suffering under the yoke of the Fraser socialist government."[100] The Society gradually dissipated throughout the 1990s and 2000s, but was revived in 2011 by a new generation of Liberal MPs, with former Howard government ministers Peter Costello and Nick Minchin as its patrons.[101]

Australian Lecture Foundation

Established by Hugh Morgan in 1981, the sole purpose of the Australian Lecture Foundation was to bring prominent intellectuals to Australia on lecture tours. Under the stewardship of Ray Evans, the Foundation provided financial and logistical support for like-minded thinkers to travel to Australia to disseminate ideas and to network with eager audiences of Australian conservatives. Speakers included American neo-conservative and editor of *Commentary* Norman Podhoretz, British socialist turned conservative historian Paul Johnson, London-based Australian political theorist Kenneth Minogue and British philosopher Roger Scruton. Economic journalist Christopher Jay described the Foundation's work as "a remarkably inexpensive method of securing exposure for particular ideas, press coverage and entree to Government and the public service."[102]

Australian Adam Smith Club

The Australian Adam Smith Club was founded in Sydney in 1981, a fusion of the Libertarian Dinner Club and the newsletter *Optimism*, with Greg Lindsay as its inaugural chairman.[103] A Melbourne branch was founded by David Sharp in 1983. Aiming "to promote and explore the further understanding of the principles and works of Adam Smith and like-minded thinkers," the club welcomed new members who were on board with its hardline economic stance. Adam Smith club members "take an uncompromising stand in the support of":

- private property
- freedom of contract
- freedom from coercion by others
- freedom of trade and enterprise in the market, both domestically and internationally
- freedom of the individual within the framework of minimal government activity
- freedom of movement of capital and labour throughout the world.[104]

The Sydney branch of the Adam Smith Club folded in the mid-1980s, leaving the Melbourne branch to carry on the name. It remains in existence to this day, producing a rudimentary newsletter called *Laissez Faire* and holding quarterly dinners. Past speakers at these dinners have included Ray Evans, Bert Kelly, Geoffrey Blainey, B.A. Santamaria, Lauchlan Chipman, Bob Day, Keith Windschuttle and Gary Johns. In 1989 Hugh Morgan received the Adam Smith Club's award for outstanding services to liberty.

Centre 2000

Centre 2000 was founded in Sydney in 1983 and was closely linked with the Australian Adam Smith Club. While the Adam Smith Club remained little more than an intimate dinner club that hosted guest speakers, Centre 2000 was determined to spread the neoliberal message through literature and public campaigns. It sold books via mail order and published a bimonthly magazine called *The Optimist* from 1985 to 1989. A program called "Sponsor an Intellect" was established, which aimed to supply schools and universities with books on free market themes. The academic advisory council for this program included Leonie Kramer, Lauchlan Chipman, Wolfgang Kasper and David Kemp. One of Centre 2000's public campaigns was "Tax Freedom Day", an attempt in 1985 to stir a tax revolt by handing out 120,000 fake banknotes with a face value of just 55.5 cents, representing the value of each dollar earned by individuals after the government takes its share.[105]

Council for the National Interest

The Council for the National Interest (CNI) was founded by Catholic intellectual and political activist B.A. Santamaria in 1985. According to Gerard Henderson, it was a front organisation that was "part of [Santamaria]'s plan to construct a new political party."[106] The group was initially concerned with defence and foreign policy issues, but in the 1990s "broadened its focus to encompass the whole range of economic, social and political issues vital to the national interest."[107] CNI board members included John Stone, Lauchlan Chipman, Leonie Kramer, former Western Australian Liberal premier Charles Court and Western Mining chairman Sir Arvi Parbo. From 1989 it published the quarterly journal *Australia and World Affairs*, which became *National Observer* in 1999 before finally ceasing publication in 2012. It aimed to "provide high-quality commentary which is not affected by contemporary political correctness or prejudices."[108] Contributors included many members of the single-issue advocacy groups discussed in this book, such as Hugh Morgan, Ray Evans, Charles Copeman, Harry Gibbs, Peter Howson, Geoffrey Partington, Keith Windschuttle, William Kininmonth and David Flint.

*

The institutions discussed in this chapter were important pillars in what came to be known as the New Right. Inspired by their ideological counterparts overseas – especially in the United States and the United Kingdom – a new generation of Australian conservatives rejuvenated their side of politics and redefined what it meant to be a conservative. They rejected the moderate conservatism of Robert Menzies' Liberal Party in favour of a radical neoliberalism that placed its faith in markets as the main guarantor of freedom and prosperity above all else.

Damien Cahill has argued that the radical neoliberal movement acted as a hegemonic force in Australia from the 1970s to the 1990s, with think tanks playing a central role. "The radical neo-liberal movement is not reducible to its think tanks," he wrote. "Movement activists sometimes operate independently of the movement's mobilising structures. The importance of think tanks, however, is they provide the movement with its organisational backbone."[109]

David Kemp was a political scientist at Monash University from 1975 to 1990, advised Malcolm Fraser both as Opposition leader and as prime minister in 1975–76, and was director of the Prime Minister's Office in 1981. During the 1980s, he was an occasional contributor to the *IPA Review* (while his brother was its editor), before he went to Canberra as a Liberal MP in 1990. As both an observer and a participant, he is as well placed as anyone to comment on the transformation of conservative politics in the 1970s and 1980s. He put it like this in 1988:

> Over the decade to 1985 something akin to a broad, though not unified, liberal movement came into existence with political and intellectual leaders, publicists and pamphleteers, journalists and commentators, policy support in the public bureaucracy and in private 'think tanks', interest group mobilization and an apparently expanding base of mass support. Comparatively isolated intellectuals became linked in a nationwide network challenging traditional conservative centres of power in both industry and the labour movement, and creating significant problems of adjustment and accommodation for each of the major parties.[110]

The neoliberals reinvigorated the IPA, fought and eventually replaced the protectionists at *Quadrant*, and created new institutions such as the CIS, Centre of Policy Studies and AIPP, among others. In doing this they laid the groundwork for the transformation of the Liberal Party's economic approach, and to a lesser extent the Labor Party's as well. As their ideas came to dominate economic debates, they looked to areas of social policy that they considered ripe for reform.

2

THE TROIKA: HUGH MORGAN, RAY EVANS AND JOHN STONE

T HREE MEN WERE AT THE HEART OF the right-wing revival of the 1980s: Hugh Morgan and Ray Evans, both of whom worked for Western Mining Corporation (WMC) for much of their professional careers, and John Stone, a former Treasury official and politician. Individually, all three were men to be reckoned with. In combination, they had the ideas, passions and contacts to exert vast and meaningful influence on Australian political life.

Hugh Morgan: establishment rebel

At first glance, Hugh Morgan is a stereotypical business establishment figure. As Patricia Howard recounted in 1993, he "can be seen most mornings in the back seat of his chauffeured Mercedes, being driven from his Toorak home to his Collins Street office, reading various office reports."[1] Upon reaching his office building, according to Gerard Henderson, "you have to gain access through a security entrance, then pass through an elaborately disguised sliding door and walk along a picture-filled passageway. The atmospherics resemble a cross between the set of a James Bond movie and an up-market art gallery."[2]

Morgan was born in 1940 and is the son of a former managing director of WMC. He attended the exclusive Geelong Grammar School before studying law and commerce at the University of Melbourne. He worked as a judge's associate in the Commonwealth Industrial Court and as a solicitor before moving into the mining industry in 1965. Despite his blue-blood pedigree, Morgan emphatically rejects the notion that he was born into privilege. With breathtaking obliviousness, the "impeccably dressed, well spoken" Morgan relayed his family's struggles to Henderson: "Hugh Morgan maintains that his parents were not well off and that, as for many of his generation, life was a bit of a struggle. His Geelong Grammar education was made possible by his grandfather who paid the hefty school fees. He worked part-time during significant parts of his Law/Commerce degree and paid board at home. In short, he was not born to great wealth."[3]

By 1976, aged just thirty-five, Morgan had become an executive director of WMC. He was appointed managing director in 1986 and chief executive officer in 1990, enduring a tumultuous reign as head of the company before finally stepping down in 2003. He is a veritable creature of the Melbourne establishment, with memberships of the Liberal Party, the Melbourne Club, the Australian Club and the Royal Melbourne Golf Club. He has had two stints on the board of the Reserve Bank of Australia (1981–1984 and 1996–2007) and has held countless directorships, chairs and honorary positions for a range of business and voluntary organisations. From 2003 to 2005 he was the president of the Business Council of Australia, an industry body comprising of the CEOs of more than 100 of Australia's largest companies. He is a director of the Cormack Foundation, established in 1988 to raise funds for the Liberal Party through large investments in blue-chip shares. The Foundation has also made donations to the IPA, CIS and Des Moore's Institute for Private Enterprise.[4]

In the mid-1970s, following the election of the Whitlam government, Morgan's interests began to take on a sharply political edge. As Sarah Burnside has shown, this period saw the "broad agreement that Australia's interests were furthered by resource development" increasingly brought into question.[5] In 1973, amid a resources boom, the Labor minister for minerals and energy, Rex Connor, commissioned the economist Thomas Fitzgerald to answer the broad question: what is Australia getting from its mineral industry? In the resultant report, *The Contribution of the Mineral Industry to Australian Welfare*, released in 1974, Fitzgerald emphasised three main elements:

The first was the scale of the taxation concessions granted by the federal government to the mining industry ... The taxation concessions greatly advantaged expanding mineral companies ... The second part was the extent of the overseas ownership of these advantaged mineral exploiters. And the third ... was the power and disposition of state governments, without any reference to the federal government, to grant great mineral rights to companies, foreign or local, which would automatically mean granting extraordinary federal taxation concessions to the expansion of those deposits.[6]

Essentially, the wealth created from mining was concentrated in the hands of a small number of companies, Fitzgerald argued; of these, many were foreign-owned, which was to the detriment of the ultimate owners of the resources, the Australian people.

To put it mildly, the mining industry – led by its peak body the Australian Mining Industry Council (AMIC, now the Minerals Council of Australia) – was not impressed. AMIC produced its own report, *Mining Taxation and Australian Welfare*, which asserted that Fitzgerald's report was "too narrowly conceived, distorted by the particular statistics selected and written without any consultation with the mining industry."[7] Morgan later described Fitzgerald's report as "the Tom Fitzgerald ambush," and identified it as a turning point for him personally and the industry more broadly: "Its effect on the Australian Mining Industry Council led to a realisation at the time that success in mining was not just a question of bog boring and firing. Success in mining was a question of political survival in a community with rapidly changing values."[8] Morgan had come to realise that industry could not simply sit back and hope that its good work would be appreciated. Businesspeople, it appeared to him, had to actively persuade the community in the same way their adversaries did, and he adopted this approach as president of AMIC from 1981 to 1983.

The Fitzgerald Report having established something of a precedent, Morgan now recognised that public opinion could not be ignored. As Ronald Libby relates, this period proved "a learning exercise for AMIC in preparation for mounting full-blown public advocacy campaigns such as the anti-land-rights campaign in Western Australia in 1984."[9] In a 1984 *Bulletin* article Morgan was still lamenting the reluctance of business to defend itself. "The private sector has yet to discover the same political *savoir-faire* and confidence which the trade union movement or the conservation movement, for example, have in such abundance," he wrote.[10] "Politicians can only accept what is accepted in the public opinion polls," he told *The Sydney Morning Herald*, "so you have to change public opinion!"[11]

One way to influence public opinion was by supporting think tanks that promoted free enterprise. After some involvement with the Institute of Economic Affairs in Britain, Morgan became convinced that similar organisations were needed in Australia. As we saw in the previous chapter, he therefore joined the IPA Council in 1978 – a position he held for more than twenty years – and raised more than $200,000 for the CIS in 1979. In 1986 Morgan was awarded honorary life membership of the CIS in recognition of his support.

It was during this period that Morgan also established himself as a prominent public figure. In a 1985 feature, Paul Sheehan waxed lyrical about his growing stature and influence:

> Hugh Morgan's eyes gleam even brighter than his hair. He is charming and unafraid. He has become, in some ways, the most important conservative figure in Australia. He is not merely a captain of industry, he is at the centre of a large and growing network of activists who are seeking to reshape the political agenda in this country. They have decided to change public opinion. They are bypassing the universities. They are even hoping to begin Australia's first private university. They are not short of money. And they have decided the issues are too important to be left to politicians.[12]

Other observers echoed these sentiments. David Kemp wrote that "in any history of the period, his will be seen as a most important role, both for his own contributions to debate and for his outstanding organizing capacity."[13] Paul Kelly described Morgan as one of the two "most influential businessmen within non-Labor politics" in the 1980s.[14] By the mid-1990s, the *Australian Financial Review* saw him as a contender for the title of ideological godfather of the Australian right.[15]

Backed by the influential chairman of WMC, Arvi Parbo, Morgan sought publicity through a number of provocative speeches on industrial relations, foreign debt, small government, Aboriginal land rights, immigration and the environment, littered throughout with religious and literary references. The "preacher" Morgan was captured in a full-page cartoon in *The Bulletin* in 1985, depicting him standing at a lectern, brandishing a Bible, atop a pile of dirt signposted "WMC sacred site. Keep Off."[16] But in his 1990 book of interviews, *Australian Answers*, Gerard Henderson detected a dissonance between the scripted and unscripted Morgan:

> I was halfway through my hour-long discussion with Hugh Morgan when it suddenly dawned on me that he had not as yet quoted from the Old Testament, William Shakespeare or Samuel Johnson. There appear to be two sides to WMC's managing director. The written Morgan is tough-minded, sometimes strident. He has an obvious message and the nature of its presentation makes it memorable and, at times, unforgettable. Then there is the spoken Morgan – also tough-minded but ostensibly moderate and discreet. The written Morgan is heavily into the works of prophets, playwrights and pamphleteers. The spoken Morgan exudes a preference for action over theory, seems more interested in art than literature and even shows some signs of agnosticism.[17]

Henderson had unwittingly stumbled upon an important fact: the scripted Morgan was not Morgan at all, but rather his fellow WMC executive Ray Evans.

Ray Evans: corporate theologian

Born in 1939, Ray Evans was given the full name Neville Raymond Evans. According to Peter Costello, he was named in honour of the British Prime Minister Neville Chamberlain, but as Chamberlain's reputation quickly went south due to his disastrous appeasement policies towards Nazi Germany, the family switched to calling him Ray.[18] After graduating from the University of Melbourne he worked for the Victorian State Electricity Commission (SEC) from 1961 to 1968, before becoming a lecturer in electrical engineering at the Gordon Institute of Technology in Geelong. In 1976 that institution's higher education courses were taken over by the newly established Deakin University, where Evans became a senior lecturer in the School of Engineering. In 1980 he was promoted to the position of deputy dean, but the following year Malcolm Fraser's Review of Commonwealth Functions – otherwise known as the "razor gang" – saw funding cuts that led to that school's abolition, and Evans was left unemployed.

In November 1981 Evans wrote to WMC's Arvi Parbo offering his services as a speechwriter. Just a week later he ran into Hugh Morgan at a CIS event in Sydney, and mentioned the letter he had written to Parbo, which Morgan happened to have in his pocket.[19] The two established an instant rapport, and Evans was offered a job at WMC in Melbourne, where he began work in April 1982. Morgan elaborated on the reason for hiring Evans in 2005: "He was hired basically because the material I had read sounded apposite to the sorts of challenges and issues that we felt needed to be addressed."[20] Evans was affectionately known as WMC's "corporate theologian," which was reflected in his penchant for quoting the Bible.[21] But his main role was to defend WMC against its enemies, and provide the material for Morgan to mount robust counterattacks. "My role was to engage in the culture wars and provide him with feedback," Evans recalled.[22] His friend Patrick Morgan went into more detail:

> Ray devised the strategy of getting Hugh Morgan ... to make a series of provocative statements (that came easily to Ray) on mining, the economy, Aboriginal matters and Australia's place in the larger scheme of things. These talks were designed to elicit howls of outraged protest from the various anti-progress lobbies, which they did. Hugh Morgan gained as a result a high media profile and had to be included, as the authorised "voice from the Right", so to speak, in all subsequent controversies in these areas.[23]

Evans was responsible for most, if not all, of Morgan's controversial addresses, and eventually wrote over 200 speeches for him throughout the 1980s and 1990s, before retiring from WMC in 2001. The combination of Evans the forceful, polemical writer and Morgan the high-profile public speaker proved extraordinarily powerful.

But where had Evans' signature brand of forthright political activism come from? Like many of his generation, Evans became politically active as a university student. He joined the ALP Club at Melbourne University, and later served as its president for one year. This "intellectual forum" had been founded in 1959 by lecturer Frank Knopfelmacher, with the assistance of *Quadrant*'s Richard Krygier.[24] Knopfelmacher, a Jewish émigré from communist Czechoslovakia, was a psychologist, philosopher and sociologist whose social democratic anti-communism had a profound influence on the political and intellectual development of many of his students. At a time when "a generation of Melbourne University students split into pro- and anti-Knopfelmacher camps,"[25] Evans was most definitely a member of the former, as Knopfelmacher's son Andrew recalled in 2002. "Although the ALP Club was ostensibly a social democratic operation," he said, "it was a tribute to his intellectual impact that current New Right operatives such as Ray Evans actually received their initial political formation and inspiration from Dad's lectures."[26] Questioned about this by journalist Andrew Cornell, Evans agreed that Knopfelmacher had been an important influence on him.[27]

Another of Knopfelmacher's students was Robert Manne, who, as we saw in Chapter 1, fought bitterly with Evans over the direction of *Quadrant* in the 1990s. Manne believes that Evans was influenced by Knopfelmacher in ways not immediately obvious. Knopfelmacher convinced those students falling under his influence that there were vital books they must read if they wanted to grasp the nature of contemporary politics. One such book was the memoirs of Arthur Koestler, the Hungarian journalist, novelist and influential political activist and intellectual. Koestler wrote memorably about his old boss Willi Münzenberg, the Comintern's most successful propagandist, who produced a succession of useful committees on the most highly charged political causes of the 1930s – the crimes of Nazism or the fascist threat in the Spanish Civil War – in the way "a conjurer produces rabbits out of his hat; his genius consisted in a unique combination of the conjurer's wiles with the crusader's dedication."[28] Manne is convinced that Evans learned about the craft of political persuasion from Münzenberg, via Knopfelmacher. Furthermore, in his role as an inspirational leader of the anti-communist ALP Club, Knopfelmacher taught students a politics of black and white, of good versus evil. "When Ray became an ideological neoliberal after the collapse of communism he translated this kind of Manichaeism to Australian history and domestic politics," says Manne.[29]

In the early 1960s Evans attended Labor Party conferences as a delegate for the Federated Fodder & Fuel Trades Union. An amusing item in *Farrago*, the Melbourne University student newspaper, recounts Evans, then sporting a crew cut, being heckled by a fellow unionist at the ALP state conference in 1962: "Sit down, you long-haired intellectual," he was told.[30] Ostensibly still on the left of the political spectrum, Evans' views on foreign policy were shifting him further and further to the right. This rightward shift became entrenched when Sam Benson, the federal member for Batman in Melbourne, was expelled from the ALP for supporting Australia's participation in the war in Vietnam. Evans followed Benson out of the ALP and went on to assist him in his successful campaign to retain his seat as an independent at the 1966 election.[31]

A powerful influence on Evans in this period was B.A. Santamaria, the infamous leading figure in the 1950s Labor Party split, and head of the National Civic Council, a conservative Catholic advocacy group. Years later Evans joked that he was "Santamaria's tame Protestant."[32] As Gerard Henderson details in his biography, Santamaria founded or was involved in an extraordinary number of political and religious organisations throughout his career.[33] One in particular was Peace with Freedom, a small group founded in 1965 in response to the increasing anti-war sentiment at Melbourne University. Members included Evans, Henderson, Knopfelmacher, Krygier and *Quadrant* editor James McAuley. In addition to being wonderful networking opportunities, involvement in such organisations served as useful models for Evans' later political activities. According to Patrick Morgan, Santamaria provided Evans with a vital insight about individuals and organisations: "Santamaria got across to Ray that in public life the individual is very ineffective. You need to form an organisation to carry out your aim, because this gives you public credibility."[34]

By now a committed political activist, Evans stood unsuccessfully as an independent candidate in Victoria in the 1969 special Senate election to replace John Gorton, who had resigned and moved to the lower house upon becoming prime minister. Evans received just 1.6 per cent of the vote. In 1971 he wrote an overwrought letter to Santamaria and other friends and colleagues, outlining his reasons for joining the anti-communist Democratic Labor Party (DLP). Evans believed that the United States was no longer committed to the defence of Australia, and that the Coalition government was being complacent about this fact. He saw the DLP as the only party that understood Australia's predicament, and likened its leader, Vince Gair, to the great French statesman Charles de Gaulle: "like de Gaulle, he knows, unlike any other senior politician, that it is only upon ourselves that we can rely for our future independence and security." Acutely aware that the DLP was dominated by Catholics, he threw his lot in with the ALP breakaway outfit nonetheless, for the sake of the nation: "I have decided that I should discount the cultural difficulties that people with backgrounds similar to mine have encountered as members of the DLP, and join up with the only Gaullists that we have."[35]

Evans' timing was poor, however. Having helped keep the ALP out of office since the mid-1950s, the DLP entered a period of inexorable decline following the election of the Whitlam government in 1972. Evans was a candidate for the DLP in the seat of Bellarine in the 1973 Victorian state election, where he received 7.8 per cent of the vote, but this was to be his last foray into electoral politics. Instead he turned to a more indirect form of political advocacy. With McAuley, Santamaria founded the Australian Council for Educational Standards in 1973, an advocacy group opposed to progressive trends in education. Evans was recruited to help run the organisation and edit its publication, the *ACES Review*, providing him with invaluable experience in advocacy group leadership, although he didn't last long in the role. Others in the organisation felt that Evans' strident editorials were too reactionary, and he was eased out of the job in 1975.[36]

Throughout the 1970s Evans was also transforming into an economic dry, largely in response to the industrial landscape he witnessed while working at the SEC and later in higher education. Patrick Morgan recalled Evans' view of the SEC, which he saw as: "a workplace in which bosses and workers had set up a cosy, closed-shop arrangement where overmanning practices and inflated salaries were endemic, all at the expense of the public. He had then moved to the Gordon Institute at Geelong which morphed into Deakin University; here he witnessed feather-bedding and rent-seeking activities (his terms) and other forms of self-protection from measurable, real-world criteria."[37] The most important influence on Evans in this period was his "mentor and hero" Bert Kelly.[38] Sharing Methodist Christian upbringings, Kelly instilled in Evans the notion that politics is a morality play – that morally righteous outcomes are more important than political or economic ones. "Bert was not really an economic rationalist as that term is now employed," Evans wrote following Kelly's death in 1997. "Bert was the great embodiment of Edmund Burke's dictum that 'politics is morality writ large' and if the application of the moral principles which had been inculcated into him from childhood led to economically sensible conclusions, that was an additional benefit."[39]

The extent of Evans' admiration for Kelly was illustrated in the considerable efforts he made to honour him in retirement and death. Following Kelly's disappointment at being dropped as a columnist in 1988 after a run of almost twenty years, Evans organised a function to honour him at the National Gallery of Victoria, attended by over 400 people. As early as 1990 he sought and received Kelly's blessing to write his biography, but wasn't able to find the time and eventually handed the task to Hal Colebatch.[40] When Kelly died, Evans delivered the eulogy at his funeral. In 2011, Evans helped his friend Bob Day establish the Bert Kelly Research Centre in Adelaide. The Centre is host to the Ray Evans Library, to which he bequeathed his considerable book collection.[41] In 2012 Colebatch's biography of Kelly, titled *The Modest Member*, was finally published, and Evans spoke at its official launch.

But back in 1982, armed with his informal political education and mentorships from Frank Knopfelmacher, B.A. Santamaria and Bert Kelly, Evans found himself in a unique role: political adviser and speechwriter to leading businessman Hugh Morgan. It was here that Evans came into his own as one of the most influential political activists of his generation.

John Stone: enigmatic intellectual

John Stone's unflagging commitment to a cause (and to winning an argument) is perhaps best illustrated by a famous tale that has become part of Canberra folklore. While he was working as a Treasury official in the 1950s, Stone would have Friday evening drinks with colleagues, academics and journalists. Here, according to former High Court Justice Dyson Heydon, "John became famous for besting journalists in argument, a skill for which they have never forgiven him."[42] On one occasion Stone became involved in a bet with two other men over which of them could win a running race to Lake George, twenty-six miles away. They decided to settle the bet right away, and after ducking home to change into his running gear, Stone set off towards his destination. He reached Lake George in first place around 5 am, another argument won.

Born in the Western Australian wheatbelt in 1929, Stone was a high achiever from an early age. In 1941 he won a scholarship to attend Perth Modern School, where he excelled in academic and sporting pursuits. He was a member of the WA Colts under-21 representative hockey teams that were national champions in 1948 and 1949. He went to the University of Western Australia (UWA) and graduated with a Bachelor of Science, with first-class honours in mathematical physics, in 1950. He was then awarded a Rhodes Scholarship and travelled to Oxford University to enrol in a Bachelor of Arts, where he graduated with first-class honours in philosophy, politics and economics in 1954.

The parallels here with Stone's later political opponent, Bob Hawke, are uncanny. Hawke was also born in 1929, attended Perth Modern School and UWA, and won a Rhodes Scholarship to study philosophy, politics and economics at Oxford. Both also served as president of the undergraduate guild at UWA. There was never any love lost between the two. "I'd have to say Bob was rather unrecognised in the intellectual stakes," recalled Stone in 1987. "I think the thing that offends me about Hawke in this area is his pretensions, and the continual harping on things like the Rhodes Scholarship, three honorary doctorates and goodness knows what. I didn't know him very well, I didn't think he was a very nice boy. He wasn't my type. He was a bit of a lair, loudmouthed, cocky and full of himself even then."[43] Hawke returned fire with his own recollections of their youthful rivalry in his autobiography, published in 1994. "Stone, whom I inherited decades later as Secretary of Treasury," he wrote, "exhibited at that early stage all the arrogance and cynical contempt for his fellows which were to characterise his distinguished career as a public servant."[44]

Returning to Australia after completing his degree at Oxford, Stone took up a position at the Commonwealth Treasury, where he remained for the next thirty years, except for the period 1967–1970, when he was in Washington DC working at the International Monetary Fund and the World Bank. In 1979 he became secretary to the Treasury, the department's most senior role. There he made his hardline position on industrial relations known when Malcolm Fraser asked him to prepare a memorandum of advice for an incoming conservative government in Britain. "Union power has become a threat not merely to economic stability," wrote Stone, "but to civil liberties and the very concept of the rule of law upon which the British society has been founded and of which it has been for so long such a notable exemplar."[45]

Stone had been initially encouraged by Fraser's strong electoral mandate and apparent economic liberalism, but like many on the insurgent New Right, he was left bitterly disappointed by the Fraser government. "How could Fraser leave office in 1983," he wrote some decades later in *Quadrant*, "with so little achieved in turning back the Whitlamite tide of destruction that he had promised to reverse?"[46] In 1983 Stone voted Labor for only the second time in his life, but things did not improve, and he resigned from Treasury in 1984 following increasing disagreement with the Hawke government over the direction of economic policy. Justice Heydon summarised Stone's outlook at this point as consisting of six propositions:

1. Governments had too much power in society.
2. The Federal Government had too much power in relation to other governments.
3. Within each government, a small core of Ministers had too much power compared to other legislators.
4. Within each executive, the public service was becoming too politicised to give independent advice.
5. Trade unions had too much power over governments and other social forces.
6. These evils could only be exposed and combated by vigorous debate, which he saw as the lifeblood of democracy.[47]

Like Evans, Stone was a great admirer of Bert Kelly, and in an obituary wrote of how he would often read Kelly's speeches on tariffs aloud to his wife late at night.[48] Stone's preoccupations both reflected some of the intellectual currents of the time and provided a blueprint for other right-wing activists to follow.

Stone took a big risk in abandoning a long and successful public service career, but he revelled in the intellectual freedom that his resignation enabled. He moved to Melbourne and took up a short-lived position as a visiting professor at Michael Porter's Centre of Policy Studies, before he became a senior fellow at the IPA in 1985. In that year he also helped found the CNI, and commenced writing regular articles on a wide variety of topics for *The Sydney Morning Herald* and *Quadrant*.

In April 1987 Stone accepted an offer to help develop Joh Bjelke-Petersen's single-rate tax policy, which was to form a key part of the Queensland Premier's ill-fated "Joh for Canberra" campaign. Many were shocked to see such a respected figure associating with a man whom much of the country regarded as a joke, and whom would only damage the Coalition's campaign to defeat Labor in the 1987 election. Stone responded in the only way he knew how: engaging in vigorous debate in defence of his position. "In the end, it is *policies* – not political parties – that I care about," he wrote in the *IPA Review*. "I see in this initiative by the Premier of Queensland, including through its effects upon the policy-forming processes of all the Federal political parties, a real chance of turning around those policies which have brought Australia to its present pass. That is why I am working for Sir Joh."[49]

Before long he had doubled down. Despite not being a member of the National Party, and never even having voted for it, Stone was in June 1987 offered the number two spot on the party's Queensland Senate ticket (behind Sir Joh's wife, Florence Bjelke-Petersen). He was subsequently elected to the Senate in July, and immediately became the leader of the National Party in the Senate. Delivering his maiden speech in September 1987, Stone wore his H.R. Nicholls Society tie, though he light-heartedly reassured other senators that "when I put on this tie this morning I had no intention of being provocative on this occasion."[50]

The "Joh for Canberra" campaign was widely blamed for the Coalition's 1987 election loss, including by Liberal leader John Howard. Nevertheless,

Stone subsequently served as Howard's shadow minister for finance, until Howard sacked him in September 1988. The sacking was ironic, in that Stone had supported Howard's controversial remarks on the need to slow Asian immigration, but then went further just as Howard was trying to calm things down. "Howard," wrote Paul Kelly, "having tolerated Stone's transgressions on indirect taxation and immigration for fourteen months, felt compelled to act."[51] Stone was philosophical: "I bore Howard himself no ill will for this. As I said in a press conference the next day, he had probably done me a favour."[52]

In March 1990 Stone resigned from the Senate in order to contest the lower-house seat of Fairfax in Queensland, a decision that left Gerard Henderson perplexed. "It seems likely that John Stone will remain an unpredictable enigma," he wrote. "Few would doubt his ability or courage. But many will query his political judgement."[53] Stone's attempt to switch chambers was unsuccessful, and this brought an end to his short career in electoral politics. After this setback Stone returned to his former role as a senior fellow at the IPA, and recommended writing articles for *Quadrant*, as well as a weekly column for the *Australian Financial Review* that ran until 1998. Since then he has been an occasional contributor to both the *Australian Financial Review* and *The Australian*, albeit with reduced frequency in recent years. Throughout the 2000s he also wrote increasingly strident articles for the CNI journal the *National Observer*.

As Dyson Heydon observed in 2010, Stone is "peppery and pugnacious" and "does not shy away from a fight. He can take it, but he can certainly dish it out." He went on to recall that "many a speaker at a *Quadrant* dinner or a Samuel Griffith Society conference or an H.R. Nicholls Society meeting will take to their graves the vivid recollection of the puzzled and frowning face of John, advancing towards the podium in order to extirpate the speaker's fallacies with the intellectual equivalent of fire and sword."[54] On the other hand, as journalist Craig McGregor found after interviewing him in 1987, he can be a model of civility: "There is a polite, old-fashioned charm about Stone: he calls everyone 'Mr', he observes all the correct rituals, his cultural style is donnish, patronising, somewhat upper class."[55] In my own email correspondence with him he was unfailingly courteous and generous with his reminiscences.

Advancing age has done nothing to dull Stone's passion for political intrigue and debate. Following the successful coup against Tony Abbott in 2015, for example, he became a ferocious public critic of Malcolm Turnbull, "a man without a conservative bone in his body, whose significant actions have long been directed to destroying the values [the Liberal Party] used to, and largely still does, stand for."[56] He urged a restoration of Abbott, or, failing that, a new leader with comparable right-wing bona fides, such as Peter Dutton. When the Liberal Party finally put Turnbull out of his misery in August 2018, replacing him with Scott Morrison, Stone remained as vigilant as ever about the influence of Liberal moderates. "Scott Morrison can claim (just) to be right of centre," he wrote in a letter to the editor published in *The Australian*, "but owes his prime ministership to all those left and far-left Liberals who previously supported Malcolm Turnbull."[57]

*

Until the 1980s, Hugh Morgan, Ray Evans and John Stone had had next to nothing to do with one another. But as we will see in the following chapters, by the middle of the decade they were ready to embark on a series of campaigns to transform political debate in Australia. Acting alone they would probably have been ineffectual, but together they were a force to be reckoned with.

3

RIGHT-WING REVIVAL: THE H.R. NICHOLLS SOCIETY AND INDUSTRIAL RELATIONS

I N HIS COMPREHENSIVE ACCOUNT OF Australian politics in the 1980s, *The End of Certainty*, Paul Kelly identified Australia's distinctive system of industrial relations as one of the five pillars of the post-Federation political consensus. "Arbitration was the greatest institutional monument to Australian egalitarianism and its quest for social order," he wrote. "Its longevity is a tribute to its ability to incorporate its opponents."[1] The Australian industrial relations system was accepted by both capital and labour and became entrenched over decades. However, during the 1980s this industrial consensus collapsed, and the H.R. Nicholls Society was a key actor in the process of creative destruction that brought the consensus to an end.

Australia's twentieth-century industrial relations system was catalysed by the depression and bitter strikes of the 1890s, and the subsequent rise to political prominence of the Australian Labor Party. As historian Stuart Macintyre chronicles, when unions' attempts to achieve wage justice through strikes were defeated, "they turned to the state as a countervailing force to the employers' industrial supremacy, seeking state power so that employers could be made to yield what they would not offer."[2] And so, arbitration courts and wage boards were established in the pre-Federation colonies through alliances of trade unionists and liberal lawyers. The latter were especially concerned with restoring peace to the community, because "the new class turmoil threatened their vision of a prosperous, orderly society."[3] They sought to end the hostilities between capital and labour by creating an independent umpire who sat within the apparatus of the state.

When the six colonies came together to form the Commonwealth of Australia in 1901, the Constitution gave the new federal parliament specific powers to make laws with respect to "conciliation and arbitration for the prevention and settlement of industrial disputes extending beyond the limits of any one State."[4] Prime Minister Alfred Deakin set about making full use of these powers in supporting the passage of the Conciliation and Arbitration Bill, which was first introduced to parliament in July 1903. Eventually passed in December 1904 following extensive debate and the fall of Deakin's government, the *Commonwealth Conciliation and Arbitration Act* created the Commonwealth Court of Conciliation and Arbitration, which was charged with settling disputes between employers and employees, or their trade union representatives. Kelly's description of the legislation accurately captures both its benevolent intentions and its adverse consequences, at least in the eyes of its critics:

> The philosophy of the Arbitration Act was that industrial relations required an umpire and could not be left to employers and employees. The aim was to remove the need for industrial action by paying workers a fair wage and guaranteeing equity across industries. The Australian system was unique because "it provided regulation not only of the process for settling disputes but also direct regulation of the outcome ... based on specific views about wage equity." This led to a system of national wage regulation and institutionalised comparative wage justice, an idea that defied the contrasting economic performance of different industries in varying regions. The Act enshrined trade union power and encouraged the growth of unions on a craft rather than an industry basis.[5]

For its critics, the system forced businesses to pay above-market rate wages even when economic conditions or employee productivity levels did not justify it. Furthermore, it entrenched the power of trade unions to dictate the terms of industrial bargaining.

The legislation required that the president of the Court of Conciliation and Arbitration would come from among the Justices of the High Court. In 1907, Henry Bournes Higgins, who had served as attorney-general in

John Watson's Labor government despite not being a member of the ALP, was appointed as the court's second president. In his first case, Higgins brought down what became known as the Harvester judgement, a decision that would go on to shape Australian wage regulation for much of the twentieth century. Indeed, Higgins's biographer, John Rickard, described it as having "won its place in Australian history books as a symbolic part of the making of the Australian nation."[6]

Higgins had been asked by the parliament to determine what was a "fair and reasonable" wage, and chose the Sunshine Harvester Works in outer Melbourne as his test case. In making his judgement, Higgins declared: "I cannot think of any other standard appropriate than the normal needs of the average employee, regarded as a human being living in a civilized community."[7] Thus, in addition to standard expenses such as rent, groceries and fuel, he included in his calculations all of those things that a family of five in such a community might require. The list included: "light, clothes, boots, furniture, utensils, rates, life insurance, savings, accident or benefit societies, loss of employment, union pay, books and newspapers, tram and train fares, sewing machine, mangle, school requisites, amusements and holidays, intoxicating liquors, tobacco, sickness and death, domestic help, or any expenditure for unusual contingencies, religion or charity."[8] Taking all of these expenses into account, Higgins determined that the basic wage for an unskilled worker should be seven shillings per day, or two pounds and two shillings per week. Australia's system of centralised wage fixation was born.

In the words of Rickard, Higgins had "placed the onus on employers and critics to either accept this standard or justify a lesser one."[9] When they weren't able to do the latter his formulation became entrenched. The combination of a minimum wage and arbitration was, as Higgins wrote in the *Harvard Law Review*, "a new province for law and order."[10] Needless to say, employers were not impressed with Higgins's judgement. Not only did they see it as conflicting with the laws of the market, leading to likely unemployment where reductions in wages might otherwise keep workers employed, but they also felt that the state was taking the side of trade unions in a class war. Eventually they came to accept the system, and were incorporated into its structures and institutions. "The duties of the state towards the community, the need to mitigate the effects of the market, the entitlement of all to earn a living wage," wrote Macintyre, "became embedded in political discourse."[11] The arbitration framework endured for the next eight decades. By the 1980s, according to Kelly, it had "become the strongest pillar of the old Deakin Settlement."[12]

But, during that decade, a combination of tenacious New Right activists and Liberal Party politicians were now determined to "turn Mr Justice Higgins on his head."[13] They did this by forming the H.R. Nicholls Society, a single-minded organisation that abandoned the principles of moderate accommodation in favour of radical confrontation.

Taking on the IR Club

When the ALP under Bob Hawke inflicted a crushing defeat on Malcolm Fraser's Coalition government at the March 1983 election, things were looking bleak for the radicals of the New Right. Hawke had come to office carrying a message of "national consensus". Prior to the election the Labor Party had struck a Prices and Incomes Accord with the Australian Council of Trade Unions (ACTU), designed to control inflation and promote employment and economic growth. Shortly after the election, Hawke invited a wider group of political, business, financial and union leaders to Parliament House for a National Economic Summit, where they discussed ways of confronting the recession. Hawke's consensus approach was anathema to the New Right, but before long they began to feel the tide was turning back their way, and two events in particular were singled out by Hugh Morgan as pivotal to the changing mood.

The first was the publication of Gerard Henderson's 'The Industrial Relations Club' in *Quadrant* in September 1983, in which he criticised the "club-like atmosphere" of Australian industrial relations, targeting government institutions, employers and unions as all complicit in prizing industrial peace over economic performance. "The IR Club exudes an ethos of complacency and self-congratulation," wrote Henderson. "Here can be found men and women who are truly reasonable and moderate. They alone understand industrial realities; they alone know how the system works;

and it is they who can do deals and fix agreements. Within the Club there is no time for confrontation. Rather, sweet reasonableness prevails. The task is to secure industrial harmony. Economic realities take what is very much second place, if that."[14] Journalist Tim Duncan said in 1989 that Henderson's article "set off the notion that industrial regulation was the basis for a new form of privilege which allowed the so-called representatives of the under-privileged, in this case the union bosses, to turn themselves into Orwellian pigs."[15]

The second event was John Stone's Edward Shann Memorial Lecture in Economics at the University of Western Australia in August 1984, which Ray Evans later described as "arguably the seminal document in the campaign for liberalising the labour market."[16] Stone's lecture was delivered shortly after he announced his intention to resign from the Treasury. Titled '1929 and all that,' the lecture drew parallels between the present state of the Australian economy and its condition on the eve of the Great Depression. In particular, Stone pointed to three problems: financial mismanagement, protectionism and ossified labour markets. He articulated his strong view that labour is a commodity just like any other, a signature neoliberal doctrine that was in plain opposition to the historically dominant Australian view that workers should be afforded protection from the vagaries of the market: "The fact is that there has been in Australia an unwillingness to view the workings of labour markets like other markets – in terms of supply, demand and price. Yet employment, unemployment and wages – the things which do attract attention and concern – are nothing more than the labour market reflections of the operation of supply, demand and price."[17] Thus, due to the influence of "that post-Federation regulator *par excellence* Henry Bournes Higgins," what should be recognised as simple economic truth was viewed as a sort of heresy. This economically damaging tradition, Stone argued, had persisted through the decades with the strong support of trade unions, the Labor Party and the industrial relations bureaucracy, working in concert. He went on to describe the problem in the strongest of terms: "The truth is that our system of wage determination today constitutes a crime against society. It is, starkly, a system of wage determination under which trade union leaders and people preening themselves as 'Justices' of various Arbitration benches combine to put young people in particular, but many others also, out of work."[18] Given his own proclivity for dramatic language, it is not surprising that Ray Evans took particular notice of Stone's lecture. Evans was especially impressed with Stone's criticism of Higgins, calling it "the most significant attack on the founder of our arbitration system since Prime Minister Billy Hughes sought to undermine Higgins in 1917."[19]

The Hancock Report and the steering committee

In July 1983 Labor's industrial relations minister, Ralph Willis, announced the appointment of a Committee of Review into Australian Industrial Relations Law and Systems, "with the aim and for the purpose of developing a more effective and practical industrial relations system in accordance with social, economic and industrial changes which have occurred and are taking place in Australia."[20] The committee was to be chaired by economist Keith Hancock, then vice-chancellor of Flinders University, and assisted by George Polites of the Confederation of Australian Industry (CAI) and Charlie Fitzgibbon of the Waterside Workers' Federation. For its critics, these appointments immediately exposed the review as a sham. Paddy McGuinness, for example, in a paper written for the CIS, questioned the make-up of the committee and pre-emptively criticised its findings: "As paid-up life members of the industrial relations club, the mutual admiration society of practitioners and experts in industrial relations, the three members of the committee necessarily start from the common presumption that the centralised system of wage fixing under the Commission has worked pretty well and is in need of only minor reform."[21] Ultimately released in May 1985, Hancock's three-volume report made 148 recommendations for change; and it confirmed the scepticism of its critics with its conclusion that "conciliation and arbitration should remain the mechanism for regulating industrial relations in Australia."[22] Many of Hancock's recommendations were in line with the submissions of the ACTU and CAI, who "were in broad agreement beforehand about the general reforms they wanted."[23] This collaboration was for the New Right further evidence of the cosy industrial relations club at work. John Howard described the report as "a product of the IR Club, by the IR Club, for the IR Club."[24] The influence of Gerard Henderson, who had joined Howard's staff in January 1984, was clear.

Though many on the right were disappointed with the Hancock Report, Ray Evans saw an opportunity and contacted John Stone in order to discuss what to do next. Evans had already been in contact with disenchanted IR Club member Barrie Purvis and a young, pre-politics Peter Costello, and by September 1985 the four men were meeting regularly to discuss industrial relations.

Purvis, at the time director of the Australian Wool Selling Brokers Employers' Federation, had a long career in industrial relations and personnel management. He was a founding member of the Industrial Relations Society of Victoria, one of the organisations identified by Henderson as being part of the industrial relations club. Initially a moderate willing to work within the system, Purvis had become fed up and developed into a "real hardhead" who was "renowned in employer circles for his bulldog-like approach."[25] He maintained the lowest public profile of these four founding members, and died in July 2014.

Peter Costello was only twenty-eight years old when he was contacted by Evans, but had already made a name for himself in industrial law, thanks largely to the Dollar Sweets case of 1985, in which he had represented that company in its dispute with striking members of the Federated Confectioners Association, and won. The Dollar Sweets dispute was especially significant because it was won in the Supreme Court of Victoria rather than the Conciliation and Arbitration Commission. As Costello recalled: "It showed that the common law had jurisdiction in industrial disputes and that civil courts could be effective where the Arbitration Commission failed."[26] An end to arbitration was in sight.

Although the four men barely knew one another, they agreed to form a "steering committee" with a view to founding a larger organisation devoted to labour market reform. Thus heralded the birth of the H.R. Nicholls Society, although it was yet to acquire that title.

The legend of Henry Richard Nicholls

The name of the H.R. Nicholls Society stemmed from an arcane piece of trivia that Evans discovered in John Rickard's biography of H.B. Higgins. Justice Higgins, as we saw above, had become the *bête noire* of employers for guaranteeing Australian workers a fair and reasonable wage in the 1907 Harvester judgement. Evans was enamoured with Rickard's biography of Higgins – reflecting on his career in 2010, he called the book his "Road to Damascus."[27] From his reading of the book he concluded that the Justice had been "a nut who, to the great detriment of his country, found himself able to give legal form and substance to his fantasies."[28] Not content with this pithy critique, he went on: "Eccentrics and nuts are always more interesting than ordinary, sane folk, and Rickard's absorbing account of Higgins, who, at least in terms of far reaching influence, must be accounted as one of Australia's most damaging and delusioned [*sic*] nut cases, reveals just how malleable Australian society was at the time of Federation."[29]

Rickard's biography related an ostensibly small historical incident that, for Evans and the steering committee, would get elevated to the status of legend. In 1911 the eighty-one-year-old editor of the Hobart *Mercury*, Henry Richard Nicholls, was charged with contempt of court after editorialising about Justice Higgins' suspect political motivations in a dispute brought before the Court of Conciliation and Arbitration. The editor described Higgins as "a political Judge, that is, he was appointed because he had well served a political party."[30] He was forced to withdraw the statement and apologise before the full bench of the High Court, although he was eventually acquitted on the grounds that his comments did not technically constitute contempt of court.[31]

This might appear to have been a rather trivial affair, and it had certainly been treated as such by historians. But for Evans and his fellow New Right activists, Nicholls' role as an outspoken critic of Higgins elevated him to the status of political martyr. "Having discovered this octogenarian newspaperman of delightful character," Evans told Paul Kelly, "we decided that he should be brought back into contemporary debate as a symbol of what was right against Higgins in Higgins's own time."[32] This canonisation of Nicholls was just one example of Evans' peculiar "penchant for historical figures apposite and sometimes opposite to the ginger group in question."[33]

We have no way of knowing whether Nicholls himself, long dead, would have approved of the organisation named in his honour, but the members of the H.R. Nicholls Society wasted little time in claiming to speak on his behalf. Stone declared Nicholls to be "keenly aware of the need to avoid the pollution of the real law, and the real courts, by the insidious incursion into them either of politicized Judges or of the administrative writ of the political executive."[34] In even more dramatic terms, John Hyde described Nicholls' editorial as concerning "the liberty of the subject faced with the tyranny of arbitrary power."[35]

At the time, these grandiose claims were met with scepticism. Labour academic Braham Dabscheck, for one, questioned whether Nicholls was an appropriate mascot, given that "his only excursion into industrial relations – if it can be called that – was his editorial criticising Higgins. He does not appear to have either participated in or influenced industrial relations in his era."[36] Labor's minister for social security, Brian Howe, was so incensed at the New Right's attempt to recruit the dead for political purposes that he commissioned a researcher at the Commonwealth Parliamentary Library to prepare a paper on Nicholls. The overtly polemical paper mocked Nicholls' transition from youthful radical to ageing, unhinged reactionary, and argued that, as an arbitrary selection from history, he was "a very slender base upon which to construct a legend."[37]

The Toorak seminar

In January 1986 the newly minted steering committee sent out letters inviting potential members to an inaugural seminar in Melbourne the following month. The seminar promised "a series of important papers ... on the legal, constitutional, economic, philosophical, sociological and industrial relations aspects of what has been called 'our Higgins problem'."[38] This term came from a speech Hugh Morgan had given to the Industrial Relations Society of Victoria in June 1984. It was appropriate, then, that Morgan agreed to deliver the opening address, which was to be "an 'in club' affair so that we can discuss these matters without restraint."[39]

The seminar was held at the stately Country Women's Association headquarters in Toorak over the 28 February–2 March weekend and attended by between thirty and forty people, whom Paul Kelly later described as "an honour roll of the free market counter-establishment of the 1980s."[40] In addition to the steering committee and Morgan, attendees included Gerard Henderson, John Hyde, Bert Kelly, Michael Porter, David and Rod Kemp, Andrew Hay of the Melbourne Chamber of Commerce and the Australian Federation of Employers, Ian McLachlan and Paul Houlihan of the National Farmers' Federation (NFF), mining executive Charles Copeman and, most provocatively, former governor-general Sir John Kerr. Stone remarked to the press that he thought that Kerr "ought to be brought in from the cold" more than a decade after his dismissal of the Whitlam government.[41] No serving politicians were invited to attend the seminar. Neil Brown, the Liberal shadow minister for industrial relations, requested an invitation, but was refused on the grounds that the organisation wanted to avoid the impression that it was a front for the Liberal Party.[42]

At the seminar, a number of papers were given on recent industrial disputes, providing businessmen and lawyers with the opportunity to share ideas about the best ways to deal with the activities of militant trade unions. Especially important in this regard were the contributions of Wayne Gilbert on the South East Queensland Electricity Board dispute, Houlihan on the Mudginberri abattoir case, and Costello on his Dollar Sweets experience. As Evans recalled in 2012, "It was primarily an attempt to set up a combined think tank and support system for people who were under attack and didn't have anywhere to turn. So what we did then was to bring together quite a wide range of people who'd been involved in different disputes. And it was a bit like a revivalist meeting actually. People, many of whom had never met each other before, sort of coming together and telling their experiences."[43]

Stone accepted his nomination as the H.R. Nicholls Society's inaugural president, but resigned in 1989, at which point Evans took over and remained in the position for the next twenty-one years. Though the first seminar received a small amount of press coverage, it wasn't until some months later that the Society achieved true notoriety, as related industrial events came to occupy media attention.

Furore

For Peko-Wallsend chief executive Charles Copeman, the H.R. Nicholls seminar was emboldening, and it inspired him to launch an almighty fight with the unions at the Robe River iron ore mine in Western Australia's Pilbara region. Having taken over the mine in December 1983, Peko-Wallsend was attempting to change work practices in order to improve productivity and profitability, but had been met with fierce resistance from the unions and local management, and the WA Industrial Relations Commission had stepped in to attempt a resolution. The Peko-Wallsend board – which John Stone had joined in May – found the Commission's orders unacceptable, and in late July Copeman took the drastic decision to sack the entire workforce of around 1200 people. The dispute continued throughout August, with staff eventually returning to work in early September. Giving his version of events the following year, Copeman claimed that productivity had doubled, and credited the H.R. Nicholls Society with having "played a vital part in giving me the encouragement to initiate what we did."[44]

For the media, the connections between the union-busting mining giant and the shadowy H.R. Nicholls Society were irresistible. In August 1986 Pamela Williams published a cover story in *Business Review Weekly* that detailed all of the main players in the campaign to take on trade unions and destroy the arbitration system. "Almost every significant union defeat over the past year," she wrote, "can be connected with members of a small group who constitute the H.R. Nicholls Society."[45] Though Stone later claimed that Williams was disparagingly referred to by members of the Canberra press gallery as the press secretary of the ACTU's Bill Kelty,[46] her article was very well sourced from H.R. Nicholls members and was the most complete account of the inaugural seminar to date. The major news-papers were soon following suit with long features on the New Right phenomenon and the numerous connections between individuals, busi-nesses and think tanks.[47]

Meanwhile, the ALP and the union movement went on the attack. Speaking on Melbourne radio, Prime Minister Bob Hawke described the H.R. Nicholls Society as "political troglodytes and economic lunatics,"[48] a phrase that did more than anything to raise the organisation's profile and has since become part of its folklore. "The thing that really gave us a big kick-along was Bob Hawke," Evans joyously recalled to me. "What did he call us? Political troglodytes and economic lunatics. Wow! What more could you want? Ha!"[49] WA Premier Brian Burke, ACTU president Simon Crean and Hawke government minister Mick Young were also forceful in their criticisms. But no one went further than ACTU official John Halfpenny, who called the group the "industrial relations branch of the Ku Klux Klan" in his Arthur Calwell Memorial Lecture at Monash University.[50] Halfpenny and *The Age* newspaper, which published his remarks, were promptly sued by Evans and Costello for defamation. Their action was suc-cessful, and both received damages. According to Evans, the cheques were signed by packaging magnate Richard Pratt.[51]

But attacks on the New Right weren't only coming from the expected sources on the left. In an extraordinary intervention, Brian Powell, the chief executive of employer group the Australian Chamber of Manufac-tures, accused members of the New Right of showing "truly fascist tendencies that make it harder and harder for us to negotiate change."[52] Powell's comments led to a war of words between employer groups, reveal-ing deep divisions between the new radicals and the old guard members of the IR Club. Geoff Allen of the Business Council of Australia claimed the New Right had "solid acceptance" in the business community, whereas the CAI's Bryan Noakes warned about "extreme views and simplistic solu-tions being suggested to solve complex problems."[53]

Amid all of this uproar, the H.R. Nicholls Society held a dinner at Melbourne's Southern Cross Hotel to launch *Arbitration in Contempt*, a hardback volume containing the proceedings of the inaugural seminar. Geoffrey Blainey gave the book's launching address, and noted the wide-spread publicity the organisation and its publication had received in the preceding weeks: "I can recall no other book of recent years whose launching has been so widely and excitedly discussed." He went on to mock the efforts of the government to turn public opinion against the Society: "The publicity has come from the very politicians who hope that the book will *not* be read. In the last year Canberra has set in motion million-dollar advertising campaigns but hardly one of those propaganda campaigns has been as effective as that directed by the Labor ministry, unwittingly, against this book."[54] More than 200 people paid $100 each to attend the dinner. The "no politicians" rule had been relaxed, and invitations were sent to sitting members of both major parties. For obvious reasons, Labor politicians had no interest in attending, and John Stone got plenty of laughs when he announced that ministers such as Ralph Willis and John Button had sent their sincere apologies.[55] But in a sign that the Society's ideas were gaining traction within the Liberal Party, Opposition leader John Howard and shadow treasurer Jim Carlton made appearances.

Howard, who had supplanted Andrew Peacock as Opposition leader in September 1985, was in an awkward position. Along with Carlton, he was a prominent economic dry in the Liberal Party, and was thus supportive of industrial relations reform. But he was also conscious of the need to appeal to the wider community. "He was trying to play to the dries in the party as an IR reformer," recalled Costello, "but he was [also] trying to play to the public as a reasonable man."[56] Associating with what was then seen as a quite radical group was fraught with political risk. According to Evans, Howard struck a decidedly uneasy figure at the dinner: "Howard was there looking like a rabbit, frightened, you know, not wanting to be photographed, not wanting to be seen there. And he somewhat reluctantly gave a vote of thanks to Geoffrey Blainey, and he was obviously torn between, 'Is this good for me or bad for me?' He didn't know."[57] Nevertheless, Blainey invited Howard back to his home in East Melbourne afterwards, where they spoke for some hours.[58]

Pamela Williams, whose *Business Review Weekly* article had kicked off the media furore about the New Right, wrote a follow-up cover story in December. This time her focus was on the role that the H.R. Nicholls Society and other business groups were playing in shaping the industrial relations policies of the Liberal Party. Despite the perception that she was a Labor-aligned journalist, Williams again managed to coax a number of

New Right figures to speak on the record about their goals and tactics. She concluded with an alarming historical comparison, drawing parallels between the contemporary Liberal Party and the ALP prior to its split in 1955: "The way the New Right has manoeuvred its way inside the portals of the Liberal Party ideology and policy-making machines is reminiscent of the sort of infiltration that took place in the ALP in the 1950s. The tactics then were similar insofar as the Industrial Groups (or groupers) moved into pressure positions in the party's branches and policy-making structure."[59] The extent to which the Liberal Party would embrace the New Right's radical plan to reform industrial relations was now one of the most pressing questions in Australian politics.

"An attempt to burn down Nauru House"

In their invitation letter sent to potential members in January 1986, the H.R Nicholls Society's steering committee declared that their broad aim was "to give new impetus for reform of our present labour market and to provide a forum for discussion of alternatives to the present regulation of industrial relations."[60] They had long been disenchanted with the state of industrial relations in Australia and felt that the time was right to gather the forces of reform and encourage open debate. "There needs to be an increase both in the tempo of the debate and of its depth and breadth of intellectual content," the letter continued. "Although it has started off well there is a risk that it may slow down and perhaps peter out."[61]

Hugh Morgan claimed that the Society had no edict, and was "only a collection of people a bit like a dining or debating club,"[62] but the group did develop its own statement of purposes, and these were excerpted in newspaper advertisements:

- To promote discussion about the operation of industrial relations in Australia, including the system of determining wages and other conditions of employment.

- To support the reform of Australian industrial relations with the aim of promoting the rule of law in respect of employer and employee organiza-tions alike, the right of individuals to contract freely for the supply and engagement of their labour by mutual agreement, and the necessity for labour relations to be conducted in such a way as to promote economic development in Australia.[63]

But what did the group really want to achieve? Especially when contrasted with the public furore the group's formation caused, these goals come across as somewhat vague and even benign. They tell us which issues the H.R. Nicholls Society was concerned with, but provide minimal clues as to where they stood in the industrial relations debate. There was undoubt-edly some deliberate obfuscation in the group's public position, but it did not take a lot of digging to find its true intentions.

The H.R. Nicholls Society's targets were threefold: the conciliation and arbitration system, centralised wage fixation and trade unions. As the title of its first publication made clear, the Society held Australia's conciliation and arbitration system in contempt. Ray Evans neatly captured the general view when he wrote in 1985 that "there are, I suppose, a number of insti-tutions that have contributed significantly to our economic decline, but in any catalogue of them the Commonwealth Conciliation and Arbitration Court, and its child the C & A Commission, would have to occupy first place."[64] Far from campaigning for reform of this institution, they wanted it abolished. Nowhere was this objective made more explicit than in an anonymous member's comment reported in *The Sydney Morning Herald* in August 1986: "It really is an attempt to burn down Nauru House [the Commission's Melbourne headquarters] and everything the Arbitration Commission stands for."[65]

The H.R. Nicholls Society did not accept what it saw as the fundamen-tal premise of Australia's conciliation and arbitration system – that employers and employees are by definition in conflict with each other and require an umpire to resolve their differences. In its eyes, the system was premised on the mistaken assumption that profit was theft: employers tak-ing for themselves what rightfully belonged to the workers whose labour produced the wealth. To Society members, the notion that there is a power imbalance between capital and labour is a myth. This is a total rejection of one of the most basic notions of the labour movement: that employees need to be protected from exploitation by powerful employers. Evans blamed such a misconception on the work of Karl Marx: "The phrase 'industrial relations' is a product of Marxism. The Marxist world is divided into classes, the working class, the bourgeoisie, and the capitalist class, and since, according to Marx, class warfare is inevitable, 'industrial relations' is, like international relations, the study of war and peace between the classes."[66] Contra the Marxist worldview, the H.R. Nicholls Society wanted employers and employees to see each other not as adversaries, but as partners in the same project of prosperity, and this could only be achieved by overturning the arbitration system. "The key to industrial relations reform," explained Gerard Henderson, "is to make it legal for employers and employees to reach their own agreements about work conditions and practices – free from the interference of trade unions or industrial tribunals."[67]

Speaking in 2012, H.R. Nicholls Society board member Des Moore ridiculed the idea that Australian workers are susceptible to exploitation by their bosses. "For the most part it's a lot of nonsense," he said. "You've got over 800,000 employers in Australia. They're competing in a labour market for the services of 11 million employees. There's absolutely no scope in general for exploitation, because we've got a competitive marketplace there right at the start."[68] In the Society's view of worker-employer relationships, once freed from the constraints of government interference, both parties would be able to enter negotiations about wages and conditions on a level playing field.

Allied with the H.R. Nicholls Society's objective to bring down the conciliation and arbitration system was a desire to end Australia's tradition of centralised wage fixation. As we have seen, the notion of a basic wage set by government goes back to Higgins's 1907 Harvester judgement. Though they had reluctantly tolerated it, many conservatives had never liked this state of affairs. The most assertive challenge to centralised wage fixation arrived in 1985 when the AIPP published *Wages Wasteland: A Radical Examination of the Australian Wage Fixing System*, a collection of essays that included contributions from John Hyde, Ray Evans, Gerard Henderson and Paddy McGuinness, and was launched by John Stone. The H.R. Nicholls Society picked up on and expanded this debate.

Recalling the inaugural seminar in his memoirs, Peter Costello wrote: "We all agreed on one general principle: that centralised wage fixation had failed and that Australia needed to liberalise and free up its industrial laws."[69]

The economic case against the minimum wage was laid out by Tasman Institute visiting fellow Peter Hartley at the Society's thirteenth conference in 1992. Minimum wage laws, he declared, "are an example of a price control. Price controls limit the volume of transactions, and distort the quality of goods or services exchanged in the market place. In the case of a minimum wage, the costs are thought mainly to take the form of reduced employment and output, while the gains accrue mainly to those who keep their jobs at a higher wage rate."[70] As Stone made clear in his 1984 Shann lecture, labour market deregulationists believe that labour is a commodity like any other, subject to the same laws of supply, demand and price. When governments interfere in this process on the side of workers, the market is distorted. As employers are increasingly forced to pay workers more than they are able, they are left with no choice but to let some staff go. The resultant unemployment is not only a disaster for the laid-off workers, it is damaging to the wider economy.

Gerry Gutman, an economic consultant and former public servant who had earlier made the only submission to the Hancock committee to propose radical industrial relations reform, identified three key problems with the Conciliation and Arbitration Commission's handling of wage fixation in Australia:

> They are the problem of how to adjust relative wages between, say, truck drivers and tool makers in a situation where there develops a shortage of tool makers and surplus of truck drivers. There is further the question of equal pay for equal work; why cannot a toolmaker be paid more when he is employed in an efficient and expanding firm than when he is employed in a loss-making and declining enterprise? And finally, there is the problem of what to do when an expanding firm makes over-award payments and the Commission is urged to see this as increased "capacity of the industry to pay" and promptly "flows it on" into its award structure.[71]

Centralised wage fixation made no allowance for the enormous variety of circumstances in different enterprises and industries. The H.R. Nicholls

Society argued that this and many other economic problems could be solved by allowing the market to determine wages.

The Labor Party tried to deal with some of these issues with the Prices and Incomes Accord, agreed between the ALP and ACTU in February 1983, just prior to Bob Hawke's election victory. In an attempt to rein in inflation and promote employment and economic growth, the unions agreed to wage restraint in return for a "social wage", such as improvements in health, education and welfare. However, the H.R. Nicholls Society saw this as simply more unnecessary government intervention, as well as setting a dangerous precedent in allowing the union movement to become a "partner in government."[72] Gutman argued that an unintended consequence of the Accord was to consign the Conciliation and Arbitration Commission to irrelevance. "Since the Accord," he said, "the Commission's main role in wage fixing has been that of rubber-stamping agreements reached between the Government and the unions."[73]

The H.R. Nicholls Society's third target – trade unions – was made patently clear when Hugh Morgan devoted his opening address to "the origin, the nature, the purpose, of trade union power."[74] For anyone associated with the labour movement, his conclusions were not pretty:

> The fundamental nature of trade unionism, its subversive challenge to the authority of the State, its jealous dislike and hostility of the family, is increasingly recognised and intuitively understood by more and more Australians ... Trade union power in Australia, and in Britain, is based on a residue of legal privilege. It is that legal privilege which has to be whittled away.[75]

For the H.R. Nicholls Society, this legal privilege had its origins in the *Conciliation and Arbitration Act*, which gave the government the power to "refuse to register any association as an organization if an organization, to which the members of the association might conveniently belong, has already been registered in the State in which the application is made."[76] Thus, those trade unions already established were given legal privilege over any other type of organisation that might like to represent workers. In the view of the Society, this made belonging to a trade union "practically compulsory,"[77] and it explained Australia's high rate of trade union membership. "We will only find out whether trade unions are important social institutions, capable of attracting allegiance and loyalty, when the monopoly privileges they enjoy, bestowed by the State, are withdrawn by the State," said Evans.[78]

Though in an ideal world the H.R. Nicholls Society would probably have liked to see trade unions disappear altogether, they were forced to accept the more pragmatic reality that unions would continue to play a role in the political and industrial landscape. They therefore tasked themselves with discussing possibilities for trade union *reform*, a subject to which the second conference, held in December 1986, was devoted in its entirety.

This theme has been returned to repeatedly throughout the Society's lifetime. Reflecting on it in 2006, John Stone was eager to claim a moral dimension for the unyielding campaign against trade unions.

> I want to emphasise that, from the outset, the Society was not solely aimed at reforming the labour market to increase productivity and raise average real incomes. It was also motivated – although this was never acknowledged by our adversaries – by a strong sense of moral outrage about the effects of trade union power, operating through the arbitral tribunals, on the lives of the less fortunate in our society. Equally strong was our sense of outrage over the widespread corruption, and even violent crime, to which trade union privilege had given rise.[79]

Stone's narrative of the H.R. Nicholls Society's history was an attempt to counter the impression that it was simply a union-busting front group for big business. The reform of trade unions was necessary not only because their pernicious and pervasive influence damaged the economy; it also gave license to criminal behaviour that would not otherwise be tolerated. As Stone and Evans had learned from Bert Kelly with regard to protectionism, such reform was a force for social and moral good, aside from its economic benefits.

The conference model

As Peter Costello told *The Bulletin* in 1986, forming the H.R. Nicholls Society was "a provocative act."[80] Extremely dissatisfied with the Australian industrial relations debate, these men set out to change public opinion by offering a sharp break from eighty years of conventional wisdom. They wanted to change the thinking both of the political class – politicians, bureaucrats, business leaders and the media – and the wider public, without whose broad support reform is exceedingly difficult. Well aware that their ideas were quite radical within the Australian context, they were embarking on a long-term campaign to shift debate.

Their efforts took two main forms. First, regular conferences were held in which guest speakers were invited to put forth various observations and arguments about Australia's industrial relations system. Second, they tried to distribute their message via publication in the mainstream and business press, as well as through submissions to various government inquiries and reviews.

One of the first questions usually asked about think tanks and advocacy groups is where their funding comes from. But a key difference between these single-issue advocacy groups and the more established think tanks is that they are inexpensive to run. The H.R Nicholls Society has always been run by volunteers, and the limited funds required are raised through annual membership fees. Initially, the cost of an annual subscription was $30. It has risen gradually over the years and at the time of writing is $85. Occasional dinners featuring guest speakers allow the organisation to raise additional funds. Those wanting to attend conferences pay their own way, which covers venue hire and associated costs, but the events barely break even. Ray Evans said in 2012 that the balance sheet of the H.R. Nicholls Society was around four to five thousand dollars, a miniscule amount compared to the multi-million-dollar budgets of organisations such as the IPA and CIS.[81]

The H.R. Nicholls Society has held conferences almost every year since 1986, including biannual conferences in most years up until 1994. Following the model set by the inaugural seminar, conferences are usually held over a weekend, with a Friday evening dinner and opening address followed by a number of papers and discussions on Saturday and Sunday. As we will see in the following chapters, the Samuel Griffith Society and Bennelong Society would also adopt this conference model.

Until his retirement as president in 2010, conferences were organised by Ray Evans, who also came up with the titles and themes. When I interviewed him in 2012, Evans was eager to stress not only the political and intellectual significance of the conferences but also the way in which they encouraged social networking:

> You form social attachments; it becomes a weekend to look forward to. It helps people form networks that otherwise wouldn't happen. It's a very important part, I think, of political life in Australia, which is outside formal membership of a political party, but which enables people who have similar views or similar concerns to get together and realise, "I'm not totally isolated." I still remember that first H.R. Nicholls conference. There were only thirty-five or forty people there, but it did have this revivalist thing about it. So in political life, as in warfare, morale is everything.[82]

But beyond the social aspect, the conferences were a serious attempt to influence political debate. Participants were typically a mix of business leaders, lawyers, academics, economists, employer advocates and consultants, think-tank researchers (often from the IPA or CIS), journalists, politicians and even the occasional trade unionist.

Inviting politicians to participate in conferences was the most direct way the H.R. Nicholls Society could influence their views on industrial relations. Obviously Labor politicians were less inclined to attend, though finance minister Peter Walsh did give a paper in 1987 that robustly defended the Hawke government against criticisms from neoliberals. Following his retirement from politics, Walsh, who was a noted contrarian in the Labor Party, continued his association with Evans through the Lavoisier Group, as we shall see in Chapter 6.

Far more important than trying to convert the enemy were efforts to lobby Liberal MPs, who were struggling to come up with a coherent industrial relations policy in Opposition. Fred Chaney, then shadow industrial relations minister and a known moderate, agreed to give a paper at the

1987 conference, but was unable to attend due to election commitments. His paper was delivered by his more hardline colleague, Neil Brown, and Evans noted that despite the paper having officially been Chaney's, Brown's advocacy was evident and appropriate for the conference.[83] Chaney then delivered a follow-up paper in 1988, but the Society made its dissatisfaction with him plain by republishing in the conference proceedings a newspaper column strongly critical of his remarks. Peter Reith addressed the 1989 conference during his first period in charge of industrial relations, marking the beginning of a hot and cold relationship with the Society. The guest of honour at the 1990 conference was John Howard, who had lost the leadership of the Liberal Party a year earlier. His awkwardness from the 1986 launch was replaced by effusive praise for the organisation's "major contribution to the industrial relations debate."[84]

When the Coalition won government in 1996 after thirteen years in the political wilderness, the H.R. Nicholls Society continued to use its conferences to critique the government and urge further workplace reform. This did not prevent Liberal politicians, including ministers Peter Reith, Tony Abbott and Nick Minchin, from becoming regular guests at these conferences. Eric Abetz, who served as employment minister during Abbott's brief prime ministership (2013–2015), first addressed the H.R. Nicholls Society in 1992, prior to entering federal politics, then returned in 2010 and 2011 as the shadow minister for workplace relations.

Since 2001 conferences have included the presentation of the Charles Copeman Medal. Named after the hero of Robe River, the medal is awarded to those considered to have, like Copeman, promoted the cause of freedom in the labour market. Peter Costello returned to the H.R. Nicholls fold in 2001 to present the inaugural medal to Barry and Moera Hammonds, owners of a Queensland shearing run who had challenged the dominance of the Australian Workers' Union in the shearing industry. In 2002 Peter Reith was honoured for his role in the waterfront dispute, just five years after he had been savaged for his timid industrial relations reforms. Paul Houlihan, former industrial director of the NFF and founding member of the H.R. Nicholls Society, won the award in 2007 for his pivotal role in the Mudginberri dispute in the 1980s. Upon his retirement in 2010, Ray Evans was awarded a Copeman for his long service to the Society. A year later it went to John Lloyd, who was appointed as the Australian Building and

Construction Commissioner by the Howard government, and given extraordinary powers to investigate union activity, especially that of the militant Construction, Forestry, Mining and Energy Union. Lloyd was later a controversial Coalition appointment as Public Service Commissioner, a position from which he resigned in June 2018 following revelations of his inappropriate correspondence with the IPA while in office.

As we have seen, the proceedings of the inaugural seminar were published and released to great fanfare in September 1986. This publication was such a success that a second print run was ordered in 1992. In the meantime, the organisation published the proceedings of each subsequent conference, albeit in a less impressive A4-sized softcover format. These publications were sent free of charge to financial members and made available for sale to others. This ceased in 1997 after eighteen volumes had been published, and since then conference proceedings have only been published online. All conferences up to and including 2012 are now archived and available for free on the H.R. Nicholls Society's website. The website was set up in the 1990s but until recently was really only a digital storage space for papers, articles and speeches. Younger members have since encouraged the use of social media such as Facebook, Twitter and YouTube. The website was revamped in 2013 and 2018, but updates have been inconsistent throughout this period.

Aside from periodic bouts of publicity generated by their conferences, members of the H.R. Nicholls Society tried to keep the industrial relations debate alive by writing regular opinion pieces and letters to the editor in the daily newspapers. From the beginning this was a deliberate strategy to influence politicians, as revealed in Peter Costello's remarks in 1986:

> Basically, we come up with ideas. The Liberals and others say, "Oh no, this is too radical for us. We have to get re-elected." So we put them out into the public debate, writing articles and so on and the newspapers publish them and gradually people begin to talk about the ideas. Then the Liberals suddenly say, "This sounds like a good idea. Who can we get to help us on this?" And the natural choice is one of us, because we've already been talking about the same thing. Sometimes the idea has lost a few bits and pieces on the way, so you write more articles and wait to see if it comes around in the public debate again.[85]

Though they have often bemoaned the hostility with which the media greeted their ideas, leading members of the Society such as Morgan, Evans, Stone and later Des Moore became go-to figures whenever the media sought comment on industrial relations issues. All four have been regular writers in the major daily newspapers over the past three decades. Their inflammatory rhetoric was doubtlessly a major selling point when it came to convincing editors to publish their columns. When I asked Evans whether his organisations have cultivated deliberate media strategies, he emphasised the importance of coming up with ideas first, after which media attention would naturally follow. "Getting people into the media is easy," he said, "provided you've got something to say about something that matters to people."[86]

Speaking in 2012, inveterate letter-writer Moore lamented the "tragedy" that, because "*The Age* swung so far to the left," his letters are no longer published in its pages.[87] He is still regularly published in *The Australian* and the *Australian Financial Review*, however, and Moore was eager to point out the importance of those papers, despite their relatively small circulation numbers. For him it is a simple equation: they are read by politicians, therefore they are important. And so, he continues to write to both papers whenever their articles pique his interest, hoping to seize the attention of politicians.

Another method of advocacy for the H.R. Nicholls Society was to make submissions to government inquiries and reviews. The organisation made written submissions to the Royal Commission into the Building and Construction Industry (2002), the House of Representatives Committee on Paving the Way to Paid Work (2003), the Fair Pay Commission's annual review of the minimum wage (2006), the Productivity Commission inquiry into Executive Remuneration (2009) and the Fair Work Act Review (2012). Given that such inquiries and reviews usually attract very large numbers of submissions from a diverse range of interests, it is difficult to believe that the Society was able to exert a huge amount of influence through such methods.

The waterfront: "Australia's most scandalous industry"

Though Prime Minister Paul Keating made some positive moves away from centralised wage fixation and towards enterprise bargaining in 1993, the H.R. Nicholls Society was never likely to be satisfied with the reforms of a Labor government. When the Coalition returned to power in 1996 they were hopeful that John Howard and Peter Reith would act decisively, especially when Paul Houlihan was appointed to the government's taskforce to help draft new industrial relations laws.[88] In introducing the government's legislation, Reith echoed the sentiments of the H.R. Nicholls Society: "The bill I introduce today represents a break with a system of industrial relations that has been based on a view that conflict between employer and employee is fundamental to the relationship and that an adversarial process of resolving disputes is appropriate to the relationship and inevitable."[89]

But the *Workplace Relations Act*, passed after extensive negotiations with the Australian Democrats, proved to be a huge disappointment to the Society. In January 1997 Evans wrote a letter to H.R Nicholls members in which he denounced the government in menacing terms: "Having achieved office, the Government put on the clothes of pragmatism and collaborated with the enemies of labour market freedom and full employment to produce an act which was falsely touted as a solution to these problems. This is an example of political betrayal which will be long remembered."[90] The letter was leaked to the press for maximum impact, and Reith suspected the involvement of his leadership rival Costello, a view he maintained in his memoirs. Though reluctant to criticise someone he admired in Evans, he felt that "on this occasion, the society was used by Costello for his own ends."[91]

The Society would not let up, however. The letter was followed in August by *Mission Abandoned*, a 10,000-word pamphlet that detailed the Society's objections to the Howard government's employment policies. Though Reith seemed unfazed by the criticisms, developments on the waterfront offered an opportunity to show that the government was serious about workplace reform.

Industrial relations reform on the waterfront had long been a concern of Australian employers and governments, and the twentieth century was replete with tense and sometimes violent confrontations on the docks. The militant maritime and stevedoring trade unions, such as the Seamen's Union of Australia and Waterside Workers' Federation (WWF) – amalgamated in 1993 to form the Maritime Union of Australia (MUA) – were widely viewed as having a stranglehold on the docks. According to Braham Dabscheck: "'Smashing the MUA' represented the end product of an ideological position which had been germinating in the minds of the opponents of Australian unionism for over a decade. Taking on and destroying the MUA, arguably one of Australia's strongest and most successful unions, would have constituted a fundamental, if not irrepairable [sic], blow to Australian unionism."[92]

Nowhere was this view held more strongly than among members of the H.R. Nicholls Society. Poor productivity standards in what Evans called "Australia's most scandalous industry" were seen as damaging to the nation's international competitiveness.[93] Economic consultant David Trebeck first outlined some bold ideas for waterfront reform to the Society in 1988. "A group of strongly motivated individuals, companies and/or organisations," he declared, "backed by a more contestable market environment and, where necessary, access to civil remedies under common law, can provide the strength and cohesion necessary to break the union power which currently exists."[94] He was supported the following year by Houlihan, who also argued for a radical approach to waterfront reform: "There is no escape from this imperative – the power of the WWF has to be broken."[95]

Trebeck and Houlihan would go on to become pivotal figures in the Howard government's attempts to challenge the power of the MUA. In June 1996 they won a government tender "to undertake a secret and comprehensive study of the waterfront industry and to develop options for tackling it."[96] In an attempt to break the MUA's monopoly on employment, Trebeck and Houlihan suggested that the government could be a catalyst by engineering a dispute, and then using the *Workplace Relations Act* and the *Trade Practices Act* to limit the union's possibilities for legal strike action. Details remained secret until a leak to Pamela Williams led to a front-page story in the *Australian Financial Review* in August 1997.[97]

ACTU secretary Bill Kelty responded by promising "the biggest picket that's ever been assembled in the history of this country" if the government dared to take on the MUA.[98]

In the meantime one of the two major stevedoring firms, Patrick Stevedores, was in secret consultation with the government and the NFF. A plan was hatched for the NFF – "whose antipathy to the wharfies was as Australian as Vegemite"[99] – to set up its own stevedoring operation and employ non-unionised labour. In response, Patrick would sack its workforce, arguing that it couldn't compete with the NFF's cheaper labour. This provocative act would cause the MUA to strike, and the resultant legal action would cripple the union financially. After details were leaked in late 1997 about an ultimately unsuccessful plan to train ex-soldiers in Dubai as a replacement workforce, Patrick and the MUA spent the first few months of 1998 in what Patrick boss Chris Corrigan referred to as a "game of chicken."[100] When MUA workers were evicted from Webb Dock in Melbourne and replaced by non-union NFF staff, the MUA responded by establishing picket lines on the docks. Finally, at 11 pm on 7 April, amid dramatic scenes complete with security guards in balaclavas and snarling dogs, Patrick sacked its entire workforce of 1400 people.

The following months saw a high-stakes legal battle in the courts, and a public relations battle on the docks and in the media. Eventually the MUA prevailed and its members returned to work, but only after making concessions that led to productivity gains on the waterfront. Thus, the outcome was bittersweet for the hardliners of the H.R. Nicholls Society. Houlihan was at first adamant that they had been comprehensively defeated, but by December 1998 he was concluding that the MUA won the battle but lost the war.[101] Though their ultimate goal of breaking the MUA's closed shop ended in failure, subsequent reforms have significantly changed the culture on the waterfront, allowing businesses to become more profitable and pass on the gains to the Australian people. For the H.R. Nicholls Society, it only served to confirm that the way to deal with militant unionism was not through compromise and cowardice, but through principled, radical action.

Work Choices: "the old Soviet system of command and control"

Principled, radical action was what John Howard had in mind when he embarked on a new round of legislative reform of industrial relations in the mid-2000s. Though Howard's commitment to workplace reform was questioned in the 1980s, by the 2000s there was little doubt that his sympathies lay with the radicals. "For Howard, deregulation of the workplace was his deepest economic faith," wrote Paul Kelly. "This cast him as a political radical. The campaign against union power to achieve a more productive Australia was integral to John Howard's character."[102] For members of the H.R. Nicholls Society, the Howard government's boldness in the waterfront dispute had made up for some of the failings of the *Workplace Relations Act*, but they were by no means satisfied.

Ray Evans urged Howard to become a "truly great prime minister" by taking radical labour market reform to a double dissolution election. "Opening up the labour market to those who are presently locked out of it will, of itself, generate huge increases in prosperity," he argued, speaking at the Society's May 2003 conference. "The surest road to such an outcome is a double dissolution election, in which one of the trigger Bills is an omnibus labour market reform Bill; a Bill which will bring to a close the Higgins legacy of detailed, intrusive and debilitating regulation and control of the Australian labour market."[103] Evans continued his lobbying with a personal letter to the prime minister, but Howard, while sharing his frustration with the obstacles to radical reform, had no intention of taking the issue to a double dissolution. He remained a political pragmatist, and an election fought on one of Labor's strengths was too great a risk.

As it happened, no double dissolution was necessary. The Coalition unexpectedly won control of the Senate at the 2004 election and almost immediately began planning further industrial relations reform. Evans was determined to ensure that the opportunity to revolutionise industrial relations was not wasted, telling the *Australian Financial Review*: "It'll take a huge amount of work to make sure the ambitions of the government are based on solid, theoretical economic grounds – and that we see off the whole industry of vested interests that have been running the show for 100 years."[104] In May 2005 "Work Choices" was announced, the government's scheme to radically overhaul the industrial relations system. Protections that workers had enjoyed under existing legislation were to be stripped away, unions more heavily regulated, and the maligned Industrial Relations Commission sidelined in favour of a new Fair Pay Commission. Not surprisingly, Work Choices faced a wellspring of opposition from the trade union movement, which launched a nationwide protest campaign, but with control of both houses of parliament the government had little trouble passing the *Workplace Relations Amendment (Work Choices) Act* into law in December 2005.

Most observers expected that the H.R. Nicholls Society would be enthusiastically supportive of the legislation, but this assumption proved a mistake. Instead, the group argued that the reforms gave too much regulatory power to the government and abandoned traditional liberal commitments to freedom and flexibility. "The tragedy is that Howard's Work Choices law, with minor exceptions, supports regulation and disparages freedom," wrote Evans shortly after the bill passed the Senate.[105] Later he went even further, likening Work Choices to "the old Soviet system of command and control, where every economic decision has to go to some central authority and get ticked off."[106] Howard, though, was dismissive of such criticisms: "Evans said that we should legislate to cut the minimum wage in the name of reducing unemployment and that, as far as possible, we should throw industrial relations to the operation of the common law. He attacked the award system and the continuing role of the Industrial Relations Commission. His attitude was politically unrealistic, as no government could possibly embrace such a radical agenda."[107] Workplace deregulation may well have been Howard's deepest economic faith, but compared to members of the H.R. Nicholls Society he was a lightweight, and they had no hesitation in telling him so.

In an apparent attempt to appease the hardliners in March 2006, finance minister Nick Minchin was secretly recorded telling his "soul mates" at the Society that though the Australian public "violently disagreed" with Work Choices, "we do need to seek a mandate from the Australian people at the next election for another wave of industrial relations reform."[108] This view was quickly shot down by Howard, which undoubtedly only reinforced the Society's view of his cowardice. Howard was scathing of Minchin in his autobiography: "He had been naïve, had broken very directly with the principle of cabinet solidarity and, worst of all, had played into the hands of the Labor Party. It reinforced a Labor argument that the Coalition had secret plans to reduce protection for Australian workers."[109]

Notably, Howard made no criticism of the substance of Minchin's remarks, only of their political implications. Ever the pragmatist, Howard knew the limits of what was achievable in the industrial relations arena. His criticisms of Minchin and the H.R. Nicholls Society seem to acknowledge – albeit implicitly – that their (and his own) hardline views were detached from mainstream Australian sentiment. Eventually the Australian people were able to deliver their verdict at the 2007 election, with many observers concluding that the Coalition's defeat could largely be blamed on the ideological overreach of Work Choices.

Today

The fortunes of the H.R. Nicholls Society have ebbed and flowed across the three decades during which it has been operational. Its influence has been variously dismissed and overstated by both supporters and detractors. As we have seen, Labor figures were quick to denigrate the group when it first emerged. But in December 1989, a confidential NSW Labor Council pre-election report was leaked to the press, and it included the following alarming pronouncements: "The likely election of the Kemps, Costellos, McLachlans, Copemans etc. combined with the Stones, Howards, Hewsons etc. essentially means the H.R. Nicholls Society will be in control of industrial relations. [...] The H.R. Nicholls Society has won the intellectual and political debate and will soon have its collective hands on the levers of power."[110] The leaking of this report was viewed as an act of disloyalty to Labor, and its authors immediately faced calls that they be sacked from the party. Evans later recalled how pleased the Society was with the attention, but lamented the fact that the predictions proved incorrect when the Coalition finally won office in 1996.[111]

Peter Costello entered federal parliament at the 1990 election, ironically representing the eastern Melbourne seat that is named after H.B. Higgins. He went on to become Australia's longest-serving treasurer in the Howard government from 1996 until 2007. In an interview in his first year in that role, he suggested that the demonisation he faced as a result of his involvement in the H.R. Nicholls Society was a spur to go into politics. "Doing all these cases in a system which I considered fundamentally corrupt and in need of great change – and then becoming the *bête noire* of the ALP and ACTU – I thought, well if that's the way you feel about it I'm going to Canberra. I'm going to fix them," he told *The Australian*.[112] According to Evans, Costello let his H.R. Nicholls Society membership lapse when the Coalition won the 1996 election so as to avoid a conflict of interest. However, Labor was still attacking Costello for his association with the Society as late as 2007. By this point he had seemingly burned his bridges with his old friends, with Stone in particular providing regular scathing assessments of Costello's record in economics and industrial relations.

Josh Bornstein, a lawyer who represented the MUA during the waterfront dispute, argued in 2000 that the Howard government's industrial relations policy was being driven by the H.R. Nicholls Society and Des Moore's Institute for Private Enterprise.[113] Just a few years later, as the Society's renewed campaign for full deregulation of the labour market got underway, an article in the *Australian Financial Review* affected surprise that the group was still in existence.[114] Following the implementation of Work Choices, the Society was again being described as an enormously influential backroom player in conservative politics. Shaun Carney described it as "the most effective political pressure group since the National Civic Council in its heyday in the 1950s and 1960s."[115] Michael Bachelard agreed, calling it "one of the most influential non-government groups in the country in the past twenty years."[116] Clearly, the perception of the extent of the H.R Nicholls Society's influence depends on the political circumstances of the time.

The failure of Work Choices was obviously a huge setback for industrial relations reformers on the hard right. But the successful passage of Labor's replacement legislation in 2009 offered an opportunity for the H.R. Nicholls Society to again prove its relevance in the industrial relations debate. The group saw Labor's *Fair Work Act* as a disastrous re-regulation of the workplace, not only scrapping Work Choices, but returning Australia to the days prior to Paul Keating's 1993 enterprise bargaining reforms. Much of the focus of recent conferences has been on the flaws of the *Fair Work Act*, but to little avail. The Liberal Party's fear of an industrial relations scare campaign was made abundantly clear when Tony Abbott kicked off his 2010 election campaign by declaring Work Choices "dead, buried and cremated," despite having defended its provisions in his book published only a year earlier.

The Society was also faced at this time with the challenge of losing the once indefatigable Ray Evans, who retired due to health problems. A dinner was held in October 2010 to honour his contribution, with tributes from Hugh Morgan, Bob Day and John Stone. Evans died in June 2014 at the age of seventy-four. He was succeeded as president by solicitor Adam Bisits, who had been on the board since 2003. Prior to his death in 2017, Bisits attempted to reinvigorate the Society, but with mixed success. In June 2011 he recruited public relations consultant Ian Hanke, a known hardliner who had advised Peter Reith during the waterfront dispute and Kevin Andrews during the Work Choices debate.[117] It was hoped that Hanke would be able to push the Opposition towards a more combative approach, but the Coalition remained wary, unwilling to risk the chance of an election victory for the sake of appeasing a minority of radicals. In 2012, Health Services Union corruption whistleblower Kathy Jackson gave the dinner address at the Society's conference, but this publicity coup later led to embarrassment, when Jackson faced serious corruption charges of her own.

The 2013 election brought renewed hope, not only because the Coalition was returned to power, but also due to the election to the Senate of H.R. Nicholls Society board member Bob Day, representing the Family First party. Day had hoped to replace the retiring Alexander Downer in the lower house in 2008, but believes Downer "pulled the ultimate swiftie" on him, and ensured he failed to win Liberal preselection. He then left the Liberal Party and joined Family First.[118] Meanwhile, though the industrial relations policy the Coalition had taken to the election was viewed as timid, the new government was seen as "potentially receptive" to the Society's agenda.[119] The most promising development came in early 2014, when Tony Abbott announced the establishment of the Royal Commission into Trade Union Governance and Corruption. But despite its intense focus on exposing corrupt elements within the union movement, the Royal Commission's final report did not manage to significantly change the terms of the debate.

There was another glimmer of hope when Malcolm Turnbull replaced Tony Abbott as prime minister in September 2015, as H.R. Nicholls Society member Kelly O'Dwyer was promoted to Cabinet. But aside from the re-establishment of the Howard-era Australian Building and Construction Commission, the Turnbull government continued to tread cautiously. Scott Morrison, who replaced Turnbull as prime minister in August 2018, has appeared a more willing combatant in the industrial relations battle. He and O'Dwyer, his industrial relations minister, seized on controversial comments by union leader John Setka to propose deregistering unions whose officials break the law.

But despite this rather conventional day-to-day political rhetoric from the Coalition, the Work Choices debate revealed an inconvenient truth for members of the H.R. Nicholls Society: though they would like deregulation of the workplace to go further, the majority of Australian voters disagree, and seem satisfied with Labor's industrial relations framework. The Society is now a lonely, marginal voice, and its poorly attended recent conferences are a far cry from what Evans described as the "revivalist" atmosphere of the early years.

Though John Howard was always sympathetic to the Society's aims, he kept the group at arms length throughout his prime ministership, keenly aware of the necessity of not appearing too radical to the voting public. Upon his retirement, Evans highlighted the importance of political debate and networking over and above any direct influence on policy: "What did we accomplish? We provided a network, a fortress complete with a magazine loaded with arguments, experiences of successful battles with trade union intimidation, and contacts where people could find help and succour. [...] What the H.R. Nicholls Society did was to raise the flag of freedom in a vital sphere in Australian life."[120] It seems fair to conclude that the Society's influence on government policy was incremental and indirect. And yet, it cannot be doubted that the H.R. Nicholls Society played an important role in transforming the debate about centralised wage fixation and arbitration, one of the pillars of the twentieth-century Australian Settlement.

4

BACK TO FIRST PRINCIPLES: THE SAMUEL GRIFFITH SOCIETY AND THE CONSTITUTION

T HE AUSTRALIAN CONSTITUTION WAS DRAFTED by delegates of the six Australian colonies at a series of Constitutional Conventions in Sydney in 1891, then in Adelaide, Sydney and Melbourne throughout 1897–1898. At this time the delegates were all British subjects, so naturally they saw the British Westminster system of responsible government as the most useful constitutional model from which to work. But they were also strongly influenced by the federalist system of the United States, in which sovereignty was divided between state and national governments.

Though the convention delegates were almost exclusively of British origin, they had also come to identify strongly with their respective colonies. As constitutional historian Geoffrey Sawer notes, most of the delegates were "State-righters." They opposed outright unification along the lines of the British system, in favour of "a federation in which there was a strong emphasis on preserving the structure and powers of the States."[1] Thus, the framers of the Australian Constitution came up with a "hybrid constitutional system," combining the two constitutional principles of responsible government and federalism.[2] The British monarchy was retained, and the colonies "agreed to unite in one indissoluble Federal Commonwealth under the Crown of the United Kingdom of Great Britain and Ireland."[3] In an influential 1980 article, political scientist Elaine Thompson referred to Australia's unique blend of both Westminster and Washington influences as "the Washminster mutation."[4]

Brian Galligan has identified three defining attributes of a federal system of government: "first, the existence of two levels of government, national and state; second, the guarantee that neither has sovereignty over the other; and third, some allocation of powers between the two."[5] Australia's founding fathers adopted three features of the US Constitution to codify this system: a Senate (sometimes known as the states' house), in which each state is represented equally regardless of population differences; constitutionally specified division of powers between the Commonwealth and states; and judicial review, whereby a court (in Australia's case the High Court) acts as a judicial umpire in disputes between the Commonwealth and states.[6]

From a federalist point of view, the two decades that followed Federation saw the High Court treating the Commonwealth and states as equal, coordinate partners. However, the High Court's judgement in the 1920 *Amalgamated Society of Engineers v Adelaide Steamship Co Ltd*, commonly known as the Engineers' case, brought radical change. This judgement is widely considered to be one of the most important in Australian history; it "has had a profound impact on the course of later decisions and has become a touchstone against which those later decisions are constantly measured."[7] At issue in the Engineers' case was the question of whether the Commonwealth had the power to legislate in industrial disputes that extended beyond the limits of one state, and for that legislation to be binding on all of the states involved. In a five-to-one majority decision, the High Court ruled that the Commonwealth did have such power, overturning a key tenet of its approach to the Constitution up until that point. For non-legal minds the case's focus on doctrines of intergovernmental immunities and reserved state powers may appear abstract and obscure, but the practical result was that the Commonwealth was increasingly permitted to move in on areas previously thought to be the sole preserve of the states. This was the significant – and for some, controversial – implication of the ruling.

Further blows to federalism came with the Uniform Tax cases of 1942 and 1957. The first case upheld four pieces of Commonwealth legislation, the obvious intentions of which were to take over the income taxing powers of the states. Though the decision did not preclude the states from raising their own income taxes, the reality was that the rate set by the Commonwealth rendered it practically impossible for the states to do so. The second case affirmed the constitutionality of the first, albeit with one minor exception. The resultant vertical fiscal imbalance, in which the states have significant financial responsibilities yet little ability to raise revenue, has left the states dependent on the Commonwealth for revenue ever since.

The strength of the Australian federal system has also been complicated by political partisanship. Since Federation, the conservative side of politics has been supportive of federalism, a position that stems from "a deep if vague understanding of the link between 'federalism' on the one hand, and notions like 'liberalism', 'conservatism' and even 'democracy' on the other."[8] That is, by balancing two levels of government, federalism serves to protect citizens from the power of a unitary state, and enhances their freedoms while maintaining order and stability. But this support has not always been as consistent as some would like. "From its very beginnings," wrote the IPA's John Roskam, "the Liberal Party's rhetorical commitment to federalism was strong. But once the party had achieved government, that commitment in practice was weak."[9] This ambivalence was captured by Robert Menzies in a 1966 speech:

> Now, I am a Federalist myself. I believe, as I am sure most of you do, that in the division of power, in the demarcation of powers between a Central Government and the State governments, there resides one of the true protections of individual freedom. And yet how true it is that as the world grows, as the world becomes more complex, as international affairs engage our attention more and more, and affect our lives more and more, it is frequently ludicrous that the National Parliament, the National Government, should be without power to do things which are really needed for the national security and advancement.[10]

Though its status as a federalist or states'-rights party has become increasingly tenuous in practice, the Liberal Party maintains its formal commitment to federalism to this day. "We believe," asserts its official platform, "in a federal system of government and the decentralisation of power, with local decisions being made at the local level."[11]

The Australian Labor Party, on the other hand, has never been shy in declaring its dissatisfaction with federalism, viewing it as an unnecessary obstruction to its social reform objectives. In a 1957 lecture provocatively titled 'The Constitution versus Labor,' Gough Whitlam, for example, outlined Labor's concerns:

> Much of the frustration, and even demoralisation, in Labor ranks in recent years flows from the fact that the Australian Labor Party, unlike the British and New Zealand Parties, is unable to perform, and therefore finds it useless to promise, its basic policies. It has been handicapped, as they were not, by a Constitution framed in such a way as to make it difficult to carry out Labor objectives and interpreted in such a way as to make it impossible to carry them out.[12]

Whitlam's view was shared by his bitter political foe, Malcolm Fraser, who in January 1975 argued that "a federalist system of government offers Liberals many protections against those elements of socialism which Liberals abhor."[13] However, for Brian Galligan, Fraser's later record in government only served to confirm that "federalism is taken for granted on the Liberal and conservative side of politics and only championed when under perceived threat from federal Labor governments."[14] Events that unfolded in the 1980s strengthened this thesis and eventually led to the formation of the Samuel Griffith Society, which, as we shall see, vowed to defend the Australian Constitution against a multitude of perceived threats.

Constitution under attack

By the late 1970s and into the 1980s, defenders of the Australian Constitution became increasingly wary of threats from the ALP. In 1979 Bob Hawke delivered the ABC's Boyer Lectures. At the time Hawke was president of the ACTU, and was widely coming to be seen as a likely future Labor prime minister. Suggesting that Australians "have come to be infatuated by an assiduously cultivated phenomenon called 'States' Rights'," Hawke's lectures were a forthright challenge to the very nature of Australia's federal system.[15] He went as far as to call for states to be abolished, arguing that they "no longer serve their original purpose and act as a positive impediment to achieving good government in our current community."[16] For John Stone, whose opposition to centralism had been building throughout the 1970s, the threat could hardly have been more explicit.

When he did eventually run as leader of the ALP in the 1983 election, one of Hawke's main election promises was to prevent Tasmania's Hydro-Electric Commission from building the Gordon-below-Franklin Dam, which environmentalists argued would destroy much of south-west Tasmania's pristine wilderness. Upon winning the election, Hawke immediately set about honouring this promise by enacting legislation prohibiting construction of the dam. The Tasmanian government, believing that this was a state matter in which the Commonwealth had no power to intervene, ordered work to continue. The Commonwealth then took the matter to the High Court in what became known as the Tasmanian Dam case. In a controversial judgement, the Court ruled in favour of the Commonwealth on the grounds that the site had been included on UNESCO's World Heritage List, and therefore fell under the Commonwealth's external affairs power, which covers international treaties. This particular course of action had actually been recommended by Gough Whitlam in the 1957 lecture cited above. "A Labor government," he asserted, "should make more use of the external affairs power to extend its legislative competence, in particular by implementing conventions and treaties, such as those made through the International Labour Organization and the World Health Organization. [...] There would seem good ground for believing that the High Court would not be prone to invalidate Commonwealth legislation in such fields."[17]

Needless to say, federalists – both inside and outside the Liberal–National Coalition – were appalled. Here was what seemed like collusion between the Labor Party and the High Court to manipulate the meaning of the Constitution to achieve transparently political ends. Nevertheless, the environmentalists had won and there was seemingly nothing that appeals to the federalist principles of the Constitution could do about it. Paul Kelly argued that this should have been a wake-up call for conservatives to unshackle themselves from the "dead weight" of federalism: "The Coalition fell victim to its states rights philosophy at a time when public opinion was behind the use of Commonwealth powers to protect the environment in the national interest."[18] Misuse of the external affairs power would later become one of the most persistent topics of discussion (and irritation) at Samuel Griffith Society conferences.

The putative attacks on the Constitution continued. In 1985 attorney-general Lionel Bowen announced the Constitutional Commission, a panel of eminent lawyers, hand-picked and provided with the following terms of reference:

> To inquire into and report, on or before 30 June 1988, on the revision of the Australian Constitution to:
> a. adequately reflect Australia's status as an independent nation and a Federal Parliamentary democracy;
> b. provide the most suitable framework for the economic, social and political development of Australia as a federation;
> c. recognise an appropriate division of responsibilities between the Commonwealth, the States, self-governing Territories and local government;
> d. ensure that democratic rights are guaranteed.[19]

Though these guidelines seemed to indicate that Labor was reconciled with federalism, constitutional conservatives remained on guard. In his maiden speech in the Senate in September 1987, John Stone warned that "few things will divide us more, and more savagely, in our bicentennial year than any action on any proposals coming forward from that Commission which seem likely to undermine the established Constitution of Australia."[20]

The Commission produced a 1200-page report with thirty pages of recommendations for constitutional reform, although most were largely speculative, with no realistic prospect of enactment. The government did, however, take some specific amendments to the people in four simultaneous referendums in September 1988. The proposals – to provide for four-year parliamentary terms; to provide for fair and democratic elections throughout Australia; to recognise local government; and to extend certain rights and freedoms – were chosen by the attorney-general for their reasonable prospects of success.[21] However, all four proposals were defeated by huge margins, with the highest national Yes vote only reaching a miserable 37.6 per cent. Even taking into account Australians' broad historical wariness of constitutional change (just eight of thirty-eight Australian referendum proposals had been passed), this was a dismal result which, for constitutional conservatives, only served to confirm that political elites were out of touch with the people. According to Stone, this comprehensive rejection did not deter the Labor Party, but forced it to shift to a "softly, softly process to achieve its ends."[22]

Over four days in April 1991 a Constitutional Centenary Conference was held in Sydney to commemorate the one hundredth anniversary of the National Australasian Convention of 1891, which created the first draft of the Australian Constitution. The Centenary Conference was presided over by Sir Ninian Stephen, former Justice of the High Court and governor-general, and convened by law professors Cheryl Saunders and James Crawford. The gathering saw academics, public servants, lawyers, politicians, journalists, businessmen and various others set out to "identify the constitutional issues that needed attention in Australia at the beginning of the decade leading up to the constitutional centenary in 2001."[23] By the conclusion of the conference the attendees had resolved to establish a Constitutional Centenary Foundation, which would, throughout the 1990s, continue a "public process of education, review and development of the Australian constitutional system, in the interests of all Australians."[24] Twelve key issues were identified:

1. The head of state
2. Guarantees of basic rights
3. Responsible government and its alternatives
4. The effectiveness of parliaments
5. Four-year terms for the House of Representatives
6. Accountability for taxing and spending
7. Voter or state initiative for referenda
8. Federalism and economic union
9. Legislative powers
10. The Aboriginal and Torres Strait Islander peoples and the Australian constitutional system
11. Judicial independence
12. Trial by jury[25]

Though the convenors of the Centenary Conference sought to avoid any perceptions of political partisanship, Stone remained unconvinced. The following week he used his column in the *Australian Financial Review* to attack the conference and its organisers. He asserted that Saunders was politically compromised by her marriage to Ian Baker, then a minister in the Victorian Labor government, and he went on to ridicule the whole enterprise, likening it to such failed 1980s projects as the Australian Bicentennial Authority and the Constitutional Commission. "Whatever public figureheads (or worse) may be appointed to this body," he wrote, "it will as usual be run by much the same bunch of centrist left-leaning lawyers who, since the previous committee of inquiry into constitutional reform disappeared into ignominy in 1988, have clearly been under-employed."[26]

Stone would later give a paper in which he elaborated on the many areas where he took issue with the Foundation. Proceeding from the hypothesis that it "bears the appearance of a constitutional termite," he interrogated how the organisation was established, how it was governed and financed, and what its leading figures – Saunders in particular – had said on constitutional matters that might draw into question their claims to impartiality. His conclusion was unequivocal: "It is a body brought into being with a purpose – to gnaw away at our constitutional foundations in the hope that, one day, the structure erected nearly 100 years ago will crumble away and a new construct, more centralist, more unicameral, and of course republican, can be put in its place."[27] Saunders remained unperturbed, continuing to lead the Foundation until its scheduled disbanding in December 2000. In a 2007 paper she downplayed Stone's position as merely that of a noisy minority, whose "sustained suspicion ... gives warning that impartiality is likely always to be a contested claim from some perspective."[28]

Discord prompts action

One interested reader of Stone's work was the young legal academic Greg Craven. Craven studied arts and law at the University of Melbourne before completing a Master of Laws in 1984. Since then he has enjoyed a successful career as a legal academic, holding positions at the University of Melbourne, the University of Notre Dame and Curtin University before his appointment as the Vice-Chancellor of Australian Catholic University in 2008. Craven has published widely in the field of constitutional law and has been a regular newspaper columnist for many years. Outspoken and independent, his career has not been without controversy, especially during his tenure as Crown Counsel to the Victorian attorney-general in the 1990s. This was seen as a "unique appointment, which straddles the role of ministerial adviser and senior public servant," and Craven was widely regarded as being at the forefront of the Kennett government's attempts to shake up the legal profession.[29]

Craven considered himself to be a constitutional conservative, so it was with some disappointment that he read Stone's attack on Cheryl Saunders in April 1991. While sympathetic to Stone's constitutional views, Craven was unimpressed with the ferocity of his attack on Saunders, who was not only a colleague at the time, but had also supervised his masters thesis in the early 1980s. As luck would have it, members of the H.R. Nicholls Society – including, of course, Stone – were due to meet in Melbourne for their tenth conference that very weekend, and one of the scheduled speakers was none other than Greg Craven. A committed federalist, Craven delivered a paper on 'Constitutional and other constraints on state governments seeking labour market reform,' in which he was extremely critical of the High Court's interpretation of the Constitution, resulting in increasing centralisation of power in Canberra: "Since the Engineers Case the general thrust of the Court's interpretation has been powered by an entirely non-legal agenda and that non-legal agenda has been the desire to expand the power of the Commonwealth, to expand the legislative competence of the Commonwealth, at the expense of the States. That is perhaps not a political agenda but an institutional political agenda."[30] This was music to the ears of members of the H.R. Nicholls Society, who, as we saw in Chapter 3, had been railing against the centralised nature of Australian industrial relations since 1986.

Craven was not only interested in arguing about the centralisation of power and the High Court, however. With Stone sitting in the front row of the audience, Craven took the opportunity to return fire on behalf of Saunders. Though the published proceedings suggest a quite polite and civilised exchange, Craven has since recalled that the live debate was much more robust. "What actually happened was, when I gave the speech – and I don't know if it's in the version of the speech published in the H.R. Nicholls proceedings – I actually had a go back at John, who I didn't know," he told me in an interview in 2015. "I said look, basically the constitutional right in Australia has always been good at attacking positions, it's never been good at putting forward any sort of cohesive constitutional philosophy."[31] Craven had lain down a provocation. Conservatives may disagree with the views of the Constitutional Centenary Foundation, but what were they going to do about it? Instead of just criticising, asked Craven, "why aren't you making that type of constitutional contribution?" His was a plea for a more organised constitutional conservatism, which he regarded as "perennially inherently disorganised," and therefore unable to effectively argue its case.[32]

To Craven's great surprise, given the forcefulness of his comments, Stone responded in the discussion period by essentially agreeing with him. Stone's remarks are published in the conference proceedings and are worth quoting at length:

> I happen to agree almost totally with everything that was said, and I urge Mr Craven in the light of that to do what some people in this room did five years ago, namely to promote a genuine debate on federalism. After all, some people in this room started a genuine debate upon the industrial relations situation in this country, the disgraceful situation which obtained in industrial relations. I would agree wholeheartedly with everything that Mr Craven said toward the end of his remarks, that federalism was probably the wave of the future and the reasons he gave for it.
>
> I suggest to him that he should consider forming a Parkes Society to promote the cause of federalism – a society for the promotion of federalism. I am sure you would get a lot of members from this room. That's a serious suggestion. I think that needs to be done and it is a society which needs to be totally divorced from governments, attorneys-general, and other people who are involved in manipulative processes and public funding.[33]

Having expected the famously combative Stone to launch into a tirade, Craven was pleasantly surprised by this constructive response. It was promptly agreed that they should begin planning a new organisation – modelled, as Stone suggested, along similar lines to the H.R. Nicholls Society, but focused on federalism and the Constitution. Such were the birth pangs of what was to become the Samuel Griffith Society.

So, throughout 1991, a number of lunch meetings were held in which the direction of the proposed organisation was discussed. Ray Evans, who by this point had taken over from Stone as president of the H.R Nicholls Society, was enlisted to help with organisational matters. Craven was not particularly interested in that side of things, seeing himself as more of a consultant: "an expert constitutional lawyer and a critical friend" who could provide advice about which topics most urgently needed to be discussed. He was particularly keen to avoid the kind of narrow, antagonistic approach that had seen the H.R. Nicholls Society characterised as dangerous radicals. In our interview about these developments, he recalled telling his fellow organisers that "if you're going to be a conservative constitutional voice you're going to have your greatest effect as a *mainstream* conservative constitutional voice. [...] You should be hitting on the things that really, really matter rather than particular hobby horses that are never going to go anywhere."[34] The extent to which this has remained the case throughout the Samuel Griffith Society's existence is debatable, as we shall see. But, at the outset, it was agreed that the focus of the group should be on the central, defining issue: "the expansion of Commonwealth power by the High Court and the general issue of federalism in all its various emanations: financial, judicial, parliamentary and so on."[35]

Sir Samuel Griffith: federalist icon

John Stone's initial "top-of-the-head thought" had been to form a federalist Parkes Society in honour of Sir Henry Parkes, commonly known as the father of Federation. However, at the first planning meeting Ray Evans suggested that Sir Samuel Griffith, "in his role as (arguably) the principal draftsman of the Constitution, and because of his subsequent role as the first Chief Justice of the High Court, would be a preferable choice." There was no disagreement.[36] The Society's original statement of purposes made plain its admiration for the distinguished politician and jurist, noting especially that "he consistently supported the rights of States against the powers of the Federal Government."[37]

Born in Wales in 1845, Samuel Griffith migrated to Australia with his family at the age of eight, where they eventually settled in Brisbane. A brilliant student, he had completed an arts degree at the University of Sydney by the time he was eighteen, before returning to Queensland to study law. In 1867 the Supreme Court of Queensland admitted him as a barrister. He entered the Queensland Legislative Assembly in 1872, serving in various ministries before becoming premier in 1883. Griffith held that role until 1888, and again from 1890 to 1893, at which point he happily retired from politics and was appointed Chief Justice of Queensland's Supreme Court. Having contributed significantly to the Federation movement throughout the 1890s, he became the inaugural Chief Justice of the High Court of Australia in 1903. (Incidentally, he was the author of the 1911 High Court judgement acquitting H.R. Nicholls of the contempt of court charge described in the previous chapter). Griffith suffered a stroke in 1917, which greatly reduced his ability to hear cases. He finally retired from the bench in 1919 and died the following year.

Known as a radical liberal reformer for much of his political career, Griffith in the 1880s even "displayed some sympathy with the emerging labour movement."[38] In 1886 he introduced a bill legalising trade unions, and his 1888 election manifesto included the declaration that: "the great problem of this age is not how to accumulate wealth but how to secure its more equitable distribution."[39] These were certainly not words to impress the H.R. Nicholls Society one hundred years later. But any reputation Griffith was developing as a friend of the working man was not to last. His views hardened during the bitter shearers' strike of 1891, in which, as premier, he dispatched the military to end the industrial dispute and oversaw the trial and imprisonment of twelve strikers on conspiracy charges.[40] His general view from then on was that employers and employees should never see each other as enemies, but rather as partners in a mutually beneficial relationship, a line that would later be loudly echoed by the H.R. Nicholls Society.

For the venerators of the Constitution now forming a new organisation in Griffith's name, it was his constitutional views that were held in the highest esteem. As Chief Justice of the High Court, Griffith fought for the federalist principles that were fundamental to the Constitution, against the more centralist tendencies of Justices Sir Isaac Isaacs and H.B. Higgins, both of whom were appointed to an expanded bench in 1906. Griffith held firm against extensions of Commonwealth power until his retirement, but just weeks after his death came the decision in the Engineers' case, "reversing a central part of the work of his chief justiceship."[41] This pivotal turning point in Australia's constitutional history has been lamented by federalists ever since.

Sir Harry Gibbs: esteemed president

Having formed largely as a reaction to the Constitutional Centenary Foundation, which was led by the highly regarded Sir Ninian Stephen, the founders of the Samuel Griffith Society sought a leader of similar stature for their own organisation. Ruling himself out due to a lack of legal qualifications, Stone proposed Sir Harry Gibbs, who had not long retired as Chief Justice of the High Court and was as federalist as they come, "a bulwark for States' rights", in the words of his biographer Joan Priest.[42]

Born in Queensland in 1917, Gibbs enjoyed a stellar legal career before joining the High Court in 1970. Upon Sir Garfield Barwick's retirement from the bench in 1981, Gibbs was appointed Chief Justice, and hailed as "Sir Harry the Healer" following Barwick's controversial tenure.[43] Gibbs served in that position until 1987, when he was forced to retire due to a 1977 constitutional amendment that required federal judges to retire at the age of seventy. Conveniently, Gibbs was a great admirer of his fellow Queenslander Samuel Griffith, whose portrait took pride of place in his chambers.[44]

Most importantly for the Society's purposes, Gibbs was a devout federalist. He dissented from the majority judgement in the Tasmanian Dam case in 1983, and later said that the use of the Constitution's external affairs power in that judgement "threatens the very basis of federalism."[45] On the question of Commonwealth versus state powers, Gibbs was unequivocal: "My view of the appropriate division of power in a federal system can be summed up in one sentence: nothing should be done by the Commonwealth that could be done equally well by the individual States themselves."[46]

Gibbs was initially cautious about involving himself with the Samuel Griffith Society, and suggested some changes to the draft statement of purposes that Stone had sent him before ultimately agreeing to become the inaugural president. He was joined on the board by Stone, Evans, Hugh Morgan, mining executive Sir Bruce Watson, and Nancy Stone, a retired research biochemist and wife of John. The bulk of the administrative work of the Society for the next two decades would be carried out by the Stones.[47]

Far from being a mere figurehead, Gibbs was also an enthusiastic participant in the activities of the Society: meticulously chairing board meetings, delivering conference papers and closing remarks, and each year composing an Australia Day message to be sent to members. In 2003, at the last Samuel Griffith Society conference he was to attend, the Society made a special presentation to Gibbs "as a testament to the respect and affection in which he and Lady Gibbs are held, not only by the Board but by our membership in general."[48] Following his death in 2005, the board resolved that they would establish a lecture in his honour, the Sir Harry Gibbs Memorial Oration, as well as devote part of the 2006 conference to an appreciation of his life and work from various perspectives. "Sir Harry Gibbs was one of the finest men it has ever been my privilege to come to know," Stone told me. "The Society will be forever in his debt."[49]

Inaugural conference

In May 1992 John Stone sent letters to about 900 people, inviting them to attend the inaugural conference of the Samuel Griffith Society in July, as well as encouraging them to apply for membership.[50] In addition to his own personal and professional acquaintances, Stone sent the letter to members of the IPA, where he was a senior fellow at the time.[51] The conference commenced with a dinner and speeches on Friday, 24 July 1992. The launching address was to be given by Gibbs, but he had to fly to London for the hanging of his heraldic banner as a Knight Grand Cross of the Order of St Michael and St George, and so his speech was delivered on his behalf by David Russell, a lawyer and prominent Queensland National Party figure.[52] A day and a half of papers and discussion followed over the weekend, divided into six constitutionally themed sessions with the following titles: 'Nine Decades of Achievement,' 'the Demands for Change,' 'the Slide into Centralism,' 'the External Affairs Power,' 'the Head of State Debate' and 'the Aboriginal Question.' Around 120 people attended over the course of the weekend.

The Society's combative approach was signalled from the outset, with warning shots fired at its opponents, especially the Constitutional Centenary Foundation. "It has been proposed that for the rest of the century there should be a process of public education and debate in Australia for the purpose of reviewing the Constitution," wrote Gibbs. "The Samuel Griffith Society must ensure that education does not degenerate into propaganda, and that the debate is not one-sided."[53] Though his speech did not once mention the Constitutional Centenary Foundation by name, no one could be in the slightest doubt as to whom he was referring.

The conference itself didn't cause an immediate stir, but this changed only three weeks later, when Governor-General (and former Labor leader) Bill Hayden gave a speech in which he warned about the "thoroughly radical agenda" of the Samuel Griffith Society. He noted that its membership overlapped with that of the H.R. Nicholls Society, and cautioned his friends on the left against complacency:

> I recall some dismissive giggles greeting the formation of that body in circles in which I once moved. "Political troglodytes and economic lunatics," one such said. It does seem, however, that there has been a most extraordinary range of radical reforms in the field of industrial relations since then, and the H.R. Nicholls Society cannot be left out of account when assessing major influences creating the environment which accommodated this change. For those reasons, I would suggest that it would be wrong to treat the formation of the Samuel Griffith Society in any other way than with serious attention.[54]

The Society had aroused an official response, but ironically, Hayden would eventually become more of a friend than foe when he joined the board of *Quadrant* in 1998 and then sided with the No campaign during the 1999 republic referendum.

Asked to respond to Hayden's remarks, Stone welcomed the opportunity for some free publicity. He argued that the Society's formation represented a groundswell of public opposition to centralisation of power in Canberra. "Little individual people ... feel helpless because they say: 'Oh, what can I do?'" he told *The Age*. "There is a growing feeling in the community for this sort of movement. Time and again, people come up and say: 'This is dreadful, why is Canberra doing this? What's it got to do with Canberra?'"[55] In a separate interview, he played down the links Hayden had made between the two organisations, stating that of more than 400 members of the new group, "just sixty are members of the H.R. Nicholls Society."[56] Journalist Geoffrey Barker accused both of paranoia and an exaggeration of their opponents' influence, arguing instead that in pluralistic Australia there are "a multitude of groups clamouring to be heard on constitutional issues, [which is] a thoroughly good thing."[57]

Following the example of its sister organisation, the first Samuel Griffith Society conference was followed some months later by the official launch of the publication of its proceedings, titled *Upholding the Australian Constitution*. Two dinners were held in November 1992, the first in Melbourne with Harry Gibbs and NSW Supreme Court Justice Roderick Meagher as speakers. Meagher's address drew front-page media attention for its "vigorous, even extraordinary, attack on certain fellow judges and other advocates of change in Australian society."[58] Chief among his targets were Justice Gerard Brennan, lead author of the High Court's Mabo judgement (of which more later), and various members of the "chattering classes," such as authors Patrick White, Manning Clark, Thomas Keneally and Donald Horne, whose principal crime seemed to be their support for an Australian republic.[59] The second launch was held in Perth a week later, with former Liberal minister and Governor-General Sir Paul Hasluck scheduled to speak. However, illness forced him to cancel and his son delivered the address on his behalf. Hasluck – who was also to become a hero to members of the Bennelong Society, as we will see in Chapter 5 – died shortly afterwards, so this turned out to be his final public statement.

Upholding the Constitution

In contrast with the brief self-descriptions developed by the other three main hard right organisations examined in this book, the Samuel Griffith Society's statement of purposes is a rather detailed 950 words. It begins with a biographical note about Samuel Griffith, then sets forth on a long-winded preamble about the role of constitutions and parliamentary and legal institutions in "maintaining civil peace and concord, and of protecting the citizen from the arbitrary abuse of power, including executive power."[60] It then goes on to extol the virtues of Australia's political institutions, but warns of their decay. In the process, it reveals the three broad objectives of the Society: defence of the Constitution, the promotion of federalism, and a restoration of the separation between the legislative, executive and judicial powers of the Commonwealth.

Upholding the Australian Constitution is the general objective from which all other Samuel Griffith Society objectives followed, and so naturally this became the title of the group's annual publication of its conference proceedings. The Society's approach to the Constitution is set out in its statement of purposes:

> The strength of our parliamentary and legal institutions, of our political conventions and modes of behaviour is, arguably, Australia's greatest asset. The Constitution which Australians drafted and accepted in the 1890's, and which established the framework of the Australian nation as a sovereign federal state, is the keystone of this structure and has served us well. It has protected our democracy, and our liberties, by providing for independent centres of political authority and the diffusion of power which flows from that. The Australian people have voted many times against proposed amendments. We must presume that they regard the Constitution, on the whole, with approval.
>
> All institutions, nevertheless, require refurbishment and repair. There is growing concern at the decline in the prestige, standing and influence of parliament, and the growing centralisation of power and authority in the executive. There is also concern at the expansion of the power of the

Commonwealth at the expense of the States, the increasing centralisation of power in Canberra, and the consequent growth of a Commonwealth bureaucracy which, in many areas, deals with matters which were originally the sole concern of the States.[61]

The second paragraph of this excerpt clearly indicates that the group is not blindly opposed to any and all proposed changes to Australia's constitutional arrangements. If there are proposals that the group sees as having the potential to restore the original, federal intentions of the founding fathers, it is willing to consider them. But, if the proposals look to move the country even further away from these foundations, they will be given short shrift. "If any changes are to be made in our Constitution," wrote Stone, "they should only occur after the widest range of thought and opinion has been canvassed."[62] In this sense, the Society saw itself as having an educational role, stimulating discussion and hoping through its efforts to "encourage a wider understanding of Australia's Constitution and the nation's achievements under the Constitution."[63]

The Samuel Griffith Society's attitude to the Constitution would eventually set it on a collision course with the Howard government. As Paul Kelly observed, Howard's approach as prime minister was unapologetically pragmatic: "He dislikes debate about abstractions or principles of governance, from ministerial responsibility to the separation of powers, and distrusts debate on governmental models."[64] This approach was anathema to the Samuel Griffith Society.

If encouraging public discussion and respect for the Constitution was the most broad objective, and at the heart of the Society's purpose, the promotion of federalism was the issue it seized on as being of the most immediate importance and urgency. As we have seen, Stone's initial proposal in April 1991 was to form a society for the promotion of federalism, and in his launching address Gibbs asserted that "federalism is the essence of the Constitution."[65] And yet, in the Society's view, the preceding seventy years had witnessed a long march towards the complete centralisation of power in Canberra, and its job was to halt, or at the very least slow, this march. Therefore, at the top of its list of priorities was "the need to redress the federal balance in favour of the States, in view of the excessive expansion of Commonwealth power and the need to decentralise decision making."[66]

Unsurprisingly, given its questionable support for federalism – and the fact that it was in government at the time – the Labor Party became the focus of early discussions. The ALP's record in government meant it was unquestionably seen as the biggest barrier to the renewal of the federal structure. So when the Coalition took power in 1996, the Society might have been forgiven for allowing itself to breathe a sigh of relief and look to the future with some optimism. At the tenth conference in 1998, legal academic Geoffrey de Q. Walker even spoke of a "new age of federalism", with global interest in it "greater today than at any other time in human history."[67]

Members of the Society were later appalled to witness the Coalition under the prime ministership of John Howard "spitting out Australian federalism like so much constitutional gristle."[68] Across a variety of government responsibilities – health, education, industrial relations, legal matters, water, tax and finance – federalists were dismayed at Howard's willingness to ride roughshod over the interests of the states. Stone made his feelings known in no uncertain terms at the Society's 2005 conference:

> Few things have been more dismaying during the six months since last year's federal election than the swelling tide of ignorant centralism rushing out of Canberra, whether it be in the field of health, education, infrastructure, rorts for rural roads, or whatever. Even the Prime Minister has not been immune from this disease, while the immature mouthings of the Ministers for Health and Education, Messrs Abbott and Nelson, have been nothing short of appalling. A friend of mine, a person high in Liberal Party circles, recently said to me that he believed that the only member of the Cabinet who had any genuine belief in federalism was the Minister for Finance, Senator the Honourable Nick Minchin.[69]

Coincidentally, the prime minister was due to give a speech on federalism just days later. Addressing criticisms such as Stone's (though without naming him), Howard was dismissive: "These fears of a new centralism rest on a complete misunderstanding of the Government's thinking and reform direction. Where we seek a change in the federal-state balance, our goal is to expand individual choice, freedom and opportunity, not to expand the reach of the central government."[70]

But the Society remained unconvinced, and things would only get worse during the subsequent Work Choices debate, as discussed in the previous chapter. So furious was Ray Evans with Howard's approach that he called him the most centralist prime minister since Gough Whitlam.[71] He would maintain this rage for the rest of his life. Upon his retirement from the H.R. Nicholls Society, Evans declared that "until the Coalition and the conservative side of the culture wars in Australia can restore federalism as an essential element of our political life, Coalition governments will have nothing to offer the Australian people that is fundamentally different from what Labor governments have been offering during my lifetime."[72]

The third key area that the Samuel Griffith Society set out to address was the increasingly blurred lines between the legislative, executive and judicial arms of government. This issue had dual elements: judicial independence and the authority of parliament. The Society argued that the independence of the courts, particularly the High Court, had been undermined by the political influence of successive governments, and sought a delicate balancing act in which judicial independence was preserved while at the same time warding off judicial activism. As legal scholar Tanya Josev has recounted, the charge of judicial activism was imported from the United States and became a convenient term of criticism for conservatives who disapproved of what they perceived to be the liberal leanings of recent High Court decisions.[73] Barrister Ian Callinan, for one, suggested in 1994 that its recent decisions left the High Court open to the criticism that it was becoming an "over-mighty Court"[74] (a view that was not forgotten by critics when Callinan himself was appointed to the bench just four years later). The Society argued that the High Court should not be influenced by the political needs of the government of the day, but, on the other hand, should be careful not to overstep its constitutional boundaries and attempt to make law itself. Greg Craven saw these priorities as going hand in hand:

> Judicial independence necessitates the independence of the courts not only from politicians, but from politics itself. Once a court embarks on a routine course of policy formulation, it inevitably becomes part of the political process, and this by definition. It therefore makes no sense to talk of the independence of the judiciary from politicians, if the judiciary has itself chosen

to be an integral part of the very political process which defines the very concept of a politician.[75]

Members of the Society had little doubt that this process had indeed taken place, and sought to make reversing it one of their key objectives.

The Samuel Griffith Society also believed that the authority of parliament had been weakened by the dominance of the executive. In line with the Constitution, the Society emphasised "the need to re-assert the role of Parliament (including that of the Speaker and President of the Senate) vis-a-vis the Executive."[76] Its position on the role of parliament was most clearly articulated by Australia's longest-serving Chief Justice, Sir Garfield Barwick, in 1995. Seeking to return to constitutional first principles, Barwick argued that "the essence of parliamentary democracy is that the Parliament is in control of the ministry at all times and independent of it."[77] He then went on to lament the damage that the party system has done to the authority of parliament, in particular the way in which individual members are not free to speak and vote according to their own (or their electorate's) preference, but must toe the party line. The result is that the executive controls the parliament, rather than the other way around. The ever-increasing power invested in the office of the prime minister was of great concern to Barwick, an issue that Stone had earlier warned about when he hyperbolically accused Paul Keating of being "not a parliamentarian, but a dictator."[78]

An "august body"

The Samuel Griffith Society made plain from the beginning how it intended to spread its message by including in its statement of purposes a specific objective: "to arrange conferences, hold meetings, publish papers, and inform people and governments in accordance with the general objectives set out above."[79] In its aim to attract a "stable membership and funding base" the Society was very successful.[80] Writing just six weeks after the inaugural conference, John Stone reported that

470 Australians had either joined or applied to join,[81] having paid an initial fee of $20 and an annual subscription of $50 (the annual subscription now costs $75). Membership numbers have remained relatively strong despite an age demographic tipped towards seniors; the 2013 president's report advised that membership stood at 384, thirty of whom had signed up that year.[82]

Stone wanted to provide a civilised, respectful and democratic contribution to debates about the constitution. He told *The Age* in 1992 that groups such as the Samuel Griffith Society were a useful way to ward off some of the noisier – and more dangerous – elements of political debate:

> I think if people are not given a vehicle by which to express their views in a democratic matter, in accordance with the best traditions of democracy, then they tend to express their views in an undemocratic manner. It's not about marching or having street marches or nonsense of that kind, or breaking up meetings to stop people speaking to students. It's not about that sort of ridiculous, adolescent, childish, basically fascist behaviour; it's about a peaceful and law-abiding process of stimulating public debate.[83]

Stone seemed to be suggesting that Australia might witness a popular uprising against centralisation of power in Canberra. Noble as his efforts to prevent such an occurrence might have been, there was little evidence that anything of that nature was imminent. And while Stone may have seen what he was doing as channelling popular anger into something productive, the fact remains that the majority of the Society's membership has consisted of a privileged elite – judges, lawyers, politicians, academics – whose concerns could hardly have been more remote from those of ordinary Australians. Given the Society's focus on legal and political matters this is to be expected, although it is not the entire story: Stone was eager to point out that tradesmen, policemen, farmers, engineers, doctors, accountants, retired military officers and teachers have also been contributors over the years.[84]

The Samuel Griffith Society has held thirty conferences since 1992, following the same weekend format as the H.R. Nicholls Society. Meticulously planned down to the minute by Stone, the conferences were usually divided into a number of constitutional themes, with multiple papers delivered on each theme, followed by discussion periods. In addition to the core issues of defence of the Constitution, federalism/anti-centralism and judicial activism, a handful of issues have been repeatedly discussed throughout the life of the Society. These include: the republic; the prospect of an Australian bill of rights; the external affairs power; the financial relationship between the Commonwealth and the states; and "the Aboriginal question," Stone's catch-all term for anything relating to Indigenous affairs. Since 2011 conferences have been broadcast on pay television and online via Australia's Public Affairs Channel (A-PAC).

Consistent with the professional make-up of the membership, Samuel Griffith Society conferences have usually been rather formal affairs, even compared to those of the H.R. Nicholls Society. This contrast was noted by Paul Houlihan at the Samuel Griffith Society's 2007 conference. "When John Stone asked me to speak to this gathering, I was a little taken aback," he joked. "I am used to the less elevated areas of the H.R. Nicholls Society rather than this august body."[85] Despite this reputation, Greg Craven has noted that there have been occasional papers that were "a little bit off centre, a little bit eccentric."[86]

The formal, civilised tone of the conferences, however, did not preclude strong disagreement and debate. While the three other organisations examined in this book might be accused of encouraging an atmosphere of furious agreement, the Samuel Griffith Society seems genuinely interested in robust debate. Andrew Norton found it refreshing in this way: "It wasn't just people who completely agreed sitting around saying, 'Yes, you're right, aren't our enemies bad?' which is how these things can often turn out. There was actually sort of serious questions about the papers being given and robust debate from the floor, and from people who are actually really serious: academic constitutional lawyers, former High Court judges like Callinan. So people were actually in a very strong position to give that argument."[87]

While its emphasis remains federalist and constitutionally conservative, dissenters from this "party line" are welcome to contribute their views at Society conferences. Some examples include journalist Frank Devine, who argued for a bill of rights at the inaugural conference; historian John Hirst, founding convenor of the Australian Republican Movement and member of Paul Keating's Republic Advisory Committee, who was invited to put the case for a republic in 1993; and, most significantly, co-founder of the Society Greg Craven, whose position on the republic gradually evolved to the point that he endorsed the model put to a national referendum in 1999. The Samuel Griffith Society was born amid disagreement between Craven and Stone in 1991, so it was perhaps appropriate that Craven's dissenting position on the republic excited a fresh round of acrimony, as we shall see.

Some moments of conflict came courtesy of Stone himself. One of those on the receiving end of his infamous ire was David Jull, minister for administrative services in the Howard government, who in 1996 argued that, for a variety of reasons, Australia's official flag should not be constitutionally entrenched. Shortly afterwards Stone used his newspaper column to denounce Jull's "truly pathetic paper,"[88] before apologising to members in the published proceedings for the way in which the paper had not measured up to "the high standards set by every previous contributor."[89]

Most conferences since 2006 have hosted the Sir Harry Gibbs Memorial Oration, established following the death of the founding president, with speakers including former High Court Justices Dyson Heydon and Ian Callinan; Bryan Pape, a barrister who unsuccessfully challenged the Rudd government's stimulus spending in the High Court; Liberal shadow attorney-general George Brandis; Federal Court judge Richard Tracey; and former NSW director of public prosecutions Nicholas Cowdery.

The other major way in which the Society tries to spread its message is via the publication of its conference proceedings in hardback volumes under the series title *Upholding the Australian Constitution*. As with the H.R. Nicholls Society, copies of the proceedings are included with membership, and are available for non-members to purchase for $30 each. Stone was editor and publisher of *Upholding the Australian Constitution* for its first twenty-one volumes, from 1992 until 2009. These proceedings would usually be published within a few months of the conference. Their format has remained consistent throughout, and Stone agreed with the proposition that they have played an important part in bolstering the organisation. "They are handsome books, with good-sized print, wide margins and an 'uncluttered' look about their pages that make them easily readable," he told me. "They are also, of course, a ready-to-hand source of not infrequent reference."[90] Greg Craven agreed that despite the uneven quality of some volumes, the proceedings have been important:

> It is remarkable how that Society has managed to assemble now, over twenty years of conservative papers and positions around the Constitution. Quite astonishing. If you get those books and you sort of line them up – and some of them are not great works of scholarship and some of them are not meant to be, I mean they're effectively meant to be polemic, and highly effective polemic – I think they have had a significant effect.[91]

All papers can also be accessed free of charge through the Society's website, which was first set up in 1997. Although it hosts a considerable amount of material, the site is rather rudimentary and updated infrequently, signalling its secondary status in promoting the work of the Society. However, the Society has noted that there is often increased traffic to the website towards the end of university semesters, indicating its usefulness to students.

Upholding was also often supplemented by Stone's newspaper columns, where he took the opportunity to promote the work of the Society, complete with a phone number for those readers who wanted to enquire about membership or order a copy of the proceedings. Since Stone's retirement, responsibility for editing and publishing the proceedings has been shared between John Nethercote and Julian Leeser, both of whom worked under Craven at Australian Catholic University. Though the format has been maintained, the timeliness of their publication has become less reliable: at the time of writing, both the 2017 and 2018 volumes are yet to be published or made available online.

Battling the "Keating–Turnbull Republic"

The 1990s saw the emergence of a serious and concerted campaign for an Australian republic. The Australian Republican Movement was founded in July 1991 by a group of prominent Australians including Thomas Keneally,

Donald Horne, Neville Wran, David Williamson and Malcolm Turnbull. Their cause was boosted when Paul Keating ousted Bob Hawke from the prime ministership in December 1991, and swiftly put the republic at the centre of his political agenda. The formation of the Samuel Griffith Society coincided with this campaign, and though John Stone was quick to point out that this was not the reason for the Society's formation, he was certain that the debate would "figure in its deliberations."[92] Indeed, the inaugural conference saw three papers given on various aspects of the republic question.

Meanwhile, an organisation with the specific purpose of campaigning against the republic, Australians for Constitutional Monarchy (ACM), was founded by another group of eminent Australians almost simultaneously. There has been considerable overlap between ACM and the Samuel Griffith Society: Harry Gibbs served on ACM's founding council; David Flint, who has served on the board of the Samuel Griffith Society and given many papers at its conferences over the years, has been ACM's national convenor since 1998; and John Stone was heavily involved in ACM's campaigning, as he recounted to the Samuel Griffith Society in 2006.

Paul Keating's election victory in March 1993 has been described as giving "the kiss of life to the republic for the first time in Australia's history as a nation."[93] Almost immediately the prime minister fulfilled a campaign promise by setting up the Republic Advisory Committee, with Malcolm Turnbull as chairman. Keating saw this appointment as an act of bipartisanship, but members of the Opposition were sceptical, and Liberal leader John Hewson declined an invitation to appoint an Opposition representative to the committee. In an address to the Samuel Griffith Society in July 1993, Victorian Premier Jeff Kennett declared his determination to oppose Keating's and Turnbull's plans, arguing that transitioning to a republic would be technically complex, divisive and could lead to the dangerous expansion of executive power.[94] The Republic Advisory Committee's report, *An Australian Republic: The Options*, was released in October and attempted to allay such concerns with an emphasis on minimal, symbolic change. Constitutional conservatives remained unpersuaded.

Samuel Griffith Society conferences over the next few years saw only occasional interventions in the republic debate. But despite Paul Keating's 1996 election defeat to monarchist John Howard, momentum towards a republic continued and, in February 1997, Howard honoured an election commitment by announcing that a Constitutional Convention would be held the following year to discuss the issue. From this point on, the Society became much more engaged in the issue. In a March 1997 address Harry Gibbs warned that if Australia were to become a republic and the powers of the governor-general transferred to a president, absent constitutional conventions that have evolved over centuries, "the President would be in the position of a dictator."[95] The 1998 conference included a post-mortem on the Constitutional Convention, in which four speakers were, in the words of Stone, "united on one point: namely, that the malformed proposal which emerged from the Convention is not merely unsatisfactory, but positively dangerous."[96]

In July 1999, with a referendum on the republic just months away, David Flint opened the eleventh conference with yet another warning about the dangers of the "Keating–Turnbull Republic."[97] The first session of the conference proper was to include contrasting papers on the republic from Greg Craven and Sir David Smith. Craven had moved from being a "pragmatic monarchist" to a supporter of a minimalist republic in which the transition could be made with as little change to the Constitution as possible. This, to put it mildly, was not a popular position in the Samuel Griffith Society. Stone, who planned the session, thought that Craven "had made a fool of himself in the course of his Republican advocacy, and I wanted his views to be exposed to someone, in David Smith, who would be competent to take them apart."[98]

Craven rather boldly told a room full of monarchists that the Convention model "should be adopted in the upcoming debate by any thoughtful constitutional conservative who genuinely wishes to preserve intact Australia's existing constitutional genius."[99] A republic of some kind was inevitable, he argued, so the model on offer should be supported in order to prevent a more radical version, such as one involving direct election of the president. Much to Craven's dismay, Smith then responded with full force, devoting half of his 4000-word paper to an attack on Craven. He questioned Craven's integrity and ridiculed his changes of position on the republic as "constitutional *Karma Sutra* [sic]."[100] Craven had expected a civilised debate, and was extremely unimpressed with Smith having so thoroughly "played the man."[101] Even Stone was taken aback by Smith's vehemence, and offered his apologies to Craven, as did a number of others. But for Craven the experience was so unpleasant that he had little association with the Samuel Griffith Society for some time afterwards.

The November 1999 referendum resulted in a heavy defeat for the republicans. Not a single state returned a Yes majority, and the nationwide Yes vote reached only forty-five per cent. The following year's Samuel Griffith Society conference included a triumphant "referendum post-mortem" session in which David Smith spoke of his pride in having helped kill off the republic,[102] Nancy Stone examined the press coverage leading up to the referendum and found it overwhelmingly biased towards a Yes vote, and Malcolm Mackerras analysed the results seat by seat and concluded that the republic was overwhelmingly supported by inner-city voters, but aroused little interest in outer-metropolitan, provincial and rural areas. The republic issue has struggled to gain traction ever since, despite periodic attempts to revive the debate.

Mabo: "the most legally indefensible decision in the High Court's history"

Another significant constitutional issue that neatly coincided with the forming of the Samuel Griffith Society was the High Court's Mabo judgement, which was handed down on 3 June 1992. In a case brought before it by Eddie Mabo and other Meriam people from Murray Island in the Torres Strait, the High Court ruled that the common law "recognizes a form of native title which, in the cases where it has not been extinguished, reflects the entitlement of the Indigenous inhabitants, in accordance with their laws or customs, to their traditional lands."[103] The doctrine of *terra nullius* – literally "nobody's land" – that had been used as a legal defence of the dispossession of Indigenous people for over two hundred years was explicitly rejected. Furthermore, the High Court opined on the morality of white settlement, describing the "conflagration of oppression and conflict which was spread across the continent to dispossess, degrade and devastate the Aboriginal peoples and leave a national legacy of unutterable shame."[104] The momentous judgement, as David Solomon has written, "can be likened to the imposition of a peace treaty on the winning side in a war that had lasted more than two centuries."[105]

The moral language of the Mabo judgement, as well as its legal reasoning, infuriated John Stone and other constitutional conservatives. Stone described the decision as "a fit of self-indulgent personal remorse, [which] overturned two centuries of settled Australian property law."[106] As there was only one judicial dissenter, staunch conservative and federalist Justice Daryl Dawson, Stone took to describing the judicial majority as the "Mabo six," whom he asserted were examples of judicial activism *par excellence*. Hugh Morgan fumed with rage at the inaugural Samuel Griffith Society conference:

> With this judgement ... the justices of our High Court have de-robed themselves. The High Court has placed itself at the epicentre of what will become, arguably, the most important political debate of the history of this country since federation; the debate concerning the territorial integrity and the effective sovereignty of Australia as proclaimed in the Commonwealth of Australia Constitution Act of 1900. It could rival the conscription debates of the Great War for bitterness and divisiveness.[107]

Though Morgan was being characteristically hyperbolic (in an address almost certainly penned by Ray Evans), his prediction was not entirely incorrect. The debates became especially heated following Paul Keating's 1993 election victory, as the prime minister set about legislating in response to the Court's decision. But over the course of the next year it was Morgan himself who caused most of the controversy, even earning a rebuke in parliament from the prime minister: "Mr Morgan has always painted himself as a thoughtful thinker on the right. He has never been thoughtful, and he has never been a thinker. What we have here is just bigotry. It is the voice of ignorance, the voice of hysteria and the voice of the 19th century."[108] In June 1993 Morgan gave a provocative address to the Victorian branch of the Returned and Services League in which he defended European settlement in Australia as "properly, lawfully, and peacefully constituted," and called for a referendum to overturn the Mabo decision.[109] At this point even his colleagues in the mining industry began to distance themselves from him.[110]

The Samuel Griffith Society held two conferences in 1993, and the consequences of Mabo were of utmost importance at both. In an echo of the H.R. Nicholls Society's emphasis on the legal privilege of trade unions, former WA Liberal leader Bill Hassell argued in July that "Mabo creates privilege – legal privilege based on race."[111] He also laid out his theory that "Mabo is but a small part of a wider agenda, which certainly includes a separate, sovereign, Aboriginal state within Australia capable of conducting international affairs."[112] Peter Connolly followed, referring derisively to "the legislation of 3 June, 1992,"[113] while fellow barrister S.E.K. Hulme felt that the judgement's reference to "a national legacy of unutterable shame" recalled the way the medieval church held the Jews responsible for the crucifixion of Jesus a millennium earlier.[114] These two papers were soon afterwards published and circulated by the Association of Mining and Exploration Companies as part of the mining industry's campaign to undermine Mabo. Further critiques of Mabo, from barrister Colin Howard and maverick Labor MP Graeme Campbell, were heard at the Samuel Griffith Society in November.

In December 1993, following the longest debate in Senate history, the Keating government's legislative response to Mabo, the *Native Title Act*, was passed into law. Critiques of the legislation were provided at the Society's next conference in July 1994. Barrister and legal academic John Forbes predicted that institutions such as the National Native Title Tribunal and the Federal Court would be biased in favour of claimants. Colin Howard was concerned that the passage of the *Native Title Act* might embolden the High Court further:

> It would be sad indeed if, on top of Mabo, the High Court became minded to arrive at further decisions of a comparably radical nature in the belief that the passage of the *Native Title Act* was in some sense confirmation of the propriety of a court, any court, taking upon itself, at the expense of the law of the land, the teaching of an ill-considered lesson in atonement for supposedly inherited guilt.[115]

Foreshadowing his future role in the Bennelong Society, the conference also included a paper by Geoffrey Partington devoted to attacking historian Henry Reynolds, whose scholarship had been cited in the Mabo judgement.[116]

Following the election of the Howard government in 1996, the future of native title law became an issue of intense focus at Samuel Griffith Society conferences. The man most frequently consulted was John Forbes, described by the Society at the time as "one of our foremost experts on the law of native title."[117] In three papers delivered between June 1996 and October 1997, Forbes developed his argument for amendments to the *Native Title Act*, conceding that the higher objective of scrapping the legislation altogether was a lost cause. In May 1997, Howard announced his "Ten Point Plan" to amend the *Native Title Act*, an attempt, among other things, to provide certainty to mining and pastoral leaseholders in the wake of the High Court's Wik judgement. The plan received general endorsement from members of the Society, though they were pessimistic about its prospects of getting through the Senate unscathed, and then surviving a High Court challenge.

But following the successful passage of the *Native Title Amendment Act* in July 1998 (albeit with 217 Senate amendments) much of the heat went out of the debate, as none of the most catastrophic predictions about native title came to pass. This did not prevent the Society from returning to the issue throughout the 2000s, however. Keith Windschuttle, by this time notorious as a revisionist historian who believed that stories of frontier violence against Aborigines had been fabricated, argued in 2003 that the High Court had relied on such fabrications as evidence in its Mabo judgement. Gary Johns, a minister in the Keating government who played a prominent role in the Bennelong Society, as we shall see in the next chapter, addressed the Samuel Griffith Society in 2012 to mark twenty years since Mabo. He concluded that despite great expectations, native title has proved to be a disappointment for Aboriginal people. John Stone returned to the topic of Mabo in a Society address in 2017, describing it as "the most legally indefensible decision in the High Court's history."[118]

Historians Andrew Markus and Bain Attwood have provided useful analyses of the conservative reaction to Mabo. Markus identified five themes, all of which, to varying extents, can be found in Samuel Griffith Society rhetoric: a focus on the devastating consequences of the decision; a preference for a non-sentimental view of history; a belief that Aborigines, far from being disadvantaged, were privileged; a view that the High Court "had betrayed the demands of their high position"; and a critical view of Aboriginal culture.[119] Somewhat more dramatically, Attwood argued that "Mabo forms part of a new historical narrative which portends for conservatives the end of (Australian) history as they have conceived it and, therefore, the end of their Australia."[120] Looking back on the Samuel Griffith Society's hysterical reaction to Mabo overall, in which it was claimed that Australia's sovereignty and territorial integrity was under threat from a separate Aboriginal state, it is difficult to disagree with this characterisation.

Today

The Samuel Griffith Society has been in a period of transition for much of the past decade, largely due to the advancing age of its founders. When Nancy Stone relinquished her secretarial role in 2004, her husband John took it on in addition to the position of conference convenor, which he had held since 1992. When he retired in 2009, the end of an era had been reached. Responsibility for conferences was passed to Julian Leeser, but in July 2016 he moved on after being elected to federal parliament as the Liberal member for Berowra in New South Wales. The presidency, which had passed to David Smith following the death of Harry Gibbs, has been held by Ian Callinan since 2011.

Stone's secretarial role was assumed in 2009 by long-time board member Bob Day and his personal assistant Joy Montgomery, based at the office of Day's Homestead Homes business in the Adelaide suburb of Modbury. Once Day established the Bert Kelly Research Centre in inner-city Kent Town in 2011, the Samuel Griffith Society became one of a number of conservative tenants, alongside the Family First political party, the Australian Taxpayers' Alliance and Senator Cory Bernardi's Conservative Leadership Foundation.[121] But Day was forced to relinquish his leading role in the Society after taking up a seat in the Senate representing Family First in July 2014. Melbourne barrister Stuart Wood has since taken over as secretary and treasurer.

In November 2016 Bob Day resigned from the Senate, ostensibly due to the financial collapse of his business. But in an ironic twist for an avowed constitutional defender, it was soon revealed that Day faced questions over whether he had breached section 44 of the Constitution, which disqualifies anyone from sitting in parliament who "has any direct or indirect pecuniary interest in any agreement with the Public Service of the Commonwealth."[122] At issue was his use of the aforementioned Kent Town property as his electorate office. Though he claimed to have "disposed of his interest in the building," and was thus not receiving a benefit in the form of rent from the Commonwealth, he remained linked to the mortgage.[123] Day denied any wrongdoing, but the matter was referred to the High Court, which ruled in April 2017 that his election was invalid.

On an intellectual level, the most intriguing outcome of generational change within the Society has been its evolving position on the issue of Indigenous constitutional recognition. In October 2007 – just days before calling a federal election – John Howard announced that, if re-elected, he would hold a referendum to formally recognise Indigenous Australians in the Constitution. Though Howard went on to lose the election, Indigenous constitutional recognition has enjoyed bipartisan political support ever since. Yet members of the Society were wary, and when Prime Minister Julia Gillard announced an expert panel to advise on the issue in November 2010, John Stone was quick to respond with mockery. "What is it about our politicians (from all sides)," he asked, "that moves them to these flights of faux-symbolic fancy?"[124] Stone's rhetoric was echoed by Gary Johns, who outlined his arguments against recognition at the 2013 and 2014 Samuel Griffith Society conferences.

In the meantime, prominent members of the Society such as Julian Leeser and Greg Craven were meeting with Cape York Indigenous leader Noel Pearson to discuss the issue more constructively. They hoped to come up with a compromise that would both uphold the Constitution and achieve reconciliation between Indigenous and non-Indigenous Australians. In April 2015 Pearson gave the launching address for a new organisation called Uphold & Recognise, the centrepiece of which was an "Australian Declaration of Recognition," a proposal co-authored by Leeser and Damien Freeman.[125] By placing the symbolic aspects of recognition outside the Constitution, the authors hope to avoid the dangers of tinkering with Australia's highest law, while still acknowledging the unique place of Indigenous people within the nation.

But when Leeser sought to advance the proposal at the Samuel Griffith Society in August 2015, his predecessor was unimpressed. Stone doesn't see the proposal as a compromise at all, regarding it "as unacceptable as the idea(s) it purported to replace."[126] He said as much in response to Leeser's paper and, he told me, was greeted with applause by the audience. While Greg Craven views the proposal as a positive example of the way in which the Society is able to "promote a deeper conservative understanding and contribution to quite complicated issues,"[127] Stone remains unmoved. "The whole 'recognition' push has been dangerous nonsense from beginning to end," he said. "It is serving as a nice little earner for all the usual suspects in the Aboriginal industry, at taxpayers' expense, but if it is ever put to a vote, which I doubt, it will go down in flames."[128]

Though it faces a number of challenges, the Samuel Griffith Society is still a relatively sturdy organisation. This is especially apparent when one compares its recent fortunes to those of the other hard right groups examined in this book. But as the Society prepared to celebrate its twentieth anniversary, Julian Leeser, perhaps concerned about its ageing and declining membership, was eager to discuss ways in which the group could become more relevant:

> I believe that the mission for the Society in its next twenty years is to move from being a learned debating society to becoming a much more direct influence in the public debate of our nation. If the values of our Society: respect for our Constitution, federalism, the rule of law, skepticism of international law and what the Americans might call "judicial modesty" are to flourish, we must do more to promote our ideas. We must build a coalition for the values of this Society in the law, in the parliaments of our nation, in academia and among students.[129]

Here Leeser seemed to be acknowledging a paradox about the Society: that while it has maintained a strong membership and held successful conferences over a long period of time, its political successes have been few and far between. From a federalist perspective, centralisation of power remains just as much of a problem as it was in the 1980s. Upon his retirement

John Stone even admitted that he and Nancy had sometimes succumbed to doubts about whether the Samuel Griffith Society was actually accomplishing anything at all.[130]

But while the fight to restore Australian federalism may to some appear to be a lost cause, Greg Craven sees it as part and parcel of the life of the conservative, in which one takes a heroic stand against the zeitgeist. "I think if you're a federalist – and I've been a federalist all my life – it's a life of constant retreat," he told me. "It's that theory of conservatism in which you're never actually going to win, but you are going to force change to be either slower or better."[131] Craven also takes heart in the belief that the public are on the side of the Samuel Griffith Society, even if they don't know it. "The true constitutional conservatives are the Australian people themselves," he wrote in 2016. "The so-called 'Con Cons' are merely the pointy, frigid tip of an iceberg of national sentiment."[132]

5

ASSIMILATION REDUX: THE BENNELONG SOCIETY AND INDIGENOUS AFFAIRS

"I begin this article with a welcome to country – a welcome to our country. So let me begin by acknowledging the traditional owners of this land: King George III and his heirs and assigns."

– John Stone, *Quadrant*, November 2017[1]

THE DISPOSSESSION OF AUSTRALIA'S INDIGENOUS people by the British began with Lieutenant James Cook's charting of the east coast of Australia in 1770, when Cook claimed the land for King George III and named it New South Wales. Later, Captain Arthur Phillip was instructed to establish a British colony in Australia. In January 1788 he arrived with the First Fleet, which comprised eleven ships and around 1350 people. The Indigenous population of the continent at this time is disputed, but the most common estimate is 750,000, and Indigenous people are believed to have occupied the land for around 60,000 years. But despite Phillip having been told "to live in amity and kindness" with the natives,[2] the arrival of the British signalled the beginning of what Charles Rowley later termed "the destruction of Aboriginal society."[3]

The next 150 years or more of Australian race relations alternated between violence and indifference towards Aboriginal people. As the anthropologist W.E.H. Stanner explained in his 1968 Boyer Lectures, many Australians were either blissfully unaware of this shameful history or were not prepared to acknowledge it. He called this phenomenon "the great Australian silence": "What may well have begun as a simple forgetting of other possible views turned into habit and over time into something like a cult of forgetfulness practised on a national scale. We have been able for so long to disremember the Aborigines that we are now hard put to keep them in mind even when we most want to do so."[4] By the late 1960s, this silence was coming to an end, thanks largely to the reassertion of Aboriginal identity and sovereignty by a new generation of black activists. In the following decades the work of many historians, anthropologists, artists and bureaucrats – black and white – brought significant attention to Australia's lamentable history of race relations.

In the post-war period up until the 1960s the most clearly articulated government policy on Aboriginal Australia was assimilation. This policy was closely associated with the minister for territories from 1951 to 1963, Paul Hasluck, though as he later pointed out, he "inherited both the word and the purpose it expressed."[5] He did acknowledge that he gave "greater precision to the idea," however, which is evident in his address to the Australian and New Zealand Association for the Advancement of Science in Sydney in August 1952. Assimilation, Hasluck said,

> means, to my mind, that we expect that, in the course of time, all persons of Aboriginal blood or mixed-blood in Australia will live in the same manner as white Australians do, that they will have full citizenship and that they will, of their own desire, participate in all the activities of the Australian community. Full assimilation will mean that the Aboriginal shares the hopes, the fears, the ambitions and the loyalties of all other Australians and draws from the Australian community all his social needs, spiritual as well as material. Whether biological assimilation goes hand in hand with cultural assimilation is a matter which time will reveal but my own guess would be that, if cultural assimilation occurs, mating will follow naturally.[6]

Historians have disagreed about the extent to which Hasluck respected Aboriginal culture and tradition, but Geoffrey Bolton makes the important point in his biography of Hasluck that the minister "was not urging that Aboriginal people should make themselves into imitation white Australians, but that they should have access to the same opportunities and rights of citizenship."[7] Hasluck refused to accept the widely held belief that Aborigines were doomed to extinction, and he wanted to see them prosper.

In practice, though, Aborigines were expected to conform to white norms and ways of living. As part of what was perceived to be an inevitable process of integration, the lifestyle that had sustained them for thousands of years was to be abandoned for their own good. While some might have lamented this break from traditional culture, the process was seen as essential to avoid a situation in which Aborigines lived as outcasts in marginal and impoverished settlements.

As historian Tim Rowse has noted, assimilation "remains an elusive category for historians", and it is difficult to pinpoint the moment when it came to an end.[8] Nonetheless, it is generally agreed that things began to shift around the time of the 1967 referendum, which proposed that two references to Aborigines in the Constitution be removed. The first was contained in section 51 (xxvi), which gave parliament legislative power with respect to "the people of any race, other than the aboriginal race in any state, for whom it is deemed necessary to make special laws."[9] The second was section 127, which stated that "in reckoning the numbers of the people of the Commonwealth, or of a State or other part of the Commonwealth, aboriginal natives shall not be counted."[10] With the support of ninety per cent of the Australian population, the words "other than the aboriginal race in any state" were removed from section 51 (xxvi), and section 127 was repealed entirely. The effect of the first change was to give the Commonwealth concurrent powers with the states in Aboriginal affairs, which had previously been the primary responsibility of state governments (apart from in the Northern Territory, where the Commonwealth had been in charge since 1911). The repeal of section 127 meant that Aboriginal people would now be counted in the census and so brought into the nation as Australians.

The 1967 referendum is commonly cited as a major turning point in Indigenous affairs, but some historians have challenged this narrative, in which "the referendum comes to stand in for, or to symbolise (in the way that myth usually does), something much more complex and diffuse."[11] Support for this interpretation comes from the fact that Aboriginal Australians were soon frustrated with the lack of progress that followed the referendum. It wasn't until 1972, under Prime Minister William McMahon – aided by the influential public servant H.C. "Nugget" Coombs – that the Commonwealth began to use its new power over Aboriginal policy. That year also saw the establishment of the Aboriginal Tent Embassy on the lawns outside Parliament House, which amplified the pressure on the Commonwealth to consider the views of Indigenous people. Meanwhile Coombs, as chairman of the Council for Aboriginal Affairs, worked to end the policy of assimilation and usher in the era of self-determination, which was formally adopted as government policy following Labor's election victory under Gough Whitlam in December 1972.

As processes of decolonisation took place around the globe following World War II, self-determination became a defining principle of the era. Historically oppressed peoples were now demanding the right to determine their own future, and official resistance to such ideas was weakening. Tim Rowse notes that for Indigenous Australians, self-determination came to involve three essential features: recognition of land rights through legislation; being counted in the census from 1971, which allowed "choice of cultural identity"; and the emergence of an Indigenous sector, in which countless organisations were created to represent Indigenous Australians and their interests.[12] Though self-determination policies were never entirely free of political controversy, they were generally adopted by both major parties until the election of the Howard government in 1996. Around this time, as Peter Sutton has documented, the liberal consensus on Indigenous affairs began to break down.[13] Nowhere was this more evident than in the emergence of a neo-assimilationist movement, which would eventually lead to the birth of the Bennelong Society, whose lobbying would have a powerful influence on the policy direction of the Howard government.

Conservatives and land rights

The conservative backlash against Aboriginal self-determination can be traced back to the first major piece of land rights legislation in 1976, the *Aboriginal Land Rights (Northern Territory) Act*, and was closely tied to mining interests. Hugh Morgan, in his capacity as the executive director of Western Mining, emerged in the 1980s as one of the most outspoken public opponents of Aboriginal land rights. He fired his first shot in an address to an AMIC seminar in Canberra in May 1984, with Labor ministers Clyde Holding, Barry Cohen and Peter Walsh present. Morgan deployed Christianity to make a moral case for mining, denigrated Indigenous spiritual and cultural traditions, and made spurious claims regarding Aboriginal cannibalism.[14] Andrew Markus described the speech as an attempt to "undermine the legitimacy of Aboriginal claims by attacking the moral basis of their society."[15] Gerard Henderson, who was in the audience, thought it "perhaps the toughest speech I have ever heard. At times you got the impression that the paint was peeling from the ceiling."[16]

The AMIC address, written by Ray Evans, was deliberately designed to be explosive. It received front-page coverage in several major newspapers. Morgan drew criticism from all corners: "The Federal Government accused him of trying to set up a divine right of miners," *The Age* reported, "church groups scolded him with biblical quotes, historians took issue with him on cannibalism and Aboriginal groups called him a hypocrite. It wasn't Hugh Morgan's day."[17] Morgan and Evans, however, were operating according to the adage that any publicity is good publicity, and in this sense their strategy could hardly have been more successful. Morgan later described it as being "like a grenade thrown at the right time in the right place."[18] They did find at least one friend in the government: the minister for resources and energy, Peter Walsh, who defended Morgan by saying that "the terms in which a case is put or exaggerated do not in my view necessarily invalidate the case itself."[19]

Ronald Libby described Morgan's speech as "an exegesis for the religious basis of mining" that had a potent effect on the mining industry.[20] Morgan had provided the industry with an ideology from which it could launch an unprecedented public advocacy campaign against proposed land rights legislation, concentrating on Western Australia. The WA Labor government, led by Premier Brian Burke, was promptly forced to abandon its support for land rights. The campaign's success, and the threat of it being taken nationwide, ended any possibility of the federal Labor government passing land rights legislation in the near future.

Later, Morgan and Evans were able to expand on their religious defence of mining by commissioning a book by Bendigo academic Roger Sworder, eventually published in 1995 as *Mining, Metallurgy and the Meaning of Life*. Meanwhile, they continued to rail against the concept of Aboriginal land rights up to and following the High Court's Mabo judgement in 1992 and the Keating government's subsequent *Native Title Act*. As we saw in the previous chapter, these issues were also being debated extensively at the conferences of the Samuel Griffith Society.

Opposition to land rights was also growing within the Liberal Party, but the need for action did not become clear until the Coalition lost the "unlosable" 1993 election, despite Paul Keating's apparent unpopularity. David Kemp, Liberal frontbencher and key member of the New Right, decided enough was enough, as Ray Evans recounted: "Kemp, realising that the Liberal Party's understanding of Aboriginal affairs was confused and contradictory, organised this dinner with Peter Howson and other senior Liberals, to see if some coherence could be brought to intra-party debates. I was invited because I had achieved some small notoriety as a fierce critic of the Mabo judgement."[21] Liberal hardliners felt that their party had become soft on Indigenous issues. Especially concerning was Opposition leader John Hewson's refusal to campaign against Mabo, despite pressure from within the party. Kemp and Evans felt that Howson in particular could do something to solve the problem.

Peter Howson: Anglican assimilationist

Peter Howson, minister for the environment, Aborigines and the arts in the short-lived McMahon government, is the most important figure in the history of the Bennelong Society. Born in London in 1919, Howson moved to Australia following World War II and soon became an active member of the Liberal Party. Following unsuccessful attempts in 1951 and 1954, he eventually won the seat of Fawkner thanks to the Labor Party split and entered parliament in 1955. He was minister for air from 1964 until 1968, but his political career suffered following the death of Prime Minister Harold Holt in December 1967. Demoted from the ministry by Holt's successor John Gorton, Howson worked to undermine Gorton's prime ministership. In March 1971 Billy McMahon took the top job.

Howson was a serious Christian who was appalled by his church's increasingly progressive attitudes towards Indigenous people. "He found the elevation, by the Anglican Church, of Aboriginal 'spirituality' into a superior kind of religious faith not just bizarre but deeply repugnant," wrote Ray Evans.[22] By the time he was given responsibility for Indigenous affairs in May 1971, Nugget Coombs had become a powerful, disrupting influence in the area, and Howson was soon "besieged by his portfolio's strong personalities."[23] Labor's election victory in December 1972 saw Howson lose his seat, and his formal political career came to what he viewed as a premature end. He refrained from active involvement in Indigenous affairs for about twenty years, "and could only sit on the sidelines watching the destruction of all the ideas and projects that I and others had set in place."[24] But following the dinner organised by Kemp in 1993, Howson and Evans began regularly lunching together and strategising a long-term campaign: "the overthrow of the Coombsian doctrine of self-determination and separatism which was destroying the lives of Aborigines all over Australia and threatening the territorial integrity of the nation."[25]

The late Christopher Pearson, conservative columnist and former speechwriter for John Howard, described Howson as "a much-loved Liberal Party patriarch" and "one of the few federal ministers to have had Aboriginal affairs responsibilities in his portfolio and to have emerged from the experience with an enhanced reputation."[26] He also argued that Howson "saw from the outset that Coombsian policy would prove disastrous and there's a sense in which his whole post-political career can be read as an act of redress."[27] This does not explain why Howson consciously chose to stay out of Indigenous affairs for twenty years, but it is certainly true of the period from 1993 until his death in 2009.

Pearson's overwhelmingly positive view of Howson does not appear to have been shared by Paul Hasluck, who reviewed Howson's political diaries for *The Age* in 1984. Hasluck suggested that Howson was a peripheral figure, "never close to the centre of power" but rather "busy on the gossip fringe of the government."[28] He even mischievously likened Howson to the vain, bungling Jim Hacker, the title character from the British television comedy series *Yes Minister*, a figure relentlessly thwarted by the public servants who are meant to be subservient to him. From the man who Howson had urged to run for the Liberal Party leadership in 1968, these were rather unkind words.

Tim Rowse, biographer of Nugget Coombs, is also no admirer of Howson, seeing in his "sustained negative reflection on Coombs" something rather pathetic:

> His diaries reveal him to be a man of limited social range. He was moved increasingly to dismay and self-pity when the spirit of the times produced monsters undreamt of over his many lunches at the Melbourne Club. Rather than try to engage intellectually with that troubling world, Howson demonised Coombs as its Machiavellian embodiment. There was a kind of innocence in this, a crippling truncation of the liberal imagination.[29]

In this description, one can't help being reminded of William F. Buckley's memorable image of the conservative standing athwart history, yelling "Stop."

The Galatians Group

The first institutional vehicle for the right's renewed enthusiasm for Indigenous affairs was the Galatians Group, which was formed by Evans, Howson and some disgruntled Uniting Church ministers in 1994. It took its name from a passage out of the New Testament's Epistle to the Galatians: "There is neither Jew nor Greek, there is neither bond nor free, there is neither male nor female: for you are all one in Christ Jesus" (Galatians 3:28). Reverend Max Champion, who became its president, interpreted this to signify a kind of human universalism, the notion "that human civilisation is constituted not by distinctions of race, class, gender or religion but by a shared body of traditions and institutions which are maintained by laws which apply to all and discriminate against none."[30]

The Galatians Group was active from 1994 until 1999, in which time it held five conferences and published its proceedings under the umbrella theme "The Churches and the Challenge of Australian Civilisation." Topics covered included Indigenous affairs, multiculturalism, social justice, education, values and the arts. While principally a project comprising members of the Uniting Church, other denominations such as Catholics, Lutherans and Anglicans were also represented.

The immediate concern of the Galatians Group was the Uniting Church's 'Covenanting statement,' in which the leadership of the Church formally apologised to Aboriginal people "for all those wrongs done knowingly or unknowingly to your people by the Church," a gesture the Church hoped would "unite us in a multi-racial bond of fellowship which will be a witness to God's love for us all and a constant challenge to the continuing racism which oppresses you and separates us in this land."[31] The Galatians Group found this "campaign to engender shame among Australians" troubling, part of a disturbing wider trend of churches being more concerned with advocating progressive politics than with preaching the Gospel.[32] At the first Galatians conference, held in Melbourne in August 1994, a variety of views were aired, all dissenting from the Uniting Church leadership's position on Aboriginal reconciliation. Conservative columnist Frank Devine promoted the conference in *The Australian*.[33]

A number of key New Right luminaries and associates addressed the Galatians Group during its short existence, including Geoffrey Blainey, Harry Gibbs, Ron Brunton, B.A. Santamaria, Peter Walsh, John Hyde and Alan Oxley. Reflecting in 2009, Ray Evans was as forthright as ever in outlining the reasons for founding the Galatians Group, calling it "a small group of Uniting Church and other clergy who found the support given by the churches to the cause of Aboriginal separatism wanting in theological soundness, and extremely distasteful in the way the work and sacrifice of the missionaries of previous generations was denigrated."[34] Patrick Morgan described it as a group for "traditionalist Protestant ministers of religion who, though in the majority in their congregations as far as their views went, were being marginalised by trendy clerics who had grabbed control of the ruling organs of their denominations."[35]

According to Peter Howson, it was through the Galatians Group that historian Geoffrey Partington was recruited to write what would become the neo-assimilationist movement's foundational text: *Hasluck versus Coombs: White Politics and Australia's Aborigines.*[36] Partington was a prolific contributor to *Quadrant* who had also delivered a paper on the Mabo judgement at the Samuel Griffith Society. Published in 1996 with a preface by Howson, his book is a manifestly subjective account of half a century of Indigenous affairs, nostalgic for Hasluck and scathing of Coombs, with very few shades of grey. The following passage provides a neat summary of Partington's thesis:

> The assimilationist policies [Hasluck] advocated were in place for less than twenty years during the 1950s and 1960s, but, on the basis of the meagre amount of available information about educational standards, employment opportunities, health, family structures, criminal offences, and so on, there is every reason to believe that this was the period in which Aborigines achieved more real progress than in any other, before or since. At the very least it had positive features which it is foolish to ignore on ideological grounds.[37]

Partington emphasised the political differences between Hasluck and Coombs, though in reality they shared a relationship of mutual respect. Reviewing a book by Coombs in 1980, Hasluck wrote that Coombs's "highly practical intelligence ... has been applied eminently for nearly forty years to several phases of policy formation and public administration in Australia and he played an influential part in shaping comment and policy on Aborigines during the 1970s."[38] Responding through a family spokesman to the media attention surrounding the publication of Partington's book, Coombs said that though he disagreed with Hasluck's policies, their relationship was "functional and cordial."[39]

Hasluck versus Coombs was launched in June 1996 at Parliament House in Canberra by the newly appointed Liberal minister for Indigenous affairs, John Herron. This apparent government endorsement of a return to a policy of assimilation proved controversial, and *The Australian* in particular seized the opportunity to highlight divisions in policy circles. Herron claimed that his launching of the book was not an endorsement, though he did describe its thesis as "exciting and interesting"; Indigenous leader Noel Pearson found it "a bit worrying that the minister is excited about such a simplistic and ideological tract."[40] A group of sixty-six academics saw Herron's involvement and *The Australian*'s coverage as "promotion and endorsement" of Partington's views and expressed their outrage in a letter to the editor.[41] Conservative commentator Gerard Henderson was also critical of the book, and of Herron for agreeing to launch it.[42] When it later emerged that John Howard had greeted Partington at the launch it was considered sufficiently newsworthy to warrant a 400-word article in *The Weekend Australian*.[43] Such was the sensitivity at the time regarding the legacy of assimilation.

In a review of the book published in *Meanjin*, Tim Rowse was critical of the way in which Partington "makes a fetish" of Hasluck, as well as the censoriousness of the sixty-six academics' letter to *The Australian*. "Such an empty and tendentious book as *Hasluck versus Coombs* could not lay the basis for a new approach to indigenous affairs by the Howard government," he wrote. He was also sceptical of the notion that Herron's launching of the book represented an alignment of interests between Partington and the government: "Partington's contribution has rather been his momentary fillip to Liberal nostalgia. The amity between author and minister at the book launch was probably the zenith of their mutual satisfaction.[44] With the benefit of hindsight we can see that Rowse was too quick to dismiss the neo-assimilationists. A political and intellectual shift was taking place, the significance of which he was not yet able to see.

Quadrant takes charge

Public support for reconciliation between Indigenous and non-Indigenous Australians was gathering pace following the publication of the report of the National Inquiry into the Separation of Aboriginal and Torres Strait Islander Children from Their Families, *Bringing Them Home*, in 1997. The neo-assimilationists were alarmed and got busy preparing their response. In February 1998, the IPA published a pamphlet by anthropologist Ron Brunton challenging the findings of *Bringing Them Home*. Under the editorship of Paddy McGuinness, *Quadrant* published two articles along similar lines in June 1999, one of which was written by Peter Howson. Meanwhile, Frank Devine, Christopher Pearson, Andrew Bolt, Piers Akerman and Michael Duffy began to air their own concerns about *Bringing Them Home* in their regular newspaper columns.

By this time it was being reported that conservatives were mounting "a calculated assault on advocates of an apology over discredited government policy."[45] When Robert Manne also warned of a conservative campaign of historical denial, Howson was dismissive. "It is fanciful to imagine such a large number of individuals with diverse views and backgrounds could mount a campaign," he wrote. "Manne seems unable to distinguish between a campaign and an obvious concern to establish the truth."[46] Meanwhile, McGuinness was converting words into action by hosting two *Quadrant* seminars on Indigenous affairs: 'Rousseau versus Reality' in August 1999 (where John Herron gave the after-dinner address) and 'Truth and Sentimentality' in September 2000, both of which received significant coverage in *The Australian*.

This period also saw the rise to national prominence of Keith Windschuttle. A former media studies academic and Marxist who had transformed into an ultra-conservative amateur historian, Windschuttle was now devoting his energies to disproving the work of Australian historians regarding massacres of Indigenous people. His argument – that there was significantly less violence than previously reported – was first developed across three issues of *Quadrant* in late 2000, and was to become a popular right-wing position in Australia's so-called history wars. His research had the strong backing of McGuinness, who, as we saw in Chapter 1, had taken over the editorship of *Quadrant* from Manne in 1998 following significant disagreements over Indigenous issues.

Windschuttle found a prominent supporter in John Howard, who awarded him a Centenary Medal in 2003 and later appointed him to the board of the ABC. Addressing *Quadrant*'s fiftieth anniversary dinner in 2006, Howard said that "of the causes that *Quadrant* has taken up that are close to my heart none is more important than the role it has played as counterforce to the black-armband view of Australian history."[47] This term – suggesting that left-wing historians had painted an unfairly negative picture of Australian history – came from Geoffrey Blainey's 1993 Sir John Latham Memorial Lecture, and its repetition was to become a feature of Howard's early years as prime minister. Windschuttle's historical revisionism was therefore warmly received. In the words of one journalist, "if Keith Windschuttle hadn't existed, John Howard would have been sorely tempted to invent him."[48]

Spurred into action by the *Quadrant* seminars, Peter Howson organised a follow-up workshop, 'Aboriginal Policy: Failure, Reappraisal and Reform' in December 2000. Those present included Evans, Brunton, Windschuttle, McGuinness, Blainey, Des Moore, Gary Johns and Geoffrey Partington, and "it was resolved that an organisation, with the name of the Bennelong Society, should be incorporated."[49] Evans later described this moment as the culmination of "eight years of continuing effort to try to find an effective vehicle for responding to the hegemony of Coombsian doctrine."[50]

Woollarawarre Bennelong: assimilationist ideal

As with all of the groups examined in this book, the name adopted by the Bennelong Society is significant. The organisation was named after Woollarawarre Bennelong (c.1764–1813), whom one historian described as "the most significant Indigenous man in early Sydney."[51] Following his capture at the behest of Governor Arthur Phillip in 1789, Bennelong served as an intermediary between his people – the Eora – and the British invaders. Dirk van Dissel's brief biographical article, published on the Bennelong Society website, relates a favourable narrative of how Bennelong learned English and adopted European behaviour and dress while residing with Governor Phillip. Van Dissel went on to conclude:

> Time and time again, Bennelong exhibited skills of determination, diplomacy and resolve that could be likened to that of an astute and seasoned politician. He was considered a vital link between the white settlers and the Aborigines because of his ability to speak both languages and behave

accordingly in both cultures. His closeness to Governor Phillip and influential Aborigines such as Colby guaranteed his position within both societies as he was the intermediary between the two different peoples. Through his own actions, Bennelong cemented his image and position as an important and influential part of the establishment of Sydney Cove during the 1790s.[52]

For the members of the Bennelong Society, Bennelong was the earliest example of successful assimilation of Indigenous culture into what would inevitably become the dominant British culture.

However, this conveniently uplifting story is incomplete. Some time around 1800, struggling with alcoholism following three years in England, "Bennelong, who had seen at first-hand the best and worst of European civilisation, chose to reject it"; he "returned to a respected position in the Eora clan networks from which he had taken temporary leave."[53] The man who was to become the Bennelong Society's poster boy for assimilation had in fact resisted it and returned to his own culture. Van Dissel appears to have deliberately left out this important coda to Bennelong's story.

Van Dissel's article also notes that Bennelong developed a taste for wine while residing with Phillip, but did not drink to excess until he spent time in England from 1792 to 1795. The focus on Bennelong's drinking habits is noteworthy. As Aboriginal anthropologist Marcia Langton has argued, "Bennelong was the first reconstruction of an Aboriginal person as a 'drunken Abo', and from there the stereotype was developed."[54] Langton sees this popular image as both reflection and reinforcement of a broader white ideology in which Aborigines are blamed for their disadvantage, while whites absolve themselves of responsibility:

> Today it remains the background and popular explanation for the extraordinary arrest rates of Aboriginal people, for the continuing removal of Aboriginal children and the continuing exclusion of Aboriginal people from employment, education, health services, rental accommodation, and a range of other services.[55]

As we will see, there are echoes of the ideology Langton identifies here in the rhetoric of the Bennelong Society.

Canberra connections

There was barely time to celebrate the Society's formation before the group was faced with a setback – though it was quickly converted into an opportunity. John Howard announced a ministerial reshuffle in December 2000 that saw Philip Ruddock replace John Herron as minister for Indigenous affairs. Herron's appointment in 1996 had itself been a product of Peter Howson's influence, and demonstrated Howard's determination to change the course of Indigenous affairs after thirteen years of Labor rule.[56] The Liberal shadow minister in Opposition had been Chris Gallus, who Ray Evans described as "a leading South Australian wet ... completely entrapped inside the Coombsian fantasy,"[57] and Gary Johns even suggested was close to the ALP Left.[58] Whether or not these views about Gallus were true is less important than the fact that conservatives perceived her that way. Howson had worked the phones to ensure Gallus didn't hold onto the portfolio in government, and Herron, with no prior interest in Indigenous affairs, was appointed. As Howson later wrote, "the slow deconstruction of separatism could begin."[59] According to Evans, Howson's influence had also been crucial in saving Herron's job when representatives of ATSIC lobbied to have him replaced in 1998: "Peter used every contact he had within the Liberal Party to rally support for Herron and, probably by a hair's breadth, Herron was saved, at least until just before the 2001 election."[60]

For journalist Tony Koch, Herron's sacking was evidence that "Howard never considered Herron tough enough to maintain his (Howard's) own hardline attitudes to Aboriginal and Torres Strait Islander people. That's the price one pays for being honest and decent, presumably."[61] This interpretation ignores the fact that Herron had been deliberately appointed in 1996 because it was felt that he would indeed be on board with Howard's outlook, which resulted in regular clashes with Indigenous leaders throughout almost five years as minister.[62] Tim Rowse speculated that "Herron's ministry may one day be recalled as one of the more grotesque episodes in the politics of Indigenous accountability."[63]

With Herron replaced by Ruddock, the neo-assimilationists no longer had someone on the inside, as it were. But on the other hand, Herron's demotion and subsequent retirement from the ministry freed him to say and do whatever he liked regarding Indigenous affairs, and he soon agreed to become the inaugural president of the Bennelong Society, launching its website at Parliament House in May 2001. Echoing Howard's pronouncements favouring practical reconciliation over symbolic gestures such as an apology to the stolen generations, his speech, which was also published in Brisbane's *Courier-Mail*, argued that "the symbolism of land rights and reconciliation, while important to the intelligentsia of the Sydney-Melbourne-Canberra axis, has little relevance to the daily grind in communities such as Port Keats, Finke and Yuendumu."[64]

Alongside Herron, the inaugural board of the Bennelong Society included Howson, Evans, Johns and Moore. Herron's role was largely ceremonial, with the other four taking on the bulk of the work. Herron resigned his position as president in 2002, following his retirement from politics and appointment as ambassador to Ireland and the Holy See. He was replaced briefly by sitting Liberal Senator Jeannie Ferris, before Johns became president in 2004. Howson remained vice-president of the Bennelong Society from its formation until his death in 2009. Moore and Evans took on the roles of treasurer and secretary respectively.

Along with Howson and Evans, Gary Johns was another pivotal figure in the history of the Bennelong Society. A Labor member of parliament from 1987 to 1996, Johns' most senior position was as special minister of state from 1994 until he lost his seat in the ALP's 1996 election defeat. In 1997 he was appointed as a senior fellow at the IPA, and he also began work on a PhD in political science, which was awarded in 2001. His post-political career has made him an outcast in Labor circles, something that doesn't appear to bother him at all. Asked about his shift to the right since leaving politics, Johns points out that he became a "right-winger" as far back as 1980, well before he entered parliament, and that political parties are simply a vehicle for one's own views. Though he insists that he was a good team player while sitting in parliament, he did feel compelled to speak out on some issues.[65]

Johns had never paid particular attention to Indigenous affairs until the controversy over mining at Coronation Hill in the Northern Territory in

1990. "It stimulated my interest in Aboriginal politics, and the falsity of it," he told me. "I thought it was intellectually quite bereft."[66] Johns was lobbied by Ron Brunton to push the government to allow mining at the site, which he subsequently did, but to no avail. Prime Minister Bob Hawke overruled his Cabinet, and Coronation Hill was incorporated into Kakadu National Park. Johns described the decision as "a result of environmental and Aboriginal myth-making and mischief-making" and "a daft way to run a nation."[67] Hawke bitterly attacked his Cabinet colleagues' "rather brutal, innate prejudice" and remained convinced that the dispute was a key element in his loss of the Labor leadership to Paul Keating six months later.[68]

Aside from a minor role in native title issues, Johns had little further involvement in Indigenous affairs until Howson contacted him in 1999 and asked him to give a paper at *Quadrant*'s 'Rousseau versus Reality' seminar. With the help of Brunton, the paper was expanded and published by the IPA as 'Reconciliation: what does it mean?' Johns later described it as "still the only paper that seeks to evaluate rather than indulge Reconciliation."[69] He gave another paper at Howson's 2000 workshop in Melbourne and agreed, at Evans' request, to get involved in the formation and administration of the Bennelong Society. From this point on he became a key player in the neo-assimilationist movement.

Johns has also been an occasional participant in the other three key hard right groups profiled in this book. He presented a paper on trade unions at the 2002 H.R. Nicholls Society conference and has addressed the Samuel Griffith Society on five occasions. While he had no formal involvement with the Lavoisier Group, he used his regular column in *The Australian* to warn against action on climate change, echoing the Lavoisier line.

The inaugural Bennelong Society board also included two Indigenous members: public servant Helen McLaughlin and singer Maroochy Barambah. A third, Fitzroy Crossing community leader Joe Ross, was named in a Bennelong press release as being on the board, but he was quick to dispute this, saying that he had been approached and asked to write something for the website, but that he "wouldn't want to be aligned with what looks like a fairly right-wing sort of think tank."[70] The most active Indigenous member of the board was Wesley Aird. The first Indigenous graduate of the Royal Military College at Duntroon, Aird has worked as an Indigenous adviser in the mining industry and as a subcontractor to the Australian government on aid programs.[71] As a strong proponent of a pragmatic approach to Indigenous development, he was introduced to Johns, who asked him to give a paper at the 2002 Bennelong Society conference. He joined the board the following year.[72]

Paradigm shift

The Bennelong Society arrived at a time of renewed optimism on the right with regard to Indigenous affairs, with conservative commentators noting with satisfaction a changing mood in the national reconciliation debate. Paddy McGuinness had sensed this new mood following the first *Quadrant* seminar in August 1999, and trumpeted it in *The Sydney Morning Herald*. "The old certainties of those who present themselves as the defenders of Aborigines are being shaken as emerging Aboriginal leaders, such as Noel Pearson and Senator Aden Ridgeway, accept that the policies of the recent past are not working satisfactorily," he wrote.[73] Journalist Paul Sheehan supported this view a year later in a report on Howson's submission to a Senate committee on the Stolen Generations.[74]

Indications of a paradigm shift also came from the left. One was the publicity surrounding Noel Pearson's discussion paper, "Our Right to Take Responsibility," first distributed in May 1999, which focused on the twin disasters in his community: binge drinking and passive welfare. According to Christopher Pearson (no relation to Noel), the Cape York leader had spoken to both Gary Johns and John Herron in 1996 about the future of Indigenous affairs. Johns advised him to "avoid the endless circuit of junkets to Geneva and instead lead his people on the ground, by example," while Herron urged Pearson to speak out about "dysfunctional communities plagued by alcohol and violence and the syndrome of welfare dependency."[75] By mid-2000 many of Pearson's proposals for reform had been adopted by Queensland's Labor government.[76] Another sign of this change in the conversation was anthropologist Peter Sutton's inaugural Berndt Foundation Biennial Lecture, 'The Politics of Suffering,' at the University of Western Australia in September 2000, in which he spoke unflinchingly about the failures of Aboriginal policy since the 1970s.

By 2001 Christopher Pearson was boasting that "the left-liberal consensus on indigenous affairs has been broken," citing a number of recent events.[77] First was the backlash against the design of the Gallery of First Australians at the National Museum of Australia, which controversially drew inspiration from Berlin's Holocaust-themed Jewish Museum. Second was a speech by Andrew Bolt highlighting financial waste within ATSIC. Pearson also noted the increased media coverage of violence in remote communities; the emergence of new, pragmatic Indigenous voices such as Joseph Elu and Marcia Langton; and the fact that the National Press Club invited Keith Windschuttle to debate historian Henry Reynolds about Indigenous massacres, rather than providing Reynolds with a platform solely for himself.

Robert Manne, an outspoken critic of the neo-assimilationists, was by now in agreement with conservatives that the Indigenous debate had shifted markedly to the right.[78] Manne was especially alarmed at the prominence given to the publication of anthropologist Roger Sandall's collection, *The Culture Cult: Designer Tribalism and Other Essays*, in April 2001. Sandall, a former editor of *Quadrant*, argued that many "spoiled, white, discontented urbanites" had been taken in by "romantic primitivism – the idealizing of social simplicity and the world of the 'noble savage'."[79] Over the course of the next two months the book was heavily featured and fiercely debated in the press. *The Culture Cult* was an academic text that the neo-assimilationist movement was able to rally behind, and the attention paid to it provided further evidence of a shifting political atmosphere.

Neo-assimilation

Let us now look more closely at what the Bennelong Society was trying to achieve. When its website went live in May 2001, the organisation announced that it was established to:

- promote debate and analysis of Aboriginal policy in Australia, both contemporary and historical;
- inquire into the causes of the present appalling plight of many contemporary Aboriginal people;
- seek to influence public opinion so that the prospects for amelioration of the condition of these people are improved;
- encourage research into the history of the interaction between Australia's Indigenous people and the Europeans and others who settled in Australia from 1788 onwards, and of the ideas through which this interaction was interpreted by both Europeans and Aborigines;
- make available to the Australian community, particularly through the Internet, the results of these activities.[80]

Much like the H.R. Nicholls Society, these seemingly benign, inoffensive goals masked the more radical nature of the group's intentions. They imply an openness to new ideas and freedom from rigid ideology that was not reflected in the group's subsequent words and actions. Anthropologist Eve Vincent attended the 2006 Bennelong Society conference as an observer and later wrote that "it's important to stress the sincerity, reasonableness and obviousness assumed within the Society about its own ideas. This internally imagined sense of itself strikes a contrast with the fanaticism that characterises the work of Society stalwarts Johns, Howson and Geoffrey Partington."[81] In our personal interview, Gary Johns told me that "of course we have a very strong view of what we think would work, but we don't have an ideological view."[82] However, there was never any real doubt in the minds of these activists that the solutions to Indigenous problems were to be found in returning to long-abandoned policies. Based on the voluminous articles and speeches produced by its members over the years, a less ambiguous version of the Bennelong Society's aims would indicate that they sought "inclusion" (read: assimilation) over "exclusion" (read: self-determination), and were hostile to land rights, reconciliation and the celebration of Indigenous culture.

In a paper delivered at the Bennelong Society's formative workshop in December 2000, Ray Evans asserted that "the central issue in Aboriginal policy, from the earliest days of settlement up until the present day, has been exclusion versus inclusion."[83] As Geoffrey Partington's book laid out in detail, the Bennelong Society saw the era of self-determination from the 1970s onwards as an unmitigated disaster for Aboriginal people. Meanwhile, the assimilation era was recalled with rose-tinted glasses, ignoring the overwhelming evidence of egregious racism and prejudice, both official and unofficial, during those years. The Bennelong Society's first objective, then, was to bring an end to self-determination and return to assimilation, though terms such as "inclusion" and "integration" were preferred because, as Evans argued in 1996, "the word 'assimilation' has been damaged by misrepresentation."[84]

Self-determination was also often equated with "separatism" and "segregation", terms that evoke objectively racist policies such as apartheid in South Africa or the "Jim Crow" laws in the United States that lasted from the 1870s until the 1960s. This flawed characterisation, and its association with a whitewashing of assimilation, was addressed by Rosemary Neill in her 2002 book *White Out: How Politics is Killing Black Australia*. "It is perverse of the abolitionists and revisionists to paint the assimilation era as a high-water mark for progress in indigenous affairs," she argued.[85] Howson could at least say that he was consistent, given that he had taken this line while still a minister. "I have felt for some time," he wrote in his diary in May 1972, "that the present policy being carried out by the Council [for Aboriginal Affairs] is to promote racist discrimination, to put the Aboriginals apart from the other Australians rather than to encourage them to become one people or one nation."[86]

One way in which conservatives tried to demonstrate the benefits of assimilation was in their fixation on intermarriage. Time and time again figures were cited regarding the high rate of Indigenous intermarriage (the most common statistic given was seventy per cent), which to neo-assimilationists revealed that Aborigines were voting with their feet by rejecting separatism and embracing integration with the wider community.

The neo-assimilationists also invoked separatism when they discussed the issues of land rights and native title, another major focus of the Bennelong Society. Land rights and native title legislation was seen as privileging Indigenous people to the detriment of everyone else, which was completely unacceptable in a democracy that prizes equality before the law. The neo-assimilationists also argued that once land was handed back to Indigenous people, they no longer had any incentive to participate in the "real economy". But the group's position on land rights was muddied by differences of opinion about whether they should be arguing for repeal or trying to work with the legislation as it stood. In a blistering attack at the 1998 Galatians Group conference, Ray Evans said that the Mabo judgement "delegitimises the British settlement of Australia by declaring the basis of settlement (the doctrine of *terra nullius*) unlawful and morally unacceptable. In doing this the High Court brings into question the authority and legitimacy of the Australian nation and consequently of the High Court itself."[87] Evans went on to argue, in his characteristically absolutist terms, that Mabo should be overturned via a constitutional referendum, so that the structure of property law could be rebuilt.

Peter Howson was also a vociferous opponent of land rights, and blamed the dysfunction evident in many remote communities on land rights legislation. He argued that by handing over to Indigenous collectives land that was once productively used for mining and pastoral purposes, economic development was being denied to Aborigines. Land rights, as currently configured, were in fact "an instrument of imprisonment for our Aborigines, and if they are to make their way in the modern world, they must break down the prison walls which were established by the Northern Territory Land Rights Act and the various state acts which followed. When Aborigines have exactly the same rights in land and mineral titles as other Australians, then they will be free; but not till then.[88] Like Evans, Howson was a land rights absolutist. Along with the return of assimilation, he saw the repeal of land rights legislation as crucial in bringing to an end "the epidemic of suicide, alcohol and drug abuse" in Indigenous communities.[89]

Gary Johns, on the other hand, took a slightly more nuanced position. On the question of what collective land rights had achieved for Indigenous people he was unequivocal: "the land rights revolution has failed."[90] He is therefore adamantly opposed to their expansion, but unlike Howson and Evans, he accepts that native title is now consecrated in law, and believes that arguing for its repeal is a waste of time: "You're not going to wipe it out, so forget about it."[91] Rather, he believes that collective land rights simply hold no relevance to young Aboriginal people, and they are likely to leave remote areas for cities and towns, which in his mind would be a thoroughly positive development.

An additional complicating factor for the Bennelong Society on the issue of land rights was the inclusion of Wesley Aird on the board. As a member of the Yugambeh people, Aird is a native title claimant for the Gold Coast area. When I asked him whether this caused tension with other Bennelong Society members, he acknowledged that some were not supportive of the notion of native title, but did not see it as a major issue because his group's claim is not about money or land, but recognition. Aird is concerned that some groups make native title claims for the wrong reasons and without evidentiary substance, and thus understands and supports those who are opposed to land rights as a source of material gain. "If a claim is made for the wrong reasons," he says, "then I think it's entirely legitimate to be sceptical or disparaging of it."[92]

Another major concern of the neo-assimilationists was the long process of reconciliation between Indigenous and non-Indigenous Australians that came on to the national agenda in the early 1990s. With bipartisan support a Council for Aboriginal Reconciliation was created in 1991 and tasked with determining the nature of a formal act of reconciliation in time for the centenary of Federation in 2001. The various options considered included a treaty, an apology for past injustices, and constitutional recognition of Indigenous Australians. This dovetailed with a number of significant events that served to highlight the unequal status of Indigenous Australians, including Paul Keating's Redfern speech in December 1992 and the publication of the *Bringing Them Home* report in 1997.

As we have seen, the process of reconciliation was challenged by the work of Howson, Johns, Brunton and Windschuttle, among others. These men were uncomfortable with the historical awakening that began in the 1960s, in which white Australians slowly began to acknowledge the tragedy that had befallen Indigenous people since 1788, and their complicity in that tragedy. They preferred Australians to view their history as one of overwhelming achievement, albeit with minor unfortunate blemishes. But even more important was the prevention of any formal acts of reconciliation that could be construed as separatist, such as those being considered by the Council for Aboriginal Reconciliation. One of their most common arguments was that symbolic gestures would do nothing to solve the ongoing problems faced by Indigenous people. Johns, for example, sees reconciliation as an ideology, "which presumes that a semi-religious act of reconciliation, a term that came from the Catholic and other churches, will solve complex policy problems."[93]

This position enjoyed the official endorsement of the Howard government, which rejected the findings of the *Bringing Them Home* report and refused to apologise to the stolen generations, instead maintaining its rhetorical focus on practical reconciliation. Rosemary Neill saw this hard-hearted attitude as being responsible for a souring of the public mood against Aboriginal Australia. "Whatever the government's immediate political purpose," she wrote, "the lasting effect of its actions was to instigate a culture of denial and recrimination that would permanently disfigure the public debate over what has become the most emotive issue in indigenous affairs."[94]

Nowhere was the culture of denial and recrimination more apparent than in the words of the Bennelong Society's two most prolific figures, Howson and Johns. In trying to demonstrate why some Indigenous communities had failed, the pair showed utter contempt for Aboriginal culture. In his final piece of published writing before his death in 2009, Howson didn't hold back. "What is held up to us as 'Aboriginal culture' is, in reality, nothing more than the culture of the concentration camp where brutality and horror are the chief attributes," he wrote in *Quadrant*. "The dances and corroborees put on for the tourists are manifestations of an ersatz 'culture' where anything goes and any story will do."[95]

Johns went even further by explicitly blaming the problems of Indigenous Australia on the failings of Aboriginal people themselves:

> The elaborate inquiries in the 1990s into Aboriginal Deaths in Custody and the Stolen Generations and in the 2000s into Aboriginal child sexual abuse came up with the same answers, that "aboriginal culture" must be respected and that "aboriginal communities" must take charge of their destiny. But what if this "solution" is the problem? What if the culture is no more than people behaving badly, a result of blighted environments, poor incentives, awful history, and an historic culture best relegated to museums and occasional ceremonies? What if these communities are hopeless, in economic terms and every other respect, and that their only rationale is that an ancient band of people once inhabited them or, more brazenly, where some remain

in the hope that through land rights they may gain a windfall from a resources company.[96]

It was this sort of inflammatory language and argument that many found troubling and offensive, and pushed the Bennelong Society to the extreme end of the debate. Noel Pearson, who was embraced by conservatives as he embarked on a campaign to end passive welfare and substance abuse, could not stomach the "irrational contempt" that poured from the mouths of what he referred to as neo-conservatives. He saw it as only serving to damage the cause of reconciliation, and hoped that compassionate conservatives would not be swayed by their arguments.[97] Johns and Christopher Pearson were quick to reveal their disappointment that such an influential Indigenous leader was not eager to join their fold.[98]

The "least cost vehicle" for the neo-assimilationist voice

In contrast to the H.R. Nicholls and Samuel Griffith Societies, both of which were established before the use of the internet became widespread, the Bennelong Society set out from the beginning to harness the power of new information technology to spread its message. When the group was formed, its members decided their primary responsibility would be the establishment of a website, which went live in May 2001. The website allowed the public to access all Bennelong Society material free of charge, including republished newspaper and magazine articles, conference papers and submissions to government. From 2009 the website also linked to the Database of Indigenous Violence, which "aims to record all instances of serious violence against or by indigenous Australians."[99] This rather morbid website was set up by James Franklin, a mathematician and philosopher at the University of New South Wales, who joined the Bennelong Society board in 2010.

Using the internet as its primary vehicle for ideas dissemination allowed the Bennelong Society to run as a very low-cost operation, meaning that recruiting members and raising money was a marginal concern. "We don't care about raising memberships, we don't care about funding, we just want a voice," Johns told me. "So we developed the least cost vehicle for the voice: website, telephone conferences once a month and an annual conference."[100] At its peak the organisation had only 150 members, each of whom paid an annual fee of $50. As we will see, this inattention to retaining members and raising funds led to the organisation's gradual decline as its leaders aged and the political debate moved on.

Despite their enthusiastic embrace of information technology, the main way Bennelong Society members sought to influence public opinion was still through opinion pieces in the major daily newspapers. With the assistance of Des Moore, Peter Howson wrote many columns for the press: tabloid and broadsheet, Murdoch and Fairfax. Moore's April 2000 Institute for Private Enterprise newsletter reflected on their success, or lack thereof, in placing articles in the papers: "*The Age* was particularly receptive, as was *The Canberra Times,* and placements were also secured in the *Australian Financial Review*, Brisbane *Courier-Mail* and *The West Australian*. Of the major papers, only *The Australian* was unreceptive – the *SMH* seemed content to rest on Paddy McGuinness' contributions."[101] This appears surprising at first. The Fairfax press (which includes *The Age, The Sydney Morning Herald, The Canberra Times* and the *Australian Financial Review*) is usually perceived as left-leaning, while the right-leaning *Australian* could normally be expected to provide a platform for prominent conservative voices. Moore hinted that the paper's broad support for reconciliation was leading it to limit debate on difficult questions regarding Aboriginal people. In any event, only a year later Moore was pleased that *The Australian* seemed to have "expanded its preparedness to publish articles that reveal the truth about the horrific conditions in the more traditional and remoter communities and that even question the primitive cultures that have been promoted."[102]

This progress continued throughout the 2000s as *The Australian* adopted a more strident tone under editor Chris Mitchell, who was appointed in 2002. Gary Johns, who had written occasional columns since leaving politics in 1996, was given a regular place on the opinion page to outline the neo-assimilationist agenda. From 2006 onwards, Wesley Aird also wrote regular columns for *The Australian* and *The Age*, allowing the

Bennelong Society to partly avoid the impression that it was a group of white people dictating to Aborigines what was best for them. It is of course difficult to quantify how much effect all of these words had on public opinion, but members of the Bennelong Society undoubtedly succeeded in getting their ideas out into the public domain, which they felt, rightly or wrongly, was not the case during the years of the "Coombsian hegemony."

Another regular outlet for the writing of the neo-assimilationists was *Quadrant*. The magazine's small circulation meant that these articles obviously reached fewer people, but they did allow the authors to develop and expand their arguments in the hope that they might be taken up by politicians and policymakers. "You literally tried to tell politicians how to think," Gary Johns relayed to me, "and give them the words they can use in public that are defensible."[103] An example he gave of this model of influence was pushing the Liberals to talk about "integration" rather than "assimilation", and he was satisfied to witness John Howard and Amanda Vanstone doing just that – changing their terminology – in the later years of the Howard government.

Members of the Bennelong Society also tried to directly influence government policy by making submissions to official inquiries and reviews. This began with Howson and Moore's submission to the Senate inquiry into the government's response to the *Bringing Them Home* report in 2000. There were also submissions from Howson to the Inquiry into the Progress Towards National Reconciliation in 2002–2003, from the Bennelong Society as a whole to the independent ATSIC Review in 2003, and by Johns to the Indigenous Economic Development Strategy in 2010.

Following the formative workshop in December 2000, the Bennelong Society held annual conferences from 2001 until 2008, which they used to try to get in the ears of politicians. The conferences adopted the H.R. Nicholls Society model, with a general theme agreed upon and people invited to give papers around that theme. They always invited the relevant ministers and shadow ministers, with Liberals usually accepting while Labor politicians rarely responded. In addition to John Herron, Howard government ministers to attend Bennelong Society conferences included Philip Ruddock, Ian McLachlan, Amanda Vanstone, Tony Abbott, Kevin Andrews and Mal Brough. The Bennelong Society wanted politicians to hear from people who had experience living and working in Indigenous communities, rather than the usual academics and bureaucrats from the major cities. Gary Johns happily admitted that these conferences were deliberately aimed at trying to influence politicians.

These representatives of government were also often asked to present the Bennelong Medal, awarded annually from 2002 to 2009 to those the group viewed as having made a positive contribution to the Indigenous affairs debate. The medal was awarded to a mix of Indigenous and non-Indigenous recipients, with particular emphasis on those who had battled against what the Society viewed as orthodox or "politically correct" thinking in Indigenous affairs. A consistent theme among Bennelong medallists was a willingness to expose Aboriginal people behaving badly. Boni Robertson, Susan Gordon and Louis Nowra took on the issue of Indigenous family violence; Dulcie and Dorothy Wilson spoke out about the alleged misuse of their culture by Indigenous women in the Hindmarsh Island bridge affair in the 1990s; Paul Albrecht was a Christian missionary who spoke openly about the problems in remote communities; Warren Mundine questioned orthodox Indigenous views about community-owned land; Mal Brough launched a government intervention into remote communities, and Bess Price caused controversy among her Indigenous peers by supporting this decision.

ATSIC: "toy parliament"

No institution better represented all that the neo-assimilationists despised about self-determination than the elected Indigenous body the Aboriginal and Torres Strait Islander Commission. Established in 1990 by the Hawke government's *Aboriginal and Torres Strait Islander Commission Act*, ATSIC's objectives were:

- to ensure maximum participation of Aboriginal and Torres Strait Islander people in government policy formulation and implementation
- to promote Indigenous self-management and self-sufficiency
- to further Indigenous economic, social and cultural development, and

- to ensure co-ordination of Commonwealth, state, territory and local government policy affecting Indigenous people.[104]

From the outset, ATSIC was opposed by conservatives because of what they saw as its inherent separatism. "If there is one thing, above everything else, that we in this Parliament should regard as our sacred and absolute duty, it is the preservation of the unity of the Australian people," remarked Opposition leader John Howard in 1989. "The ATSIC legislation strikes at the heart of the unity of the Australian people."[105] Upon coming to government in 1996 the Coalition wasted no time in cutting $470 million from ATSIC's budget. Meanwhile, John Herron was soon on a collision course with the organisation he oversaw, prompting outrage when he warned of "storm clouds on the horizon."[106] Philosopher Raimond Gaita thought Herron's approach to ATSIC contained "a zeal that suggested he could barely wait to attack this bastion of Aboriginal privilege."[107]

Appearing on Alan Jones's radio program in May 1997, Howard agreed with a talkback caller's complaints about waste in Aboriginal affairs. He then boasted about his government's cuts to ATSIC, and his wider resistance to the "Aboriginal industry":

> I agree with that first caller. There is a lot of anger in the community. There's a feeling that millions of dollars have been wasted in the Aboriginal affairs area. I mean, just remember … that I'm the Prime Minister who took money out of the ATSIC budget. … I'm the bloke that's been under constant attack from Aboriginal leaders since the time I became Prime Minister for being insensitive to their situation. … Now, it's all very well, and I can understand why people feel like that but I want to get the record straight, any suggestion that we have perpetuated the Aboriginal industry is wrong.[108]

The Bennelong Society was also scathing of ATSIC, seeing it as wasteful, unrepresentative of Indigenous people, and even corrupt. "From its inception it was based on a fundamental contradiction," wrote Peter Howson, "the idea that a body elected by Aborigines could spend, every year, hundreds of millions of taxpayers' funds, allocated to it by the Commonwealth Parliament, without being accountable to the parliament."[109] Gary Johns belittled it as a "toy parliament,"[110] while Wesley Aird declared: "if ATSIC were a listed company, I would have sold my shares years ago."[111] They were encouraged, then, when the government announced an independent review of the organisation in November 2002. The Bennelong Society made a brief submission to the review committee, arguing that ATSIC promoted division and was a well-intentioned failure.

The review committee's report was handed to the government in November 2003. The following March, while the government was still considering its response, Opposition leader Mark Latham announced that a Labor government would abolish ATSIC and replace it with an organisation that devolved power to communities.[112] With a major political obstacle removed, John Howard promptly took his opportunity, abolishing ATSIC and replacing it with an advisory body, the National Indigenous Council. This was despite the fact that the government-appointed review panel had not specifically recommended ATSIC's abolition, but rather urgent structural change. But Howard was adamant: "We believe very strongly that the experiment in separate representation, elected representation, for indigenous people has been a failure," he said, echoing the language of the Bennelong Society's submission to the review.[113] "To the government," wrote Jane Robbins, "ATSIC was the embodiment of an undesirable form of self-determination and it was quick to take the opportunity to remove it."[114]

The fifteen-year experiment in Indigenous self-government was formally dissolved in June 2005. Naturally, the Bennelong Society was thrilled at the demise of this institutional emblem of self-determination, but it was not about to become complacent. Writing in *Quadrant*, Howson commended this "long delayed but most welcome" abolition of an elected body representing First Nations Australians, an event of "major importance both historically and politically." And in the same breath, he reiterated his ambitions to help change the course of Indigenous policy: "there is still much intellectual ground to be recovered before new policy directions can offer hope for the future, particularly for the 50,000 or so children and teenagers now living in the remote communities; sociopathic ruins from which they have to be rescued."[115] This leads us directly to another of the Bennelong Society's major policy interventions.

Remote communities and the
Northern Territory Intervention

When Indigenous disadvantage is spoken of, reference is more often than not being made to remote communities, the majority of which are located in the Northern Territory and Western Australia, and to a lesser extent Queensland and South Australia. Many of these communities have been plagued by poor standards of health, education and employment for decades. As we have seen, the neo-assimilationists laid the blame for this situation on self-determination policies that kept Aborigines trapped in communities that offered no prospects, and too often led to violence and despair.

Peter Howson devoted considerable attention to the problems in remote communities in his submission to the Senate Inquiry into the Progress Towards National Reconciliation in 2002–2003. He questioned whether the government should continue to provide services for remote communities, and proposed incentives and subsidies for people to leave. His submission is worth quoting at length:

> The Committee needs particularly to consider whether the Government should continue to provide extensive services, including housing, that encourage Aborigines to stay in communities where limited employment opportunities are available. The more that facilities and welfare are provided to these communities, the less inclined the residents will be to make the integrationist moves that provide the basis for an improved life style and for securing real employment. The road to reconciliation is most likely to be found through measures that encourage what is now a desperate need for increased integration.
>
> Accordingly, a better alternative might be to examine ways of helping the residents of these communities to move to areas where employment is more likely to be obtained and small businesses established. Possibilities might include the provision of larger housing and employment subsidies in more populated areas and of higher subsidies for educating children outside such areas.[116]

The Bennelong Society continued pushing this barrow for the next few years, with numerous articles and conference papers discussing the problems of remote communities and questioning their viability. In 2004 Indigenous affairs minister Amanda Vanstone opened the Society's annual conference with a warning about the viability of remote communities. "Many of the remote communities have limited economic potential and people are trapped there because they have no education," she said. "We must stop pretending, and we must sit down with communities and tell it like it is. The economy in many of these communities is a long way short of supporting the current population. With a rapidly growing population the prognosis is even worse."[117]

But it was Vanstone's successor, Mal Brough, who was able to put words into action on this front. In June 2007 he announced the Northern Territory National Emergency Response, the Howard government's drastic attempt to protect Aboriginal children from harm. Though widely seen as a desperate attempt by the government to halt Kevin Rudd's election-year momentum, what became known as "the Intervention" was also seen by many as a necessary response to the findings of the NT government's Inquiry into the Protection of Aboriginal Children from Sexual Abuse, published in the *Little Children are Sacred* report. But it was also strongly reflective of Bennelong Society thinking, especially the idea that Aborigines need to escape the violence perceived as prevalent in remote communities. It also raised questions about the viability of the communities themselves. John Howard described the Intervention as having "overturned thirty years of failed Indigenous policy based on the doctrine of separate development."[118]

When the Labor Party came to power in late 2007, many left-leaning Australians – Indigenous and non-Indigenous – anticipated a new beginning in Indigenous affairs following the hardline approach of the Howard years. However, apart from Kevin Rudd's apology to the Stolen Generations, with its repudiation of Howard's stubborn approach, there was no major shift in policy direction. Jenny Macklin was the minister for Indigenous affairs throughout the entire Rudd/Gillard era and has since spoken with pride about her focus on practical measures to get children to school and adults to work.[119] Most controversially, the Intervention was continued, albeit with minor concessions to public concerns about some of its more draconian measures, such as the suspension of the *Racial Discrimination Act*. Gary Johns later applauded Macklin for standing up to the "professional welfare advocates" of the left.[120]

When I asked Johns whether he thought that the Bennelong Society had any influence on the Howard government's decision to launch the Intervention, he was uncertain. Brough had attended a couple of conferences and Johns had met him in his office to discuss Indigenous issues prior to the Intervention, where he urged him to think about the long-term consequences of his policies. But he found it impossible to state with certainty whether his lobbying had a significant impact.[121] The Bennelong Society's support for the Intervention was unequivocal, however, and its 2008 conference was devoted to appraising its impact and looking ahead to the future viability of remote communities. Brough was awarded the Bennelong Medal for his efforts, with Keith Windschuttle offering the highest praise: "In the history of Aboriginal affairs, Mal Brough has been the most effective political figure since Paul Hasluck."[122] The medal was awarded the following year to Bess Price, one of the most prominent Indigenous supporters of the Intervention.

Today

The emergence of the Bennelong Society coincided with two important developments in Australian debates around Indigenous affairs. First, upon being elected as prime minister in 1996, John Howard was determined to change direction from what he saw as Paul Keating's obsession with Australia's past "blemishes." In what became one of his most memorable phrases, Howard said he wanted "an Australian nation that feels comfortable and relaxed about three things: about their history, about their present and the future."[123] The other development was the rise of a new type of Indigenous leader – exemplified by such figures as Noel Pearson, Marcia Langton, Warren Mundine and Sue Gordon – who tried to shift the focus away from rights and onto responsibilities, especially regarding issues around welfare, education and substance abuse.

Having lamented the dominance of the old-guard leftist Indigenous leadership for many years, conservatives were quick to embrace this intellectual shift.

Because of these separate but overlapping developments, it is difficult to come to a definitive conclusion about the influence of the Bennelong Society. What cannot be in doubt is that the organisation was an important player in the wider changes that took hold of the Indigenous affairs debate throughout the 1990s and 2000s. The group consistently advocated for a neo-assimilationist approach, and what were once the niche views of a small minority gradually became mainstream, both within the halls of Parliament House and among the wider community.

It is difficult to disagree with Des Moore, who is absolutely certain that there is now widespread acceptance that the self-determination policies associated with Nugget Coombs were a failure, and that the Bennelong Society was instrumental in this shift.[124] That is, the Society was probably most influential at an intellectual level. At the political level things are more complex, but the Bennelong Society was surely important. Its radical push for the complete abandonment of self-determination made Howard look more measured as he tried to change the policy approach, and Labor was unable or unwilling to turn back the tide after coming to power in 2007.

When Peter Howson died in February 2009, and with Ray Evans and Des Moore devoting considerable energy to the issue of climate change through the Lavoisier Group, Gary Johns was left to do much of the Bennelong Society's work on his own. He continued to write about Indigenous issues, and also arranged for Bess Price to give the inaugural Peter Howson Lecture in December 2009, which was later broadcast on ABC television.[125] However, no further conferences were held, and the lecture turned out to be the Bennelong Society's final public event. Johns's book *Aboriginal Self-Determination: The Whiteman's Dream* was published in 2011. The book was launched by Mal Brough, who enthusiastically endorsed it as an "extraordinary contribution to Australia and Australian literature" that "should now be read by every academic, every university student, every policy maker and every bureaucrat."[126] Johns later described it to me as a way of closing off the era.[127]

Finally, in November 2011 it was announced that the Bennelong Society would fold due to lack of interest. The website was taken down in early 2012 and major articles transferred to a dedicated page on *Quadrant*'s website. Johns said that the organisation had "basically just withered away," adding that "it's not as if there isn't work to do, it's just that there's not a lot of energy in that area any more."[128] Evans, though appreciative of the considerable amount of work Johns had put in, told me that the death of Howson was the principal reason for the group's decline.[129] Wesley Aird felt that the organisation had become a little stale, with the same board members and regular contributors saying the same things year in, year out, and hence was supportive of the decision to disband.[130]

When I posited to Johns that, given the changes that had occurred throughout the 2000s, it had perhaps been a victim of its own success, he was not prepared to rest on his laurels:

> We were happy that the debate had shifted, but if there had been more of us and we had more time we would have kept the Bennelong Society going. Because there's a lot more work to be done, we're a long way from home yet. No, it was really a matter of those players [i.e. Howson and Evans] at that time had died, got too old, had other things to do. And if someone else wants to revive Bennelong, that's up to them ... I don't have any interest in reviving it particularly.[131]

But Johns had given a hint as to what the future might hold with regard to Indigenous affairs in his letter to members announcing the disbanding of the Bennelong Society. "The debate about the recognition of Aboriginal people in the Constitution should be of major concern," he wrote.[132] As Australia moved closer to a referendum on Indigenous constitutional recognition with apparent bipartisan support, his concerns became more pressing. In June 2014 he and other former members of the Bennelong Society launched a new organisation called Recognise What? and a book of the same name. Its stated objective was "to encourage debate on any proposition to be put to the Australian people, by way of referendum, on the question of recognition of Aboriginal people in the Constitution."[133] Johns described the proposals of the Expert Panel on Constitutional Recognition as "radical and foolish."[134] Though he claimed that Recognise What? "is not running a No case, rather a minimalist Yes case," Johns nevertheless called on the government to fund a No case.[135] When Greg Craven referred to him as an anti-recognition activist in December 2016, Johns replied that he is in favour of recognition, but that "a dignified mention in a preamble to the Constitution, that there was an Aboriginal people on this continent at the coming of Europeans, is the maximum recognition consistent with the historic facts."[136] But by this time the recognition cause seemed to have lost momentum, as had the opposition to it. In early 2017, the Recognise What? website disappeared from the internet.

6

JUNK SCIENCE AND ALARMISM:
THE LAVOISIER GROUP AND
CLIMATE CHANGE

T HE SECOND HALF OF THE TWENTIETH CENTURY saw increasing global awareness of the environmental destruction being caused by human activity. Conservationists had some major successes compelling governments to take notice of their concerns, and action was gradually taken to slow or reverse particular elements of the damage. The Lavoisier Group was formed as a reaction to Australian government efforts to tackle what is now widely accepted as the planet's most pressing environmental problem: climate change caused by human activity.

One of the pioneering works of modern environmentalism was Rachel Carson's *Silent Spring*, which was first published in 1962 and quickly became an international phenomenon. The book was principally focused on the damaging effects of pesticides, especially on birdlife. Carson's identification of the health and environmental impacts of the spraying of dichlorodiphenyltrichloroethane, or DDT, in the United States eventually led to its worldwide ban a decade later. But Carson's concerns were wider. She raised philosophical objections to the ways in which modern scientific advancements allowed humans to make dramatic and unprecedented changes to the ecological makeup of the earth. "Only within the moment of time represented by the present century," she wrote, "has one species – man – acquired significant power to alter the nature of his world."[1]

These concerns about the damage humans were doing to the earth were soon combined with alarm about overpopulation. Such alarm had a long history. In 1798 Thomas Malthus published *An Essay on the Principle of Population*, which warned about the consequences of exponential population growth. Though his worst predictions never came to pass, the 1950s and '60s saw a resurgence in Malthusian thinking. In May 1968 biologist Paul Ehrlich published *The Population Bomb*, a book whose alarmism did nothing to prevent it from becoming a bestseller. "The battle to feed all of humanity is over," the book began. "In the 1970s and 1980s hundreds of millions of people will starve to death in spite of any crash programs embarked upon now."[2] Ehrlich went on to advocate various forms of population control, some more coercive than others.

Meanwhile, ecologist Garrett Hardin gave a lecture in June 1968 titled "The tragedy of the commons," in which he argued that the human race was heading towards destruction because, for the individual, the benefits of resource consumption outweigh the costs. That is, the gains are privatised while the negative effects are shared, so there is little incentive for each of us to reduce our consumption. "Ruin is the destination toward which all men rush, each pursuing his own best interest in a society that believes in the freedom of the commons," said Hardin. "Freedom in a commons brings ruins to all."[3] For Hardin, the situation was so dire that he believed the freedom to breed should be relinquished.

The increasing environmental awareness stirred up from these seminal interventions led to the emergence of several North American environmental advocacy groups, such as the Environmental Defense Fund (founded in New York in 1967), Friends of the Earth (San Francisco, 1969) and Greenpeace (Vancouver, 1971). These organisations quickly developed into global networks, providing local activists with institutional backing for their campaigns. Governments also began to take notice and felt compelled to respond. In the United States, President Richard Nixon established the Environmental Protection Agency in 1970, and many other countries soon followed suit with similar government agencies or departments. At the international level, the United Nations Conference on the Human Environment in Stockholm in 1972 led to the creation of the UN Environment Programme, which coordinates environmental activities across the globe. Finally, the publication in that year of *The Limits to Growth* by the international think tank the Club of Rome reinforced for many the urgency of the environmental crisis.

In Australia, environmental activism took off in the 1970s. The Australian Conservation Foundation (ACF), a nationwide conservation body, had been founded in 1965 with Chief Justice of the High Court Sir Garfield Barwick as president, but activists soon became frustrated with the conservative approach of its leadership, and splintered off into smaller groups. By 1970 an ACF directory listed more than 350 voluntary conservation organisations in Australia.[4] In 1971 the Builders Labourers Federation, led by a new cohort of union officials influenced by the growing environmental movement, supported the campaign of a local residents' group by instigating "green bans" to prevent inappropriate development in Sydney's Hunters Hill. This fusion was new and transformational, as activist historians Drew Hutton and Libby Connors observed:

> The reverses of the late 1960s and early 1970s would, on their own, undoubtedly have pushed nature conservationists into more militant campaigning modes, but the urban environmental campaigns of the early 1970s, drawing on traditions of left-wing and working-class struggle, helped establish the picket, the blockade, the rally, and other confrontational activities as integral parts of green movement tradition and mythology. They also established the possibility of a link between the ideological and organisational forms of the Australian Left, including a number of trade unions, and the newly emerging environmental movement.[5]

In 1972 the world's first green party, the United Tasmania Group, was formed during the ultimately unsuccessful campaign to save Lake Pedder from flooding by Tasmania's Hydro-Electric Commission. The 1970s also saw the formation of Australian branches of international organisations such as Friends of the Earth and Greenpeace. These groups were at the forefront of significant – and increasingly militant – environmental battles in the years to come.

During the 1980s environmental discourse was increasingly globalised. Governments became aware that environmental threats did not respect national boundaries, and that coordinated approaches were required. A good example was ozone depletion, which was caused by the use of chlorofluorocarbons (CFCs) in aerosol sprays and air-conditioning units. Though individual nations such as the United States, Canada and Norway had made efforts to limit their use of CFCs in the late 1970s, it wasn't until the 1985 Vienna Convention for the Protection of the Ozone Layer that a global response was put in place. The subsequent 1987 Montreal Protocol on Substances that Deplete the Ozone Layer provided for the phasing out of CFCs and has since been ratified by every country on Earth.

Following these effective international collaborations, attention turned to an even greater threat: global warming. Scientists had theorised about the possible ramifications of the release of greenhouse gases into the atmosphere since the nineteenth century, but the threat did not capture public attention until Dr James Hansen, then head of NASA's Goddard Institute of Space Studies, testified before a US Senate committee during the baking hot American summer of 1988. As he recalled in 2009, Hansen declared "with ninety-nine per cent confidence, that it was time to stop waffling: Earth was being affected by human-made greenhouse gases, and the planet had entered a period of long-term warming."[6]

Conservative British prime minister Margaret Thatcher, whose professional background in chemistry led her to take questions of science seriously, was also alert to the danger that global warming presented. In September 1988 she gave a speech to the Royal Society in which she emphasised the importance of well-funded research in order to identify the risks of global warming and deal with them appropriately. Thatcher was confident that science and technology could adapt and provide solutions to the problem, without the need for "repression of human activity by the state," which she perceived as the preferred approach of her political opponents.[7]

Later that year the Intergovernmental Panel on Climate Change (IPCC) was established by the World Meteorological Organization and the UN Environment Programme. In the words of the UN General Assembly, the IPCC would "provide internationally coordinated scientific assessments of the magnitude, timing and potential environmental and socio-economic impact of climate change and realistic response strategies."[8] Its First Assessment Report, published in 1990, was pivotal in leading to the UN Framework Convention on Climate Change (UNFCCC), the ultimate objective of which was the "stabilization of greenhouse gas concentrations in the atmosphere at a level that would prevent dangerous anthropogenic interference with the climate system."[9] This groundbreaking global agreement was negotiated and signed at the Rio de Janeiro Earth Summit in June 1992, and entered into force in 1994. These global efforts to combat climate change alarmed environmental sceptics the world over, and Australia was no exception. The alarm of a particular group of Australians associated with the New Right would eventually lead to the formation of the Lavoisier Group.

Conservatives and the environment

For activists on the right, a fusion between the old left, represented by working-class trade unions and their associated political parties, and a new, environmental left was a frightening prospect. Events in Australia throughout the 1970s and '80s had proved to them the importance of countering such a threat. But first, it was critical that the threat itself be defined and understood. John Stone attempted to do just this in a pamphlet published by the IPA in 1991. Here he identified three major themes of the environmental movement:

- resistance to change and, often allied to that, suspicion of economic development (which necessarily involves change) and technology in general;
- recurring predictions of disaster which, ten or twenty years later, are seen to have been unfulfilled, but which are then either replaced by new doomsayings or, more shamelessly in some cases, by simply making the same old predictions anew;
- the influence of elitism – that is, the tendency for an already favoured few to protect the environmental pleasures which they personally already enjoy by demanding that we sacrifice the potential capacity for the many ever to aspire towards doing likewise.[10]

Stone also expressed his objection to the "increasing tendency for some scientists ... to advance their views into the realms of social or political debate," the result of which was "to lower public trust in the objectivity of scientists, and the standing of scientists in the community, more generally."[11] Developing a theme that has run throughout Stone's career as a political activist, in which he sees left-wing activism as a threat to democratic processes, he cites a speech by ACF director Phillip Toyne: "It is clear that Mr Toyne wishes to see a wholesale process of environmental law-making, including Constitutional change designed to widen even further the powers of central government in Canberra in that regard."[12]

The IPA pamphlet also featured an essay on climate change by American environmental scientist Fred Singer. Announcing himself as "a genuine sceptic about greenhouse warming," Singer argued that there was no scientific consensus on climate change, and that sceptical views were ignored by the media in preference for the catastrophic scenarios presented by some scientists.[13] He concluded that global warming was both imaginary and hyped, exploited by those "who are desperately anxious to impose on us an international regime that would restrict the use of energy, that would tell us how to live."[14] Singer was described in 2005 by *Mother Jones* magazine as "a godfather of global warming denial,"[15] and has received funding from oil giant ExxonMobil.[16] He was also involved in campaigns to deny the impacts of tobacco smoking, acid rain and ozone depletion.[17] Nonetheless, as we will see, fellow climate change denialists now routinely echo many of the arguments in Singer's short essay for the IPA.

Unsurprisingly, both Hugh Morgan and Ray Evans have long been enormously antagonistic towards environmentalism. As the Cold War was drawing to a close, Morgan warned his colleagues in the mining industry that environmentalists were the new communists:

A generation or two ago the great cause for the revolutionaries was socialism, or its Bolshevik variant, communism. As Gorbachev and Deng Xiao Peng [*sic*] (amongst others) have conceded, socialism is a disaster. [...] The road to power, for ambitious revolutionaries, is no longer the socialist road. But the environmentalist road today offers great opportunities for the ambitious, power seeking revolutionary. [...] The Environmentalists are unrelenting in their attack on private property, constantly asserting that property rights must be subject, more and more, to political discretion, in order to preserve and save the environment.[18]

One of Evans' earliest publications was a 1980 *Quadrant* essay on intellectuals' ideological opposition to industrial and technological development throughout history. A lifelong Christian, he has described himself as a Genesis 1:28 man. That is, "man is top of the heap," and has dominion over the Earth and all that lives upon it.[19] Evans believed that Christianity was being superseded by environmentalism as the religion of the upper classes in the West. "It is a form of religious belief," he wrote, "which fosters a sense of moral superiority in the believer, but which places no importance on telling the truth."[20]

Regarding climate change, Evans proudly told me that it took him "about five minutes to realise the whole thing was a scam," and that scientific organisations and politicians had either been duped or were in on the deception: "I kept up with all the scientific stuff, and I met all the main players, and the extraordinary thing was the degree to which what was obviously bullshit, complete bullshit, was swallowed – I don't know if it was swallowed, but certainly sworn to – by the CSIRO, the Bureau of Meteorology, Malcolm Turnbull."[21] Evans believed that the IPCC Assessment Reports were based on junk science, "nonsense which the EU and its green friends in other countries have been parading as the advice of 2500 eminent climate scientists."[22] Asked to explain why he thought such learned people and institutions would accept the reality of climate change if it was so obviously a hoax, Evans' answer was characteristically unorthodox. Having earlier told a Galatians Group conference that the modern left's emphasis on social justice had its genesis in the millenarian doctrines of the middle ages, he now attributed predictions of ecological catastrophe to the same source: "I've come to the view, and it's nothing you can prove, that what we have here is an acute case of millenarial fever. And I've been reading a book on the history of Europe from nine hundred and something to eleven hundred, that period, and I was shaken by the degree to which millenarial fever became a real social scourge."[23] Evans held a genuine belief that people in positions of power had lost the ability to think rationally about social and environmental problems, leading to the implementation of potentially disastrous policies. He therefore committed himself with the utmost urgency to halting this trend.

The Kyoto Protocol:
a threat to sovereignty

The Kyoto Protocol was the first legally binding international agreement on climate change. Following two years of negotiations, it was adopted at the third Conference of Parties to the UNFCCC in Kyoto, Japan, in December 1997. The agreement committed most countries to greenhouse gas emission cuts of around eight per cent against 1990 levels by 2012. Throughout the negotiation process, however, the recently elected Howard government worked to undermine the prospects of a meaningful agreement. "If it could not prevent international agreement on mandatory reduction targets," wrote Clive Hamilton, "it was determined to gain special concessions for Australia."[24] In the latter aim it was successful, with Australia eventually permitted an increase in emissions of eight per cent, based on the argument that its heavy reliance on fossil fuels would make an emissions cut an unfair burden on Australia's economy. This significant concession was achieved with the help of right-wing activists and think tanks from Australia and the United States.

As has been thoroughly documented by sociologists Aaron McCright and Riley Dunlap, the 1990s saw conservative think tanks in the United States mobilise against action on climate change.[25] Ray Evans had watched with interest and hoped to harness similar forces in Australia. In November 1996 he attended a meeting at the headquarters of the libertarian Competitive Enterprise Institute (CEI) in Washington DC. Together with a number of representatives from American oil and energy companies, Evans strategised ways in which Kyoto could be undermined.[26] There the seeds were sown for two conferences. The first, 'The Costs of Kyoto,' was held in Washington in July 1997. The second, 'Countdown to Kyoto,' followed a month later in Canberra. Institutional support for the Australian leg came from another American think tank, Frontiers of Freedom, and Monash University's Australian APEC Study Centre, chaired by former diplomat and international trade consultant Alan Oxley. In addition to a number of prominent American climate deniers, attendees included deputy prime minister and leader of the

National Party Tim Fischer and environment minister Robert Hill. John Stone acted as rapporteur.[27] A follow-up conference, 'Kyoto: The Impact on Australia,' was held in Melbourne in February 1998. Evans described these conferences as very important in bringing together like-minded people who hadn't had the chance to meet. "So once again you get this business of social networking," he said, "which I emphasise can't be overlooked."[28]

For Evans, Kyoto was more than just wasteful environmental policy – it was a threat to sovereignty. He took up this theme with gusto as the Kyoto debate progressed. In May 1998, just two days after Australia became a signatory to the Protocol, Evans spoke at a CNI dinner in Melbourne. He described Kyoto as "the gravest threat to our sovereignty since the Pacific War of half a century ago."[29] He also gave an indication as to what he intended to do about preventing such a calamity, stating that "unless there is a major political offensive against the Federal Government, but more particularly against the Minister and the Department of the Environment, we shall probably ratify the Protocol in due course."[30] Evans continued with the "threat to sovereignty" theme in Samuel Griffith Society conference papers in 1999 and 2000, where he elaborated on Kyoto in even more apocalyptic terms:

> Why should the Kyoto Protocol, of itself, presage a new imperialism? What distinguishes it from every other international treaty which Australia has ratified? The difference between Kyoto and every other international treaty is this. If Kyoto is brought into effect the economic dislocation which must follow its implementation will be unprecedented in modern times. It will be equivalent to the famines of the early 19th Century in its disruptive power.[31]

Needless to say, at this point dissuading the Howard government from ratifying Kyoto went to the top of Evans' list of political priorities.

Support from a Labor maverick

It wasn't only those on the conservative side of Australian politics who viewed environmentalists with disdain. The most prominent figure from the Labor Party to hold such views was Peter Walsh. Having long taken an interest in the politics of the environment, the issue of climate change now came to occupy Walsh's mind more than any other.

Walsh was born in 1935 on a farm in the wheatbelt of central Western Australia (coincidentally, less than fifty kilometres from where John Stone was born). He had formed strong political views at a young age: belief in progressive taxation, "absolute horror" at capital and corporal punishment and, later, strong opposition to conscription and Australia's involvement in the Vietnam War.[32] These views helped to deliver the young Walsh into the Labor Party. But much like Gary Johns (who described Walsh as his "great hero"[33]), Walsh's decision to join the Labor Party was a product of his particular circumstances, and his subsequent political development revealed a figure far to the right of most of his party colleagues.

Elected to the Senate in 1974, Walsh served as Minister for Resources and Energy (1983–1984) and Minister for Finance (1984–1990) in the Hawke government before retiring from politics in 1993. A strong proponent of mining and development, Walsh believed that Labor was "infiltrated and/or unduly influenced" by green extremists in the 1980s.[34] He was aghast when his colleague Graham Richardson experienced a green conversion and worked to convince the government to back environmental causes in return for electoral preferences. (For his part, Richardson thought Walsh "a fundamentally cantankerous personality who was always smarting over something."[35]) Walsh was especially disgusted when Cabinet agreed to restrictions on logging in Tasmania, saying that Labor betrayed its blue-collar base, "not for any valid environmental reasons, but to appease bourgeois Left and middle-class trendoids in the gentrified suburbs of Sydney and Melbourne."[36]

Given these views, it came as no surprise that Walsh also doubted the science of global warming and was prepared to believe the worst about the scientists involved. His 1995 memoir invoked the Cold War to explain what he saw as their alarmist predictions: "Although some scientists, eager for research funds, jumped on the politically correct greenhouse band-wagon," he wrote, "the extremists care not a fig for scientific truth or human welfare ... Their objectives are to 'empower' themselves and indulge their ideological hostility to industrial capitalism. Their targeted villains have always been in North America, Western Europe and Australia, not the real environmental vandals of Eastern Europe and the Soviet Union."[37] He attended the 'Countdown to Kyoto' conference in Canberra in 1997, and reported in the *Australian Financial Review* that evidence presented there "showed scaremongering is moving from media beat up to scientific fraud."[38]

Though they weren't exactly on the same wavelength at the beginning, Walsh's involvement with Ray Evans and Hugh Morgan stretched back to the 1980s. As we saw in Chapter 5, Walsh offered qualified support for Morgan's controversial AMIC address in May 1984. In 1987, having told parliament that the H.R. Nicholls Society was "an extremist right-wing organisation aimed at abolishing the rights of workers,"[39] Walsh was invited to address the Society's third conference, and gave a paper on abuses of power in contemporary Australia. He also addressed the Galatians Group in 1996 and the Samuel Griffith Society in 1997 and 2000. Given this history with the emergent hard right, when a prominent figure was needed to become the president of a new organisation concerned with climate change, Walsh seemed ideal. "Peter Walsh came on board and he was very, very good. He was incredible, he opened doors you couldn't imagine," Evans told me.[40]

Antoine-Laurent Lavoisier: scientific iconoclast

Evans chose to name his latest advocacy group after eighteenth-century French scientist Antoine-Laurent Lavoisier, commonly considered to be the founder of modern chemistry. Born in Paris in 1743 to a wealthy noble family, Lavoisier was educated in the sciences, philosophy and law at the

Collège Mazarin. Elected to the French Academy of Sciences in 1768, he became a *fermier général* – a tax collector on behalf of the royal government – in order to finance his scientific research. Through his insistence on precise measurement he discovered both oxygen and hydrogen, and his research led to the demise of the phlogiston theory of combustion.

A liberal social reformer, Lavoisier participated in the revolutionary assemblies in 1789, and later played a leading role in establishing the metric system. His earlier role as a tax collector for the Ancien Régime did not endear him to the revolutionaries, however. He was attacked in print by the radical journalist Jean-Paul Marat in 1791, before being denounced as a traitor and executed by guillotine in 1794 during Maximilien Robespierre's Reign of Terror.[41]

For Evans, three things in particular stood out about Lavoisier. First, he attended the only school in Paris that taught sciences and mathematics as well as literature and history. "It was this originality," states the Lavoisier Group's website, "which determined Antoine Lavoisier's destiny to become the founder of modern chemistry."[42] Second, he took on the scientific establishment of the time and refused to accept the legitimacy of their methods and data, much like a small minority of scientists do today regarding climate change. Third, he was attacked and executed by the left – so he was not only a courageous scientific iconoclast, but also a political martyr.

This identification with martyrdom is also a characteristic of the Galileo Movement, a related climate denial group founded in 2011 by two Noosa retirees, Case Smit and John Smeed. This group takes as its role model the great Italian physicist and astronomer Galileo Galilei (1564–1642), who famously challenged the teachings of the Catholic Church by arguing that the Earth revolved around the sun, and was tried for heresy by the Roman Inquisition. "Taking his name," declared Smit and Smeed, "we honour his integrity and courage in championing freedom and protecting science. He replaced religious doctrine with solid observable data."[43]

The Galileo Movement's patron is Sydney radio broadcaster Alan Jones, and its former manager, Malcolm Roberts, is a conspiracy theorist who was elected to the Senate in 2016 representing Pauline Hanson's One Nation party.[44] The Galileo Movement's list of "independent advisers" includes a number of Lavoisier members, such as Des Moore, meteorologist William Kininmonth, mathematician/engineer David Evans, and geologists Bob Carter, Ian Plimer and David Archibald. Archibald has worked in oil exploration and joined the board of the Lavoisier Group in 2007. He told its members shortly afterwards that despite the sinister conspiracy against them in this life, martyrdom awaited in the next: "My reward for this work, as it is for every member of the Lavoisier Society [sic], will be in Heaven, for the Forces of Darkness control the science journals, government departments, public institutes and universities. They reward each other for concocting ever more fantastic apocalyptic visions. It is as if all the biology journals were edited by creationists."[45] Archibald's extreme views are not limited to climate change. He was a candidate in the 2016 federal election representing the far-right, anti-Islam Australian Liberty Alliance, and in the 2017 WA election for Pauline Hanson's One Nation.

Inaugural conference

In addition to Walsh as president and Evans as secretary, the founding board of the Lavoisier Group was entirely composed of mining and energy industry figures. Ian Webber was a director of WMC and Santos (an oil and gas producer); Harold Clough ran Clough Engineering and was also a director of the IPA; Bob Foster was an engineer at Shell and BHP; Bruce Kean was chairman of Oil Company of Australia and chief executive of Boral; and Peter Murray was awarded a Medal of the Order of Australia (OAM) in 1992 for his "service to mining and the community."[46] The inaugural conference, titled 'Kyoto and the National Interest,' was held in Melbourne in May 2000, with speakers from both sides of politics, from business, from the scientific community, and two representatives from the National Farmers' Federation. Shane Rattenbury – then working for Greenpeace, but since 2008 a Greens member of the ACT Legislative Assembly – observed the conference and reported there being about sixty people in attendance, describing them as "classic Melbourne

Establishment, mostly male and over fifty."[47] Walsh set the tone of the event by handing out a page-by-page critique of a CSIRO report and questioning the organisation's claims to political independence. "The modern CSIRO," he said, "is not based on science but on politics."[48]

Hugh Morgan was enlisted to give the conference's opening address. The text of his speech strikes one as fairly tame by Morgan's standards. Declaring his full support for the objectives of the Lavoisier Group, he championed the right to challenge accepted scientific views without being accused of heresy. "It is an important part of the scientific process to continuously challenge scientific opinion as new information and new theories are put forward," he said. "Without challenge in science, doctrine prevails."[49] But as Rattenbury relates, Morgan was unable to resist the lure of controversy entirely, invoking Nazi Germany by referring to the Australian Greenhouse Office's discussion papers on emissions trading as "*Mein Kampf*-declarations."[50]

Self-taught science blogger John Daly followed Morgan's address with a presentation titled 'Global warming: science serving politics.' This paper was said to have caused a Damascene conversion for Tony Staley, former minister in the Fraser government and Liberal Party president from 1993 to 1999. Staley was due to give the conference's keynote address the following day. "We had John Daly run through his standard presentation and Staley was just knocked over," said a Lavoisier insider. "He'd never heard this before. And he opened his presentation the next day saying, 'Well, I mean we're all transformed now aren't we?'"[51] As a close and trusted friend of John Howard, Staley became vital to efforts to influence the government's climate policies. Alan Oxley, who we encountered earlier as Evans' co-organiser of anti-Kyoto conferences in 1997–1998, also gave a paper at the conference in which he argued that the Kyoto Protocol was a chimera, with fundamental flaws that made it unworkable.[52] The inaugural conference came to a close with a searching question from Peter Walsh: "Can we mobilise a countervailing pressure group to counteract the green extremists?"[53]

The Labor Party was represented at the conference not only by Walsh, but also by his son-in-law, Gary Gray, who was national secretary of the ALP from 1993 to 2000. In 2001 Gray joined Woodside Petroleum as a senior executive, before entering parliament in 2007. According to Frank Devine, Gray told the conference that because global warming was becoming an article of faith for young people, "any campaign against ratification of the Kyoto protocols based on denying greenhouse was doomed to failure."[54] As we will see shortly, the Lavoisier Group took little heed of this advice.

Speaking in 2012, Ray Evans held hopes that Gray would "make history" and switch to the Liberal Party in order to hold his seat at the 2013 election. "Gary's a very, very smart fellow," he said. "He'd hold the seat as a Liberal candidate, he won't as a Labor candidate."[55] But this rather fantastical idea did not materialise. Even worse for Evans, Gray retracted his earlier views on climate change upon being appointed as resources and energy minister in 2013. Admitting that he had once described climate science as a "middle-class conspiracy to frighten schoolchildren," Gray was now aligned with his party, which had introduced a carbon tax in 2011. Asked in 2013 by the ABC's Emma Alberici whether he was a climate sceptic, Gray responded emphatically that he wasn't. "No, I'm not. I was. I was. I was a vocal climate sceptic. And as national secretary of the Labor Party I said things that frankly, Emma, nowadays embarrass me when I hear it played back. [...] I attended the inaugural meeting of the Lavoisier Group and I counted and still count as friends members of that organisation. I just don't agree with them anymore.[56]

Climate science heretics

Few of the key players in the Lavoisier Group mentioned so far held any relevant scientific qualifications, though this did little to erode their confidence in questioning the science of climate change. Still, the appearance of scientific rigour was important, so scientists known to dissent from the consensus view were required, as they had been in the US.[57] Clive Hamilton has noted that in Australia, "there are only four such sceptics with anything resembling scientific credentials – Bob Carter, William Kininmonth, Ian Plimer and Garth Paltridge."[58] All four have been associated with the Lavoisier Group to greater and lesser degrees, and the first three deserve particular attention because of their prominence and devotion to the cause.

Bob Carter's scientific expertise was in geology and earth sciences, as well as palaeontology, and he held adjunct professorships at the University of Adelaide and James Cook University in Townsville. He was a scientific adviser and emeritus fellow at the IPA, and a senior fellow at the Heartland Institute in the United States, a global leader in climate denial. A leak in 2012 revealed that he was receiving a monthly payment of US$1667 as part of a Heartland program to pay "high-profile individuals who regularly and publicly counter the alarmist [anthropogenic global warming] message."[59] Though Carter did not deny that global warming had occurred in the final decades of the twentieth century, he argued that it was not caused by human activity. He also argued in 2006 that there had been a pause in temperatures since 1998, and that "a sudden natural cooling is far more to be feared, and will do infinitely more social and economic damage, than the late twentieth century phase of gentle warming."[60]

Carter claimed to be an apolitical scientist only concerned with evidence, but this didn't stop him from stepping into the political arena. In December 2006 he made submissions to the US Senate Committee on Environment and Public Works, arguing that the debate around human-caused global warming involved "McCarthyism, intimidation, press bias, censorship, policy-advice corruption and propaganda."[61] At a town hall meeting in rural Queensland in 2009 he urged his audience to take their concerns about carbon pricing to Canberra: "You have to beat down the door of every voting senator. [...] The Liberal senators have to be convinced this bill's got to be defeated a second time."[62] In 2010 Carter published *Climate: The Counter Consensus*, which developed at length his argument that global warming is no longer a scientific problem. "Rather, and as the IPCC and its supporters had always intended," he wrote, "since at least the turn of the twenty-first century global warming has been primarily a social and political issue."[63] The book received a glowing review in *Quadrant* from Ray Evans. Carter died in January 2016, aged seventy-three. Many tributes were offered from the international network of climate denial, as well as from Australian friends Ian Plimer, Clive James, Joanne Nova, John Spooner, Gary Johns, Andrew Bolt and Jennifer Marohasy.[64]

William Kininmonth was probably the scientist most closely associated with the Lavoisier Group. A retired meteorologist, he worked for the Bureau of Meteorology for thirty-eight years and was head of its National

Climate Centre from 1985 to 1998. He later established his own consultancy, the Australasian Climate Research Institute. These biographical facts lent an air of legitimacy to Kininmonth's claims to climate science expertise, but a closer look revealed his credentials to be rather thin. In January 2012 Kininmonth was one of sixteen signatories to an opinion piece in *The Wall Street Journal* arguing that global warming is no cause for panic, and he was described as the "former head of climate research at the Australian Bureau of Meteorology."[65] Climate blogger Graham Readfearn sought more information from the Bureau about the National Climate Centre's work during Kininmonth's tenure, and was advised that it "mainly centred on climate database management and climate monitoring activities" and "had no formal role in undertaking or directing climate change research."[66]

Kininmonth was a member of Australian delegations to international climate conferences in the early 1990s, but throughout that decade became suspicious "that the science and predictions of anthropogenic global warming had extended beyond sound theory and evidence."[67] Since 2001 he has consistently argued that climate change is a natural phenomenon not influenced by human activity. In November 2002 the Lavoisier Group published his pamphlet 'Climate change: a natural hazard,' described on its website as "a veritable Exocet missile aimed at the Kyoto establishment."[68] Two years later it was expanded into a book of the same name and, in an apparent coup, launched by Kininmonth's former boss at the Bureau of Meteorology, the highly respected John Zillman. However, Zillman made it clear that he did so with reservations: while agreeing with some parts of the book, he also chided Kininmonth for going too far in his criticism of climate modelling, suggesting that he "for whatever reason, misinterprets and/or misrepresents some important aspects of the science of climate change that are now pretty well understood."[69] Zillman later told *The Age*: "I won't be expecting to be invited back as a regular."[70]

Another Lavoisier Group favourite was Ian Plimer. Like Carter, Plimer's main area of expertise was geology. He was professor of geology at the University of Melbourne when he gave a paper on the science behind Kyoto at the inaugural Lavoisier Group conference, and later became professor of mining geology at the University of Adelaide. His work in the field of mining geology has been rewarded with various mining industry directorships. Plimer came to public prominence in the 1990s as an energetic critic of creationist Christians. In 1994 he published *Telling Lies for God: Reason vs Creationism*, a 300-page scientific refutation of creationist beliefs. Plimer was particularly irritated by Allen Roberts, an archaeologist who claimed to have found evidence of Noah's Ark in eastern Turkey. In 1997 Plimer alleged in the Federal Court that creationist material distributed by Roberts was misleading and deceptive under the *Trade Practices Act*. Billed as a belated sequel to the 1925 Scopes Monkey Trial, where a Tennessee man was charged with teaching Charles Darwin's theory of evolution in a state high school, Plimer's case eventually failed on the grounds that Roberts' activities did not constitute trade or commerce.[71]

Having fought against religious belief in one field, Plimer turned to what he saw as another example of foolish superstition, lamenting that "global warming has become the secular religion of today."[72] Such views led to Plimer becoming one of the Lavoisier Group's most cited Australian scientists. Ray Evans also had a hand in Plimer's greatest commercial achievement, the 2009 publication of *Heaven and Earth: Global Warming, the Missing Science*. Anthony Cappello of Connor Court Publishing had been in discussions with Evans and the IPA's John Roskam about publishing something on climate change. Evans mentioned this to Plimer, who was searching for a publisher at the time, and "the rest is history," as Cappello says.[73] *Heaven and Earth* has sold more than 100,000 copies and has become something of a bible for climate deniers both in Australia and overseas. The book's Melbourne launch was hosted by the IPA and featured an address by Arvi Parbo, the former chairman of WMC and close associate of Morgan and Evans.

Obfuscation, denial and delay

Ray Evans made the intentions of the Lavoisier Group plain in his letter of invitation to its inaugural conference in 2000, declaring that "the science behind global warming is far less certain than its protagonists claim" and "the economic damage which Australia would suffer if a carbon tax ...

were imposed would be far, far greater than is currently appreciated in Canberra."[74] The immediate aims of the group were then outlined on its website shortly afterwards. They were:

- to promote vigorous debate within Australia greenhouse science and greenhouse policy;
- to ensure that the full extent of the economic consequences, for Australia, of the regime of carbon withdrawal prescribed by the yet-to-be-ratified Kyoto Protocol, are fully understood by the Australian community;
- to explore the implications which treaties such as the Kyoto Protocol have for Australia's sovereignty, and for the GATT/WTO rules which protect Australia (and other WTO members) from the use of trade sanctions as an instrument of extraterritorial power.[75]

The only change to these points was made in 2008, when they were slightly amended to reflect the diminishing significance of the Kyoto Protocol, and instead focus on the consequences of decarbonisation.

For critics, however, this was seen as window-dressing, and did little to disguise the Lavoisier Group's campaign of obfuscation and deception. Clive Hamilton found the Group to be "immune to argument," and summarised its convictions the following way:

- There is no evidence of global warming.
- If there is evidence of global warming, then warming is not due to human activity.
- If global warming is occurring and it is due to human activity, then it is not going to be damaging.
- If global warming is occurring, it is due to human activity and it is going to be damaging, then the costs of avoiding it will be too high, so we should do nothing.[76]

More succinctly, Guy Pearse, a former Liberal Party staffer and lobbyist turned climate whistleblower, has described the strategy as "a devastatingly effective formula: deny and delay – and deceive along the way."[77]

The obvious first step in preventing any action on climate change was to deny the existence of a problem in the first place. After all, why cut carbon pollution when it causes no harm? But given the overwhelming weight of scientific evidence refutes such a claim, to make it requires either deliberate deception, or the belief in a vast international conspiracy involving scientists, politicians, bureaucrats and environmental activists. Lavoisier Group members have not been strangers to either of these approaches.

Using a dataset of 1372 climate researchers, a 2010 US National Academy of Sciences study found that "97–98% of the climate researchers most actively publishing in the field surveyed here support the tenets of [anthropogenic climate change] outlined by the Intergovernmental Panel on Climate Change, and ... the relative climate expertise and scientific prominence of the researchers unconvinced of ACC are substantially below that of the convinced researchers."[78] Aware that such findings damaged their credibility in the debate, climate sceptics focused their efforts on emphasising the prominence of those who questioned the broad scientific consensus. In the process they helped to feed a public narrative that scientists were divided on the issue, when in reality there existed a remarkable level of agreement among experts.

This campaign strategy of denial and obfuscation was comprehensively exposed by Naomi Oreskes and Erik Conway in their 2010 book *Merchants of Doubt*. Oreskes and Conway relate how industry groups and think tanks have delayed or prevented action on issues such as tobacco smoking, acid rain, the hole in the ozone layer and global warming using the maxim "doubt is our product."

> First they claimed there was none, then they claimed it was just natural variation, and then they claimed that even if it was happening and it was our fault, it didn't matter because we could just adapt to it. In case after case, they steadfastly denied the existence of scientific agreement, even though they, themselves, were pretty much the only ones who disagreed.[79]

The strategy was immediately familiar to any observer of the Lavoisier Group.

A variety of dubious scientific arguments were used as part of this campaign. William Kininmonth argued that recent global warming "can be attributed to natural phenomena," not human activity.[80] Bob Foster believed that there was a simple reason for climate change being over-looked by the IPCC: the sun.[81] Another common theme was to present carbon dioxide as an innocent, non-polluting victim of political debate. Blurring the distinction between the naturally occurring element essential to all life on Earth and the emissions produced by the burning of fossil fuels, Ray Evans argued that carbon "has been cast as a symbol of mankind's malevolent behaviour towards the planet, and it has been demonized accordingly."[82] Hence the theme of a 2007 Lavoisier Group workshop: 'Rehabilitating Carbon Dioxide.'

A more controversial method of denying climate science was to make allegations of corruption. This preparedness to embrace conspiratorial thinking is one way in which the Lavoisier Group stands apart from the H.R. Nicholls, Samuel Griffith and Bennelong societies. Key figures such as Evans, Morgan and Walsh are on the record as having described global warming variously as a hoax, a scam or a fraud. The conclusion to Evans' 2006 pamphlet, 'Nine facts about climate change,' typified these assertions:

> The global warming scam has been, arguably, the most extraordinary exam-ple of scientific fraud in the postwar period. So many people, and institutions, have been caught up in the web of deceit, master-minded by environmental activists working through NGOs and their manipulation of the IPCC pro-cesses, that the integrity of Western science is seriously at risk. The unravel-ling of this web will result in the loss of reputation for many individuals, but more importantly, in the restructuring of those scientific institutions in Aus-tralia and elsewhere which have tied their reputations to that of the IPCC.[83]

This line of thinking received a fillip in November 2009 – just prior to the UN Climate Change Conference in Copenhagen, Denmark, where a suc-cessor to the Kyoto Protocol was to be developed – when the email server of the University of East Anglia's Climatic Research Unit was hacked. Sceptics claimed that the emails revealed that scientists were manipulat-ing data in order to advance the theory of global warming. The scientists involved refuted this, and argued that emails had been selectively edited and taken out of context to distort their content.[84] Multiple investigators in the United Kingdom and the United States agreed, finding no evidence of fraud or misconduct, but the "climategate" scandal continues to be an article of faith for climate sceptics, confirming all that they had previously suspected about the allegedly corrupt climate establishment.

Attempts to deny the science were often successful in clouding the climate change debate in doubt, especially for lay people, but most politicians and policymakers remained persuaded by the more authoritative work of eminent climate scientists. The next step for climate deniers, then, was to prevent or delay action by warning of the catastrophic social and economic consequences of reducing carbon emissions. Ironically, this involved countering the arguments of global warming "doomsayers" with their own hyperbolic predictions of the disasters that preventative action would portend.

In September 1999 it was reported that the Commonwealth Treasury had prepared a paper on a carbon tax. Evans responded by describing it as "a unilateral act of self-mutilation."[85] The following year the Lavoisier Group warned the Joint Standing Committee on Treaties that "with the Kyoto Protocol we face the most serious challenge to our sovereignty since the Japanese Fleet entered the Coral Sea on 3 May, 1942."[86] In a 2008 essay on "the chilling costs of climate catastrophism," Evans declared that the "warmists" were presenting us with two equally absurd options: either abandon all fossil fuels as sources of energy or "return to the living standards which were characteristic of Britain and North America in the eighteenth century, before the Industrial Revolution."[87]

In 2009 the Lavoisier Group published *Back to the 19th Century*, a collection of essays by Evans, Tom Quirk and Alan Moran warning of the potential consequences of the Rudd government's Carbon Pollution Reduction Scheme (CPRS). Elevating his rhetoric even further, Evans suggested that Labor's climate agenda represented an existential threat to Australian democracy: "a collation of fantasy and deceit, coupled with an ambit claim for political power which is unprecedented in Australian history and which justifies the use of the term 'coup d'état'. The discretion which is vested in the minister is breathtaking. The use of regulation rather than legislation to impose the will of the salvationists upon the people brings back the ancient claim of kings 'The law is my mouth'."[88] Such language was undoubtedly designed to frighten politicians and the public about the potential negative consequences of climate action. It appears desperate and even irrational, but it was at times effective.

Web of denial

Like the single-issue advocacy groups that came before it, the Lavoisier Group used traditional methods to publish the writing of its members – the major daily newspapers and *Quadrant* magazine. The latter became especially important after Keith Windschuttle became its editor in 2008; a succession of climate-themed articles by Lavoisier Group figures began appearing in *Quadrant* from then onwards. Ray Evans said that Windschuttle "was very keen to get this issue [climate change] up and running, and he did with great effect."[89] Evans alone penned eight such articles published between 2008 and 2012. Other authors included Bob Carter, William Kininmonth, Garth Paltridge, Tom Quirk and Tim Curtin.

But as Robert Manne has noted, these traditional methods of lobbying and campaigning were in the 2000s trumped by the internet as "the most effective denialist media weapon."[90] Like the Bennelong Society, the Lavoisier Group was born in the internet age, and its founders saw the world wide web as a vital tool to disseminate its message. "Arguably the most important activity undertaken by the Lavoisier Group is the maintenance of our website," Peter Walsh told the group's annual general meeting in 2007. "We continue to publish important pieces which either impact upon the climate change debate or inform our membership and the wider public about the progression of that debate."[91]

The internet was even more important for the Lavoisier Group than it was for the Bennelong Society, because it allowed the organisation to plug into a "global web of climate denial."[92] Venturing into this network, one is confronted with a bewildering number of think tanks, websites, blogs and industry front groups, all repeating the same messages. Guy Pearse argues that there has been "continuous collaboration over the years between Australian and US neoliberal think tanks, industry associations, polluters and politicians. They are in constant contact and working in tandem. The AIGN, the IPA, Lavoisier and the APEC Studies Centre have been at the heart of the action, as have various multinational corporations. The American players are in the thick of the lobbying here, and Australian interests are similarly enmeshed in the US."[93] As we have seen, Ray Evans was already familiar with key climate deniers in the United States thanks to his work with the CEI in the 1990s opposing the Kyoto Protocol. A links page was added to the Lavoisier Group website in 2001 and included a variety of sites, including the CEI, the Cato Institute, Fred Singer's Science & Environmental Policy Project, JunkScience.com and the Greening Earth Society.[94] In 2002 the Cooler Heads Coalition – a global network of climate denial organisations founded by the CEI in 1997 – described the Lavoisier Group as "the principal intellectual and organizational opposition in Australia to Kyoto and was organized by our colleague, N. Ray Evans of Melbourne."[95] The Lavoisier Group joined the Cooler Heads Coalition in 2004.[96]

As the number of climate denial organisations and individuals within Australia proliferated throughout the 2000s, the internet became increasingly vital as a tool of communication and coordination. Central to the network of denial was the IPA. In 2005 the IPA established the Australian Environment Foundation (AEF), which described itself as "a not-for-profit, membership-based environmental organisation having no political affiliation."[97] Its questionable environmental credentials and links to industry groups were quickly exposed, however.[98] The AEF was initially chaired by climate blogger Jennifer Marohasy, who wrote, following Evans' death in 2014, that he had taught her how to win an argument "by forcing your opponent to engage with you on the detail."[99] The AEF established the Australian Climate Science Coalition in 2008, whose Scientific Advisory Panel included Bob Carter, Ian Plimer, William Kininmonth and others closely associated with the Lavoisier Group.[100] The IPA's centrality to this network was confirmed by John Roskam in 2010, when he told *The Sydney Morning Herald*: "Of all the serious sceptics in Australia, we have helped and supported just about all of them in their work one way or another."[101]

A key method of advocacy for the Lavoisier Group was to lobby politicians, both formally and informally. This began almost immediately with a written submission to a Senate inquiry into proposed renewable energy legislation in July 2000 and, the following month, a submission to the Joint Standing Committee on Treaties' Inquiry into the Kyoto Protocol. This inquiry, which aimed to determine whether ratification of the Kyoto Protocol was in Australia's national interest, was chaired by Liberal MP Andrew Thomson. Thomson had given an impromptu address at the Lavoisier Group's inaugural conference in May, in which he informed attendees about the government's plans to establish the Kyoto Inquiry.[102]

In addition to its written submissions, the Lavoisier Group was represented at the Kyoto Inquiry's public hearings by Evans, Walsh and Bob Foster. They were joined by international guests Sonja Boehmer-Christiansen and Richard Lindzen, whose travel costs were paid by the Lavoisier Group.[103] Boehmer-Christiansen has since 1998 been the editor of *Energy & Environment*, described by Michael Mann as "the home journal of climate change denial."[104] Lindzen was a professor of meteorology at the Massachusetts Institute of Technology and consultant to oil and coal companies. Ross Gelbspan has written of how Lindzen infuriates his adversaries with his "excruciatingly argumentative style that at times seems relentlessly obscurantist and self-contradictory."[105] One is reminded here of Evans' advice to Jennifer Marohasy: force your opponent to engage with you on the detail.

This philosophy was also demonstrated in 2007–2008 during the Garnaut Climate Change Review. In April 2007 economist Ross Garnaut was commissioned by Labor Opposition leader Kevin Rudd, along with all state and territory governments, to conduct a study into the potential impacts of climate change on the Australian economy. The Lavoisier Group submitted around 170 pages of testimony to the Review, and separate submissions were also entered by Peter Walsh, Bob Carter, David Archibald, Des Moore, Sonja Boehmer-Christiansen, Fred Singer and Tim Curtin. None of this enormous amount of material seemed to persuade Garnaut, however, who concluded that Australia should commit to carbon emissions reduction targets and implement an emissions trading scheme. The Labor government, elected in November 2007, set about doing just that.

The Lavoisier Group had much more success influencing the direction of climate policy in the Howard years. Guy Pearse has documented in great detail how John Howard and his ministers were captured by fossil fuel interests and their associates. Though the Lavoisier Group was just one of many actors in this capture, it played a central role. In Pearse's view the most important figure was Hugh Morgan, having been told by an energy industry source that

Hugh Morgan has driven the Minerals Council, Hugh has driven the Business Council, Hugh has driven the Australian Aluminium Council, and

Hugh is behind the Lavoisier Group and all the rest of it. He has used the power of Western Mining, the mining industry and the aluminium industry, and the BCA; and privately, he has direct access to the Prime Minister. But he also had direct access to the former prime minister, Paul Keating. You know, of all industry leaders, he would have been the most powerful without any shadow of a doubt.[106]

Not only did Morgan directly lobby the government; he also used his enormous influence within the business community to push a number of companies and peak bodies to adopt sceptical positions on climate change. That way Howard could be seen to be listening to a variety of views, when in fact the big polluters had created an echo chamber of climate denial. While claiming to be an agnostic rather than a sceptic, Howard's language on climate change often mirrored that of the denialists. "For many, it has become a substitute religion," he wrote in his memoir. "Most of the mass media has boarded the climate-change train; arguments to the contrary are dismissed as extremist. Moral bullying has been employed to silence those who question the conventional wisdom."[107]

The Group's less successful efforts to influence the climate policies of the Labor Party were not for a want of trying. Peter Walsh, a legendary figure to many in the ALP, was vital to these efforts. A "senior Lavoisier office-bearer" informed Pearse: "We have a good following in the Labor Party ... Walshy has been a fantastic president and he's given us entree to the Labor Party because he's still got a fan club in the Labor Party and quite an effective one too ... Walshy has access to anybody he wants to see apart from the Labor Left."[108] While a few Labor figures stood out as sympathetic to the arguments of climate sceptics – Gary Gray, Martin Ferguson and Bill Ludwig, for example – the majority accepted the expertise and advice of mainstream climate scientists. In order to pursue and potentially achieve its aims, the Lavoisier Group would need to focus its lobbying efforts on the Coalition.

The Lavoisier Group kicked off with the aforementioned 'Kyoto and the National Interest' conference in May 2000, and followed it up with another, 'Kyoto: Dead or Alive?' in September 2001. A 'Rehabilitating Carbon Dioxide' workshop was held in 2007, and a forum titled 'The Solar System and Earth's Climate' in 2008, but that was all. In contrast with the

H.R. Nicholls, Samuel Griffith and Bennelong societies, a schedule of annual conferences was not consistently maintained. Instead, following the media attention surrounding the launch of William Kininmonth's *Climate Change: A Natural Hazard* in 2004, the Lavoisier Group attempted to promote its cause in the corridors of power via a series of publication launches featuring sympathetic politicians.

In May 2006 the Lavoisier Group sought to make a splash in Australia's political epicentre with the launch of Evans' 'Nine lies about global warming' at Parliament House. Though the pamphlet was a mere thirteen pages long, it was nevertheless launched by Liberal Party backbencher Russell Broadbent. Broadbent's main claim to fame in politics was as one of a handful of government MPs who challenged John Howard's hardline asylum-seeker policies. But his involvement in a campaign against a proposed wind farm development in his electorate was what attracted Evans to him. In offering Broadbent his thanks at the launch, Evans said that the MP "has been attacked and ridiculed by the chattering class press, and Victorian ministers, for taking seriously the concerns and fears of his constituents."[109]

That launch barely caused a ripple in the media, however, so the Lavoisier Group returned to Canberra in February 2007 for the launch of another Evans pamphlet, 'Nine facts about climate change.' This time Arvi Parbo gave the launching address at a function hosted by another Liberal backbencher, Dennis Jensen. Jensen holds a PhD in materials science from Monash University and was a research scientist and defence analyst before entering parliament. He is also an outspoken climate change denier, as he revealed in his maiden speech to the House of Representatives in 2004, where he accused "the global warmers" of wanting to "not only bet our economy but, more likely, significantly damage our economy on a theory that will probably go the way of the flat earth theory: restricted to a few adherents who have become totally divorced from reality."[110] With politicians from both major parties in attendance – Jensen, Broadbent and Nick Minchin from the Liberals; Martin Ferguson, Craig Emerson and Dick Adams from the ALP – the media now took notice of Lavoisier activities. Ferguson acknowledged the political risk of keeping such company when he remarked: "I don't know about global cooling, but I'll know about global warming in the Labor Party caucus if I don't watch my Ps and Qs this afternoon."[111]

For Evans' third climate publication the Lavoisier Group travelled to Adelaide and Perth in early 2009, where 'Thank God for carbon' was launched by Senator Cory Bernardi and Dennis Jensen respectively. Bernardi, a controversial member of the Liberal Party's hard right who quit to form his own Conservative party in 2017, had been an open climate denier since the publication of his 2007 article 'Cool heads needed on global warming', in which he claimed that "climate change is the latest incarnation in a thirty-year-long claim that mankind is destroying the planet."[112] Evans used both events to try to exert influence on the Liberal Party. Noting that Bernardi's appearance might upset some of his more moderate colleagues, Evans hoped that "when push comes to shove, those of you who are here today, and are in a position to influence opinion within the Liberal Party, will support Cory with all your strength."[113] At the Perth launch Evans paid Jensen a heartfelt tribute "for keeping the flag of scientific integrity and commitment to reason flying high within the Federal Parliamentary Liberal Party."[114] Finally, in November 2009, amid an almighty battle within the Coalition over emissions trading, National Party senator Barnaby Joyce launched the Lavoisier Group's collection *Back to the 19th Century*.

Lobbying against Kyoto

As we saw earlier in this chapter, opposition to climate change action among conservatives crystallised around the question of whether Australia would ratify the Kyoto Protocol. In September 1998 it was revealed that the Australian government had decided it would not ratify unless the United States did so too. Given that the US Senate had in 1997 unanimously passed a resolution rejecting any climate treaty that would impose mandatory emissions reductions and/or harm the American economy, US ratification was looking increasingly unlikely, despite President Bill Clinton's support. The Howard government was in effect committing to indefinite delay, but this seemingly favourable outcome provided little succour to the likes of Evans, who continued to devote his energies to campaigning against ratification.

Just as the Lavoisier Group was forming in 2000, divisions within the government on Kyoto ratification were deepening. On one side was the environment minister, Robert Hill, whose negotiation of Australia's lenient reduction targets had been widely praised by his colleagues, but whose commitment to Kyoto made him the subject of much criticism at the Lavoisier Group's inaugural conference. Leading those opposed to Hill was the minister for industry, science and resources, Nick Minchin, who has since argued that fears about global warming are part of an extreme left plot to "de-industrialise the western world."[115] Minchin was a willing participant in what Clive Hamilton described as the Lavoisier Group's "systematic campaign designed to muddy the waters on climate science and to pressure the Federal Government into a volte-face on its undertakings at Kyoto."[116]

According to Guy Pearse, throughout this period Hill was "progressively undermined on greenhouse policy by his colleagues, chiefly Howard, Minchin, John Anderson, Alexander Downer and Wilson Tuckey."[117] When Howard reshuffled his ministry following the 2001 election, Hill moved from environment to defence. Pearse views this as a deliberate sidelining of Hill, but Hill himself told me that the portfolio switch was his own initiative. "I had been the longest-serving environment minister, had achieved most of my reform agenda and thought the portfolio would benefit from an infusion of new blood, and ideas," he said.[118]

Hill's replacement was veteran right-wing warrior David Kemp. Kemp was welcomed by the business community as likely to be more sympathetic to their concerns about Kyoto than Hill.[119] He was also, given his involvement with the H.R. Nicholls Society and IPA, an ostensible ally of the Lavoisier Group. Though Kemp had no formal links with the Group, he and Evans discussed climate issues privately, wherein Kemp warned Evans against unrealistic demands: "Ray you are a purist, I have to live in the real world."[120] Perhaps inevitably, Kemp proved a disappointment, with Evans later writing that he had "alienated many of his old friends and supporters by adopting the rhetoric and arguments of the green ideologists who staff Environment Australia."[121]

Meanwhile, international developments were favouring the Kyoto sceptics. Republican candidate George W. Bush won the 2000 US presidential election over the Democratic Party's dedicated climate activist Al Gore.

Within months of taking office President Bush announced that the United States would not ratify the Kyoto Protocol while much of the developing world remained exempt from its requirements. The Australian government now had a powerful ally making similar arguments about the potential economic damage Kyoto could do, and on World Environment Day in June 2002, Howard unilaterally announced that Australia would also not ratify. Kemp was reportedly stunned.[122] Hugh Morgan, though, was quick to praise the prime minister in *The Australian*, reminding readers of the "economic dislocation, rising unemployment and political upheaval" Australia would have faced if legally bound to meet its Kyoto commitments.[123]

By late 2006, Howard was confidently quoting the words of Peter Walsh in parliament to mock the climate policies of his Labor opponents. But his confidence was misplaced. As he recounts in his memoir, he was facing a "perfect storm" of events that would dramatically recast the Australian climate debate.[124] In addition to the record-breaking drought conditions across much of eastern Australia, the Victorian bushfire season began early. Al Gore's climate change documentary *An Inconvenient Truth* – described by Evans as "bullshit from beginning to end"[125] – hit theatres and Gore arrived in Australia on a promotional tour, while in the United Kingdom the Stern Review on the Economics of Climate Change was released. Global warming was now an issue at the forefront of voters' minds. When Kevin Rudd took over the leadership of the Labor Party in December 2006, he placed action on climate change at the centre of his agenda, in a calculated attempt to expose Howard as out of touch. Rudd's first official act as prime minister following his 2007 election victory was to ratify the Kyoto Protocol.

The Lavoisier Group may not have prevented ratification but it had certainly succeeded in delaying it. The irony of the entire campaign was that Australia continued to meet its Kyoto targets throughout, without any demonstrable damage to the economy. The Lavoisier Group's warnings of social and economic catastrophe were proven to be mere hyperbole. Accepting that he had been outmanoeuvred on the issue, Howard dismissed Rudd's ratification of Kyoto as "feel-good politics at its best," but warned that persuading the public to accept an emissions trading scheme would prove much more difficult.[126] Carbon pricing was to become the next battlefield in which the Lavoisier Group would start lobbing grenades.

Declaring war on the Liberal Party over carbon pricing

Ray Evans related to me that in 1999 he was told that "the three top mandarins in Canberra had decided that we were going to have a carbon tax and we'd have to get used to it." "Not if I can help it, you're not!" was his defiant response, and he was true to his word.[127] In May 2003 Peter Walsh wrote to John Howard on behalf of the Lavoisier Group, reminding him of the wisdom of his Kyoto decision, and warning him of bureaucrats' desires to implement an emissions trading scheme (ETS).[128] In July that year, with some ministers concerned that the government lacked a climate policy of any material consequence, a proposal for an ETS reached Cabinet. However, against the advice of senior ministers Peter Costello, David Kemp, Ian Macfarlane, Warren Truss and Brendan Nelson, Howard rejected the proposal.[129] In 2007, increasingly desperate as an election defeat looked ever more certain, Howard changed his mind and backed the idea, but it was too late to save his government. Support for an ETS remained Coalition policy until events took a dramatic turn in 2009.

Malcolm Turnbull, who became leader of the Liberal Party in September 2008, was committed to action on climate change. As environment minister in 2007 he had argued unsuccessfully in Cabinet for Kyoto ratification. Now, as leader of the party, he was prepared to provide support for Labor's Carbon Pollution Reduction Scheme (CPRS). Members of the Lavoisier Group were alarmed. In December 2008 Evans wrote to Andrew Robb, taking him to task for the "Liberal Party's current state of hopelessness and helplessness" under Turnbull.[130] Robb was then the shadow minister assisting Turnbull on emissions trading design, but also a climate sceptic.[131] Evans challenged him to take up the fight against emissions trading: "If you really wanted to change opinion on this issue you'd be getting advice from leading world scientists who could come out here and explain the fraudulent nonsense which the IPCC has been peddling. You'd be getting people from the power industry to explain how decarbonisation will affect electricity supplies and electricity prices. It's marvellous how a bit of determined leadership can generate support."[132]

As we have seen, Evans continued to rally climate sceptics within the Liberal Party at the launches of 'Thank God for carbon' in early 2009, and the Coalition became increasingly divided over the CPRS as the year progressed. When the legislation was defeated in the Senate in August, the widespread expectation was that Turnbull would negotiate amendments that would facilitate its passage later in the year. But events – and his party – were soon beyond his control. In Evans' recollection, the pivotal incident came "when Tony Abbott, at Beaufort, in that famous meeting on the 30th of September 2009, said after a lot of sort of pushing, that it [climate science] was absolute crap, then it was away."[133] Abbott had been largely supportive of Turnbull's position, but a conversation with Minchin the day after the Beaufort event left him resolute: the CPRS had to be defeated.[134] Despite the increasing pressure on his leadership, Turnbull refused to back down, going on radio the same day to declare: "I will not lead a party that is not as committed to effective action on climate change as I am."[135]

In November the ABC's *Four Corners* broadcast 'Malcolm and the Malcontents,' which focused on the Coalition's internal war over climate change, with sceptics such as Minchin, Cory Bernardi, Dennis Jensen and Barnaby Joyce featuring heavily. The program included footage of Bernardi's speech at the Adelaide launch of 'Thank God for carbon,' and Joyce introducing Bob Carter at a town hall meeting in rural Queensland, revealing the extent to which climate sceptics had infiltrated Coalition ranks. Minchin – described in the program as "the godfather of the Liberals' climate sceptics" – invoked the authority of sceptical scientists such as Carter, Garth Paltridge and Ian Plimer, and encouraged his colleagues to speak out in defiance of their leader.[136] This especially riled Turnbull, who later said that "Minchin effectively declared war on the party in that *Four Corners* interview."[137]

Later in November the CPRS bill was denounced by Minchin in the Senate and, most dramatically, by Andrew Robb in the Coalition party room. Turnbull's leadership was now under siege, and when it was put to a ballot on the first day of December, he lost to Tony Abbott by one vote. Having admitted to Turnbull he had been "a bit of a weathervane" on the CPRS, Abbott was now in lock step with the climate sceptics.[138] "By then," he later recalled, "my view was that the ETS could be characterised as a giant tax:

creating a huge slush fund, providing massive handouts and spawning a vast bureaucracy."[139] Evans called Abbott's victory "an important event in the Anglospherian struggle between the warmists and the sceptics, and in the long term, it means that any attempt to decarbonise Australia on the grounds that carbon dioxide is a pollutant, is bound to fail."[140]

Hugh Morgan told a meeting of the Lavoisier Group the following year that "in the fortnight before this ballot on December 1, the Coalition parliamentarians experienced a deluge of emails, faxes and letters in an unprecedented and spontaneous wave of rank-and-file hostility to what was happening in Canberra."[141] Evans also said that it was the work of rank-and-file Liberal Party members, but there can be little doubt about the Lavoisier Group's involvement in marshalling the campaign. *The Sydney Morning Herald* reported that Australia's climate denial network "was instrumental in nurturing the deluge of climate sceptic emails that helped to convince Liberal MPs to dump Malcolm Turnbull."[142] In its naming of Evans as among the top fifty most influential people in politics in 2012, *The Australian* described his clout as having "reached a spectacular crescendo" during the Liberal leadership crisis.[143] Finally, Andrew Norton gave the Lavoisier Group a backhanded compliment when I asked him about its influence in 2012:

> The grumpy old men of the right actually ran a pretty effective campaign, which exploited existing vulnerabilities. They really did help transform the debate in that critical moment back in 2009, when they really helped stir the Liberal backbench to the point where the leadership effectively changed over the issue. So I think even though they're probably not that intellectually strong, their activism was very, very important in changing the Coalition's stance on this, and that had a huge domino effect.[144]

Today

In late 2008 Ray Evans was boasting of the climate denial movement's gains. "The sceptics are growing in confidence and becoming emboldened," he told

The Canberra Times. "In terms of morale, the atmosphere in the blogosphere is very cocky."[145] But following the remarkable sequence of events that culminated in Turnbull's downfall as leader of the Liberal Party in 2009, it was perhaps inevitable that the Lavoisier Group would enter a period of decline. Peter Walsh had already stood down as president in October 2009, replaced by Hugh Morgan. Ill health forced Evans to reduce his political activities from 2010 onwards. The Lavoisier Group was now essentially operating without its two most energetic and inspirational figures.

Having given up on trying to pass the CPRS in April 2010, Kevin Rudd was ousted from the prime ministership by Julia Gillard in June. A virtual tie in the August election left Gillard leading a minority government, backed by a formal alliance with the Greens. Despite this, Morgan appeared hopeful that Australia would soon be back on the right track when he surveyed the year's events in a report to the Lavoisier Group's annual general meeting in November. "A resolute Commonwealth government could ameliorate this situation greatly," he said, "provided it acted in complete defiance of the Greens and of the chattering class opinion which is still locked into Gaia worship."[146] But in February 2011 Gillard announced, with the support of the Greens, that a carbon tax would be introduced, outraging the Opposition and much of the community. The legislation passed both houses of parliament in November. Tony Abbott's subsequent campaign against the carbon tax was ruthless and ultimately successful. The Coalition won a landslide election victory in September 2013, and the tax was repealed the following year.

And yet throughout this period of high drama in climate politics, the Lavoisier Group remained virtually silent, lacking the personnel to continue the fight. When Evans died in June 2014, management of the Lavoisier Group's website was transferred to the Bert Kelly Research Centre, but updates have been few and far between. Walsh also passed away in 2015, at the age of eighty. The climate denial network lives on in Australia through other groups and individuals: the IPA, the Australian Industry Greenhouse Network, the AEF and various other lobby groups, blogs and websites; however, in March 2016 John Stone likened the Lavoisier Group to the Bennelong Society in that it had "gone out of existence to all intents and purposes."[147]

In August 2016, "inspired by the Brexit decision of the British people to withdraw from the increasingly dictatorial grasp of the EU bureaucracy," an international group of climate sceptics formed the "Clexit" campaign.[148] Led by former prime minister and president of the Czech Republic Václav Klaus and eccentric British aristocrat Christopher Monckton, both intimately familiar with the Australian climate denial scene, Clexit aimed to prevent ratification of the UN climate treaty agreed to in Paris in December 2015. Lavoisier Group figures among its founding members include Morgan, Stone, David Archibald, Alan Moran, Ian Plimer and David Evans.[149]

Given the centrality of climate change to the political upheaval that Australia has experienced over the past decade, there can be no doubt that the Lavoisier Group's role has been important. But, as this chapter has shown, it has not acted alone. Its members have spread their political campaigning and lobbying among a variety of organisations, sharing the workload while maximising results. They also have not sought to advertise their influence, providing politicians with an alibi when they are accused of getting too close to major polluters. Guy Pearse's analysis is worth quoting at length here:

> The influence of the Lavoisier Group and the other think tanks is informal and behind the scenes. Often ministers adopt the arguments of the IPA, the CIS and the APEC SC in public statements without attribution. They enthusiastically attend the greenhouse denial and delay conferences organised by the IPA, CIS and APEC SC. Support for the Lavoisier Group is generally at arms' length due to their slightly more extreme views on the science. Even so, most politicians and functionaries attending Lavoisier events are drawn from Liberal and National party circles, their attendance is usually kept quiet … To the think tanks, it matters little whether they are credited for the arguments as long as their ideas are picked up. As one senior player inside the Lavoisier Group confidently stated to me, the main thing is that there "is an understanding in cabinet that all the science is crap."[150]

In 2012 Des Moore told me that he thought the biggest change that had come about in recent years – thanks to the efforts of the Lavoisier Group and others – was that sceptics were no longer demonised and relegated to the fringes; they were now part of the mainstream debate. "I think the change has been that whereas three or four years ago people who were sceptical about global warming were regarded as being rather eccentric and way out on the right wing of politics," he said in our interview. "… we are now recognised as having a good case […] I think the sceptics are still in a minority but there's been a big shift of opinion and a preparedness to publish material that is of a sceptical origin."[151] This shift became even more explicit when Malcolm Turnbull returned to the leadership of the Liberal Party – this time as prime minister – in September 2015. Despite his long-held view that action on climate change was necessary and urgent, he was unwilling or unable to make even minor changes to the government's climate policies – policies that are widely viewed by scientists, environmentalists and economists as inadequate. The grip that climate sceptics had on his party was too strong. Eventually, they got their wish and ousted Turnbull from the leadership once again.

7

AN ANATOMY OF REACTIONARY CONSERVATISM

A new organisational form

T HE H.R. NICHOLLS SOCIETY, Samuel Griffith Society, Bennelong Society and Lavoisier Group emerged from a New Right milieu that was relatively united in its political outlook. But these four particular single-issue advocacy groups were different from the think tanks, publications and institutions that preceded them in a number of important ways. The first and most obvious characteristic that set them apart was their focus on a single policy area. Instead of taking a generalised approach to a broad array of issues, Ray Evans decided that what was needed, first in the case of industrial relations, was an organisation solely devoted to an issue that could narrow its focus in order to achieve concrete goals. As he told me: "The great advantage of the H.R. Nicholls Society was the very, very narrow focus. We didn't have to worry about anything else. [...] It's a great advantage to be able to focus on an issue which does require strong focus over a period of time."[1]

These organisations are often referred to as either think tanks or interest groups, and while it is true that they contain characteristics of both, it is important to explain why neither categorisation is sufficient. The think tanks discussed in Chapter 1 bear little resemblance to the organisations created by Evans and his associates. Think tanks are generally equipped with multiple staff who are paid to produce research which, it is hoped, will influence public policy. While the single-issue advocacy groups also aimed to influence the political process, they had no significant research capacity beyond what their small number of unpaid volunteers were capable of producing. Thus, most of their material tended to be polemical in nature, whether it was produced by members of the groups themselves, or outsiders who were sympathetic to the cause.

Single-issue advocacy groups also cannot simply be categorised as interest groups. Political scientist John Warhurst describes an interest group as "an association of individuals or organisations which attempts to influence government and public policy without seriously seeking election to Parliament."[2] Also referred to as pressure groups, lobby groups and non-government organisations (NGOs), interest groups differ from think tanks in that they are usually direct representatives of a particular industry, sector or social movement. Examples from the production side of the economy include business groups such as the Business Council of Australia, the Australian Industry Group and the Australian Chamber of Commerce and Industry, labour representatives such as the ACTU, and those from the agricultural sector such as the National Farmers' Federation. Interest groups also represent professions such as doctors (the Australian Medical Association) and lawyers (the Law Council of Australia), and various other sectors such as military veterans (the Returned and Services League), pensioners and welfare recipients (the Australian Council of Social Service), and consumers (the Australian Consumers' Association, now known as Choice).

Despite denominational differences, religious groups often pool their resources into peak bodies such as the National Council of Churches and the Australian Federation of Islamic Councils. Similarly, Australia's enormous diversity of ethnic publics are represented by myriad ethnic community groups, which then combine their resources into state-based community councils and the national umbrella group, the Federation of Ethnic Communities' Councils of Australia. The large number of Indigenous interest groups have in the past decade combined to form the National Congress of Australia's First Peoples. Other interest groups have emerged out of the various social movements that grew to prominence in the second half of the twentieth century: environmental groups (Australian Conservation Foundation; Friends of the Earth; Greenpeace), feminist groups (National Council of Women; Women's Electoral Lobby), homosexual rights groups (Gay and Lesbian Rights Lobby), and animal protection groups (Animals Australia; Royal Society for the Prevention of Cruelty to Animals).

All of these groups can be seen to represent the potentially quite broad material or ethical interests of a particular industry, sector, community or social movement; whereas the defining attribute of all four single-issue groups, conversely, is the way in which they bring a purely ideological approach to distinct policy areas. Though they may have drawn some support from the wider community (particularly from the business community, in the cases of the H.R. Nicholls Society and Lavoisier Group), they cannot be said to represent anyone specifically, apart from the ideologues that make up their small memberships.

Single-issue groups with demonstrable political impact have been rare in Australia, which is what makes these four so distinctive. One exception is the anti-abortion group Right to Life Australia, which practices what it calls "punishment politics," targeting pro-choice politicians in marginal seats with negative campaigns. Josh Gordon of *The Age* believes this strategy "partly explains why Australian politicians seem so keen to pander to fringe groups on the hard right."[3] However, the four advocacy groups examined here have shown little interest in electoral politics, aside from their obvious general preference for conservative parties, and they have no history of using punishment politics to achieve their aims.

It should be noted that, unlike in Australia, single-issue advocacy groups in the United States have harnessed their political success and grown into much larger movements. The National Rifle Association of America (NRA), was founded in 1871 and operated for a century as a recreational association for hunters and sporting shooters. But in the 1970s the NRA dramatically shifted its focus towards fighting gun control legislation, and is now seen as "the most powerful single-issue lobbying group in Washington."[4] Another example is Americans for Tax Reform (ATR), an anti-tax organisation founded by Grover Norquist in 1985. Its flagship project is the Taxpayer Protection Pledge, "a written promise by legislators and candidates for office that commits them to oppose any effort to increase income taxes on individuals and businesses."[5] By 2011 an overwhelming majority of Republican members of Congress had signed the pledge, leading *The New York Times* to identify the group as "the single biggest reason the federal government is now on the edge of default."[6] The successes of the NRA and the ATR despite considerable public opposition confirms John Warhurst's view that "pressure-group politics reward intensity and energy rather than majority opinion."[7]

The goals of ATR were taken up in Australia with gusto by Tim Andrews, who is at the forefront of a new generation of conservative activists. Andrews worked as an associate at ATR from 2008 to 2010, before returning to Australia and forming the Australian Taxpayers' Alliance (ATA) in 2012. The ATA has strong connections to the IPA, CIS, H.R. Nicholls Society and Samuel Griffith Society, and has launched campaigns on tax relief, free speech, the 'nanny state' and carbon pricing. In 2017 Andrews established the annual Ray Evans Memorial Oration. The inaugural speaker was Hugh Morgan, followed by Andrew Bolt in 2018.

Old white men

When Ray Evans was asked about the lack of women among the "pinstriped suits and greying heads" at the $100-a-head launch of *Arbitration in Contempt* in 1986, his glib explanation was that "we did not think that people could afford to pay $200 so we did not invite wives."[8] A striking element of the four Australian single-issue advocacy groups was their gender imbalance. Though this asymmetry may not seem particularly surprising, an analysis of the material on their websites confirms the remarkable extent to which the organisations were completely dominated by men. Of 187 speakers at H.R. Nicholls Society conferences between 1986 and 2015, thirteen were women (seven per cent). The Samuel Griffith Society had a similar imbalance, with fifteen women out of 202 speakers between 1992 and 2016 (seven per cent). The Bennelong Society performed the best of the four, with eighteen women out of eighty-five contributors between 2000 and 2011 (twenty-one per cent). The Lavoisier

Group returned to par, with six women out of 86 contributors between 2000 and 2015 (seven per cent).

Though all four organisations were guilty of sidelining the views of women, the Lavoisier Group seemed to attract the most comment on the issue. Paul Pollard of the left-wing think tank the Australia Institute was an observer at its conference in September 2001 and concluded that "the typical Lavoisier Group supporter is over sixty and male, lives in Melbourne, was a scientist or engineer who worked for a large mining company, and has conservative views. The ABC is 'in the enemy camp', announcements that a politically incorrect view is about to be put are greeted with guffaws, and to a man the human race is 'man'."[9] Melissa Fyfe of *The Age* attended a Lavoisier Group book launch in 2004 and found that among an audience of fifty people there was just one woman.[10] In the realm of climate conversations, such observations have been proven to be more than just anecdotal. Scholars in the United States studied ten years' worth of public opinion data and confirmed that "conservative white males are more likely than are other adults to espouse climate change denial."[11]

The question of racism is a more difficult one to make definitive judgements about. With his 1984 AMIC address, Hugh Morgan shamelessly revived (if it had ever died) a long tradition of the denigration of Indigenous people and culture within elite Australian society. He did so not behind closed doors, but out in the open, so that he could reach the widest audience possible. With the support of Evans, he continued his race-based fear campaign during the Mabo debate in the early 1990s. As we will see below, Morgan was confronted with some serious business difficulties around this time that partially forced him to tone down his public remarks; however, members of the Samuel Griffith Society and Bennelong Society were only too happy to take up the campaign of denigration of Aboriginal culture through the 1990s and 2000s.

As the public face of the Samuel Griffith Society, John Stone's views on Indigenous issues always drew plenty of attention. Stone had form on race, having controversially called for a reduction in the level of Asian immigration in 1988, a position that saw Gerard Henderson resign from the H.R. Nicholls Society.[12] Following the September 11 terror attacks on the United States in 2001, Muslims became the central focus of Stone's racial fears. In a widely criticised column, Stone argued that Australia's immigration policy "should have everything to do with whether those concerned are capable of assimilating to Australia's basically Judeo-Christian culture" and that he had the "gravest reservations" about further Muslim immigration.[13]

Stone's views about Indigenous people and culture must be viewed in this context, in which "Judeo-Christian" culture is self-evidently preferable to any alternatives. While he was usually careful to focus on the legal implications of the Mabo judgement and the policy mistakes of Australian governments with regard to Indigenous affairs, his negative opinion of Aboriginal culture was plain to see. As time passed, his language became less guarded and more contemptuous: "The less said about the violence-racked, female-oppressive, sexually predatory cultures of the Australian Aboriginal the better," he wrote in *The Australian* in 2010.[14]

This poisonous view of Indigenous culture was de rigueur at the Bennelong Society. But not only did Bennelong members deny being racist – they asserted that racism was virtually non-existent in Australia. At the Bennelong Society's formative workshop in December 2000, just one participant accepted the view that past government policies were "postulated on the basis of the inferiority of indigenous people."[15] Meanwhile, Peter Howson described Aboriginal life prior to European contact in the terms of Thomas Hobbes's *Leviathan* – "solitary, poore, nasty, brutish, and short"[16] – and Gary Johns condemned Indigenous culture as "best relegated to museums and occasional ceremonies."[17] As Stephen Gray wrote in a review of Johns' book *Aboriginal Self-Determination*, this attitude "runs in a direct line from nineteenth-century views of the 'aimless, root-eating, alligator-egg-sucking existence' of traditional Aborigines doomed to die out."[18]

Johns continued to air his provocative views about Indigenous people after the disbanding of the Bennelong Society. In December 2014 he used his column in *The Australian* to argue that women receiving welfare benefits should be forced to use contraception, a measure he admitted would doubtlessly "affect Aboriginal and Islander people in great proportions, but the idea that someone can have the taxpayer, as of right, fund the choice to have a child is repugnant."[19] Later, as he hit the promotional trail for a book devoted to the same subject, he said that many poor, Aboriginal women were being used as "cash cows." That is, "they are kept pregnant and producing children for the cash."[20] These views came under particular scrutiny after the Turnbull government appointed Johns as head of the Australian Charities and Not-for-Profits Commission in 2017. Appearing before a Senate Committee in October 2018, Johns was challenged by a Labor Senator about his views, before being referred to the Indigenous affairs minister for further investigation.[21]

If the attitudes of Morgan, Evans, Stone, Howson and Johns do not constitute racism, it is difficult to know what does.

The pivotal partnership

At the beating heart of all four single-issue advocacy groups was the extraordinary partnership of Hugh Morgan and Ray Evans; none of them would have existed without it. As we saw in Chapter 2, Evans wrote to Arvi Parbo in 1981 seeking a job at Western Mining Corporation. The core of his pitch was that he could be an effective culture warrior for the company. "The culture wars I now believe to be embedded deep in Western Civilisation," wrote Evans. "The culture wars are fought out in every institution. We see them in the churches, within political parties, in the media, in the universities and in corporations."[22] Parbo passed the letter onto Morgan, who met with Evans and "was impressed with his literary skills, unswerving political instincts and historical knowledge."[23] Morgan offered Evans a job, beginning what Evans described as a "twenty-year seminar" at WMC.[24] The partnership was successful despite the contrasting social status of the two men. Morgan is a dyed-in-the-wool Toorak blue-blood, as Melbourne establishment as they come. Evans, on the other hand, seemed uninterested in the trappings of wealth. Even as a well-paid WMC executive, he continued to reside happily in the modest suburb of Newport, in Melbourne's west.

Evans brought to WMC a remarkably distinctive approach to historical, cultural and political debates. He was a devotee of countless unfashionable causes (for example, he preferred the imperial to the metric system, and maintained a belief that New Zealand might still become the seventh state of the Australian Commonwealth), and the odds stacked against him often seemed insurmountable. But when his advocacy did achieve results, he was left conflicted. "Because he was such a tireless advocate for unfashionable causes, some of them began to generate support, perhaps even become popular," said Peter Costello. "I suspect that secretly he did not approve of his success. 'Worse is better,' he was fond of saying."[25] Evans' view was that the culture wars are eternal, and one should never accept compromises or be satisfied with partial victories. His friend Patrick Morgan reflected on this aspect of his personality after his death: "Many people thought him an extremist, but in fact he had the intellectual capacity to take his views to their logical conclusion. In this sense he was a purist, and an idealist. This made him on any particular issue basically unsatisfiable."[26]

As we saw in Chapter 2, as a result of the formative lessons of Frank Knopfelmacher, Evans was a keen student of the political and cultural successes of the left, and he passed these lessons on to Morgan. "If you think you have been outmarshalled," said Morgan, "the first thing is to go and study the opponent who has been so successful."[27] With Parbo's backing, they transformed the culture of WMC, as Tim Duncan captured in his 1985 profile of the company and its key personnel:

> Hugh Morgan's industry colleagues say that there is no corporate figure like him. But they also say that no other executive director has a chairman such as Sir Arvi Parbo and, in any case, there is nothing quite like their Western Mining Corporation. One could be forgiven for wondering whether Western Mining is a mining company, a speech factory, a first-class public entertainment service – or, simply, a political party that got lost in the desert, began to dig for gold to pass the time and found uranium and God in that order.[28]

Unusually for a business leader, speech-making became a regular part of Morgan's role throughout the 1980s and early 1990s. And these were no ordinary speeches. They were filled with references to Evans' intellectual obsessions: the Old Testament, William Shakespeare, Edmund Burke, Samuel Johnson, and much more besides. According to Duncan, much of this content was new to Morgan, "thus facilitating what Morgan himself accepts has been a rapid but essential humanities education."[29] His critics were sceptical, however, and the limits of this shotgun education were sometimes exposed. Gideon Haigh's 1993 profile of Morgan related an anecdote from an anonymous "Melbourne conservative writer" in which Morgan made frequent references to German philosophy. "Hugh was talking about Nietzsche, but he kept pronouncing it as Nitz-ski," the source, now revealed to be Robert Manne, told Haigh.[30] Former NSW Supreme Court judge Hal Wootten was quoted in the same article describing Morgan's learnedness as a "pseudo-intellectual pose."[31]

But the most distinctive characteristic of Morgan's speeches was their deliberate courting of controversy. Morgan eagerly embraced this aspect of his public role, seeing himself as a kind of free speech martyr. "If I have to be a sacrificial lamb in the interests of debate, I don't care," he told *The Sydney Morning Herald*.[32] Duncan described Morgan and Evans' work as "a public affairs icebreaker for industry in general and the mining industry in particular."[33] Within WMC, however, there was some concern about the reputational damage being done to the company. Morgan recalled that "staff did express concern and on occasion made deputation to Ray expressing great worry for the company and would he please mend his ways." But Evans knew he had a powerful protector in Morgan. "Ray suggested they come and see me if they had a problem. I never heard directly from them but the corridors spoke loudly of apprehension."[34]

In turn, Morgan had his own powerful protector in Parbo, whose friendship and loyalty he would be forced to call upon when he became embroiled in two corporate scandals at the height of his participation in the Mabo debate. In July 1993 WMC was found by the NSW Supreme Court to have trespassed on land rich in copper and gold deposits, the exploration rights for which were held by the much smaller company Savage Resources. WMC was forced to relinquish its claim on the deposits and pay Savage's legal costs. An internal review later found Morgan largely responsible. He was excluded from the company's executive share plan for two years and ordered to minimise his involvement in outside activities, but mining analysts were surprised that he was not forced to resign. "At any other company, heads would have rolled," said one, "but all Hugh Morgan received is an effective slap on the wrist."[35]

Worse was to come with regard to Morgan's corporate reputation. In January 1994 a Canadian court rejected WMC's appeal against an earlier judgement that it had engaged in a civil conspiracy against Canadian mining company Seabright Resources. WMC had taken Seabright over in 1988, but its assets turned out to be virtually worthless. Instead of accepting the loss and moving on, Morgan initiated court proceedings, arguing that WMC had been misled by Seabright. The Canadian court savaged WMC's abuse of process. "Under Mr Morgan's leadership, Western Mining has been responsible for two gross acts of corporate misbehaviour," read a blistering editorial in the *Australian Financial Review.* "The board should protect its own position by dealing with this problem decisively. More controls over Mr Morgan are not good enough. He should go." [36] Again, he managed to survive what was undoubtedly the nadir of his career.

Most commentators attributed Morgan's good fortune to the influence of Parbo. Born in Estonia in 1926, Parbo arrived in Australia in 1949 after spending time in refugee camps during World War II. Bill Morgan, Hugh's father, gave a penniless Parbo a job at WMC in 1956, "a break for which the hard-working young Arvi would remain eternally grateful." [37] When Hugh joined the company in 1976, Parbo took the young man under his wing. Given this long and close relationship, it is easy to see why Parbo may have been reluctant to dismiss Morgan, despite the internal and external pressure to do so. "Parbo is said to even remain supportive," it was reported in early 1994, "of Morgan's right to public commentary on issues such as Aboriginal land rights and the environment even when other directors have voiced their concerns." [38]

Parbo's retirement from the WMC chairmanship in 1999 meant that Morgan and Evans were no longer protected. In 2001, shortly after Robert Manne had described him as "the *éminence noire* of the ideological right in Australia," [39] Evans left the company. "What have I done since joining? I've been a soldier in the culture wars," he said in his farewell remarks. [40] Then, after years of battling internal opponents, Morgan announced his own retirement in March 2002. The twin retirements signalled the end of a remarkable two decades for the company.

Morgan returned to the political fray when he was elected president of the Business Council of Australia in 2003. In seeking the role Morgan had tried to reassure business leaders that he would refrain from inciting controversy, but his uncompromising maiden speech led some to conclude that Evans was still writing his scripts. Evans was asked whether this was the case, and his reply – "I shouldn't comment on that, I don't think" – was as good an admission as any.[41] Though no longer formal business associates, their close relationship continued until Evans' death in June 2014.

The extent of Evans' influence on the Australian right was illustrated by the outpouring of tributes from his friends and allies following his death. He was "much more than a public intellectual," John Stone wrote. "He was first and foremost a man – possessed of all those manly virtues of which one of his heroes, Margaret Thatcher, spoke."[42] Andrew Bolt admired Evans "for his wisdom, sound instincts, courage, indomitable cheerfulness and deep cultural and historical knowledge."[43] Roger Franklin, online editor of *Quadrant*, described him as "a gentleman of the old school, someone who stood by his principles without stooping to personal abuse and vilification, as do so many of his enemies and critics on the left."[44] The IPA's James Paterson wrote that "Australia has lost one of its greatest champions for freedom,"[45] and his boss, John Roskam, lauded Evans as more politically influential than the overwhelming majority of state and federal MPs. "In some way or another," he wrote, "Evans was involved in, and helped shape, the course of every major policy debate in Australia of the last thirty years."[46] Gerard Henderson agreed, describing him as "one of the most influential Australians of his time" and "an example of the fact that you do not have to be a big name to have a big influence."[47]

Evans' death was noted in the Australian parliament by Victorian Liberal Senator Scott Ryan, who spoke of the inspiration he gave to others to fight for their beliefs. "His passion, intellect and organisational capacity," said Ryan, "would ensure he was the driving force behind a range of groups, all comprised of volunteers who came together for no reason other than belief in a cause."[48] Bob Day and Hugh Morgan gave heartfelt eulogies at his funeral, reflecting on Evans' political influence as well as their close friendships with him. "Wearing his trademark HRN tie, Ray was an enormous presence at literally hundreds of important and what seemed at the time not so important events which have helped shape our country into the nation it is today," said Day. "He was my teacher, my mentor, my friend and my hero."[49] Morgan celebrated "a friendship and professional association of which I could not have imagined would be of such impact on my life. [...] Ray's influence upon events particularly in the outcome of the culture wars will continue to have a lasting impact upon Australian society. His career as an advocate is without peer in our generation."[50]

Government relations

John Warhurst has distinguished between two types of political lobbying. Political/outside work "involves putting pressure on governments through influencing and mobilising public opinion," often via the mass media. Persuasive/inside work "involves putting arguments to politicians and public servants," often via formal committee hearings and public submissions.[51] The four single-issue advocacy groups used both, but the latter was especially productive for them. Notwithstanding David Kemp's frankly bizarre claim that through the H.R. Nicholls Society "the silent majority of Australians have heard their authentic interests being promoted and some of their deepest beliefs expressed,"[52] all four organisations were made up of business and political elites, and this background was reflected in their ideological preoccupations. Naturally, their lobbying efforts were concentrated on governing elites.

The New Right gathered momentum in Australia in part as a response to the perceived failings of the Fraser government. Following Malcolm Fraser's defeat in the 1983 federal election, New Right activists set about remaking the Liberal Party in their own dry image. As Paul Kelly noted, this factional and ideological turmoil damaged the party in the short term, but helped to provide a direction for the next Coalition government:

> Many of the New Right figureheads were or became Liberals – Hugh Morgan, Peter Costello, Charles Copeman, Ian McLachlan. But the New Right was never hostage to the tactical requirements of the Liberal Party. Herein lies the key to the ambivalent impact which the New Right had on Australian politics during the mid-1980s. Its influence damaged the Opposition in electoral terms, but the New Right's pyrotechnics were successful in moving the

debate in favour of labour market deregulation. Its success was reflected in the fact that in 1990 there was no New Right; the 1985 extremists had become the 1990 Liberal Party mainstreamers.[53]

The H.R. Nicholls Society and other institutions of the New Right gained considerable traction and attention throughout the 1980s, but their hostility towards the governing Labor Party from 1983 to 1996 meant that they had little influence on government policy. This changed dramatically with the election of the Howard government in 1996. After that point, Morgan, Evans and their associates began to have real political impact.

Hugh Morgan has enjoyed a long and close relationship with the Liberal Party as a whole, and with John Howard on a personal level. Since the late 1980s he has been a leading fundraiser for the party through the Cormack Foundation. As CEO of Western Mining he approved $650,000 in donations to the Liberal Party and $85,000 to the National Party during Howard's prime-ministership, in addition to his own personal contributions of more than $50,000.[54] Morgan believed that a speech he gave in January 1984, strongly critical of Bob Hawke, led to his position on the board of the Reserve Bank not being renewed later that year.[55] But when ACTU secretary Bill Kelty resigned his seat after Howard's victory, Morgan was appointed again. He remained on the Reserve Bank board throughout most of the Howard years, finally vacating his seat in July 2007. Morgan was said to be a "frequent guest" of Howard during this period, to whom he enjoyed "unparalleled access."[56]

In 2002 Morgan was awarded the Companion of the Order of Australia (AC) "for service to business and trade development, to the mining industry in Australia and internationally, particularly through leadership in the formation and evolution of sustainable development policy, and to the community through cultural and educational research activities." Morgan was also awarded the Centenary Medal, established by Howard in 2001 as part of the centenary of Federation celebrations. Ray Evans was another recipient, as were a number of their advocacy group associates, including Peter Howson, Gary Johns, Ron Brunton, David Trebeck, Greg Craven, Peter Walsh, Arvi Parbo and Ian Plimer.[57]

An important element of Howard's political success was his rhetorical commitment to "getting the balance right," on both a macro and micro level. He had come to power promising to govern "for all of us," in supposed contrast with Labor, which he derided as concentrating on sectional interests at the expense of the mainstream.[58] "Governments exist to represent the values and aspirations of the mainstream of the Australian community," he told an audience of Liberal students shortly after becoming prime minister.[59] In a 2006 speech he argued that the secret to Australia's success was "our sense of balance."[60] On policy issues this meant listening to all interested parties, then navigating a way through that allowed him to appear as if he was governing from the centre. Because the four single-issue advocacy groups were commonly perceived to be outside the political mainstream, Howard was careful to avoid the perception that they wielded significant influence, despite his obvious sympathies with many of their objectives. Thus, he sometimes failed to deliver the sorts of outcomes that they could wholeheartedly support.

The H.R. Nicholls Society's response to the Howard government's first attempt at industrial relations reform set the tone for the relationship for the next decade. The government sold its *Workplace Relations Act* as a reasonable compromise between employer flexibility and employee protections that, as Howard reflected, brought "more balance to our industrial relations system."[61] The H.R. Nicholls Society hardliners were not interested in compromise. They felt betrayed because the legislation did not go far enough, and attacked the government ferociously. It is difficult to imagine Howard being too worried about this criticism. With attacks from the left (trade unions and the ALP) a given, additional attacks from the right conveniently matched his vision of governing from the centre.

Howard came dangerously close to undoing this self-image in 1998, when the government – led by industrial relations minister Peter Reith – sided with radical anti-union forces in the waterfront dispute. The battle divided Australia, but most were relieved when the dispute was settled, not least the Howard government, which managed to avoid conspiracy charges. Howard scraped home in the election held just three weeks later, despite losing the popular vote. Nevertheless, John Stone thought the dispute "was as significant as Thatcher's 1984 confrontation with Britain's coal miners. Here, as in Britain, the union's defeat has resulted in a huge increase in productivity."[62]

Howard's strategy of balance finally fell apart with Work Choices, when he was seen as moving too far to the radical right, though he disputed this characterisation. "Howard has made much of the need for balance, of finding and holding the moderate, consensual middle," wrote Judith Brett. "But with WorkChoices he handed the middle ground to Labor."[63] This time, friendly fire from the H.R. Nicholls Society provided no succour. Ray Evans did not accept the narrative that the radicalism of its industrial relations reform cost the Coalition the 2007 election, but he nevertheless concluded in 2010 that the Liberal Party had internalised that narrative, and was "now imprisoned by John Howard's cancerous legacy of WorkChoices."[64]

Of the four groups, the Samuel Griffith Society probably had the most cause for disappointment with the Howard government, despite Howard's successful efforts to derail the republic and roll back native title legislation. Howard's centralisation of power was the Society's number one complaint, and the prime minister did very little to placate his critics on this front. There was also the issue of Howard's long and complicated relationship with John Stone. The two first worked together when Howard was Malcolm Fraser's treasurer and Stone was secretary to the Treasury. Recalling this period, Howard described Stone as "the brightest public servant with whom I ever dealt,"[65] but the pair fell out over the 1982 Budget. Stone later became involved in the "Joh for Canberra" campaign – which many blamed for Howard's election defeat in 1987 – then served as Howard's shadow minister for finance, until he was sacked in September 1988 amid a furore over the rate of Asian immigration.

Given all this history, it is fair to say that when Stone later became a regular critic of Howard's centralisation of power and lack of regard for the Constitution, he was not a disinterested observer. However, Stone has always maintained that he holds no grudge against Howard. When Howard gave a speech defending his government's record on federalism in 2005, Stone responded with a scathing critique in *The Australian*. But even in this moment of apparent rage he went out of his way to declare his general approval of the prime minister. "I am no zealous Howard hater," he wrote. "Indeed, I have been among his most loyal supporters."[66] In his final assessment of Howard's prime-ministership, Stone counted Howard's attitude towards the federal foundations of the Constitution as one of his most significant failings, but still concluded that "despite the many valid criticisms that can be made of him, nevertheless John Howard has a strong claim to having been Australia's greatest prime minister."[67]

On Indigenous issues, the views of the Howard government and the Bennelong Society were tightly aligned. Not a word of the following excerpt from Howard's autobiography would be out of place in Bennelong Society literature: "I did not have a politically correct approach to Aboriginal issues. I did not believe in separate development for the Indigenous people of Australia. It remains my opinion that the best way of helping Indigenous Australians is to include them within the mainstream of the Australian community and endeavour, as far as possible, to ensure that they share the bounty of our prosperous nation."[68]

Howard's emphasis on balance and on serving the mainstream was again important when it came to Aboriginal affairs, a point on which both his critics and supporters agreed. "In grappling with the past, present and future," wrote Indigenous leader Mick Dodson in 2004, "Howard has often used Geoffrey Blainey's image of a 'pendulum' that has swung out of balance and now favours the interests of Indigenous Australians and other minority groups over the core interests and values of the mainstream."[69]

The Bennelong Society emerged out of an organised campaign to deny the Stolen Generations, an endeavour that received significant support from Howard and his first Indigenous affairs minister, John Herron. Howard was adamantly opposed to a depiction of Australian history as "little more than a disgraceful record of imperialism, exploitation and racism."[70] He infamously refused to offer a government apology to the Stolen Generations, and his belligerence on this issue dogged his entire prime-ministership, but he could always rely on the Bennelong Society's full support.

This close alignment was noted by Gary Johns in his final assessment of the Howard government's record on Indigenous affairs. Johns recalled that the Bennelong Society's second conference in August 2002, when Herron was its president, was titled 'Celebrating Integration.' Shortly afterwards, Herron resigned from the Senate, and in his final parliamentary address spoke proudly of the changes he had helped to bring about. "Separatism," he said, "as promoted by those who wish to live off the cause rather than for it, has no place in a modern, democratic, vibrant multicultural Australia … We are now celebrating integration."[71] Or, in the words of Mick Dodson, "classic assimilation."[72]

In the Howard government the Lavoisier Group could hardly have found a more willing partner in the battle against action on climate change. Upon election, Howard immediately changed Australia's policy direction, weakening and undermining the Kyoto Protocol at every stage, before eventually refusing to ratify the agreement. "In acting with the Bush administration to block progress toward a global agreement, the stance of the Howard government is criminally irresponsible," wrote scientist and conservationist Ian Lowe in 2004.[73] Guy Pearse's *High & Dry* has documented in painstaking detail the extent to which the government worked hand in hand with climate deniers in industry, think tanks and the bureaucracy to delay or prevent climate change mitigation policies.

And yet, ever the purist, Ray Evans was not satisfied. He viewed the environmentalist movement as an existential threat to the West and would not countenance even a slightly more nuanced view. "Instead of maintaining a constant opposition to the environmentalists, within and without the Liberal Party," he wrote, "Howard sought to appease them when he thought it was necessary."[74] Against all evidence, Evans argued in 2009 that Howard gave in not to climate deniers such as himself, but to climate activists on the left, diminishing his legacy in the process:

> The great gains made by the Greens and their supporters throughout the country between 1996 and 2007, to the point where Australia is now on the brink of enacting legislation, based on "perverted science", which will seriously impoverish the nation, is the great stain on John Howard's record. If the legislation is passed and Australia consequently enters into a period of sustained economic decline, he will be seen as the political leader who could have turned the tide, but completely failed to do so.[75]

It is important to note that this was written when Malcolm Turnbull was leader of the Liberal Party in Opposition, a time of despair for Evans. He was later pleased that the party turned back towards climate denial under Tony Abbott, but remained vigilant to his last breath, always alert to the environmentalist threat.

Sympathetic publications

The support of various media outlets was an important aspect of the successes of the four advocacy groups, and three particular publications helped to boost the New Right insurgency during the 1980s: News Limited's national newspaper *The Australian*, and magazines *The Bulletin* and *Quadrant*. Some background on these publications and their relationships with the emergent hard right is illuminating.

Rupert Murdoch established *The Australian* as the country's only national broadsheet in 1964. At this time Murdoch's political views were broadly left-wing, and *The Australian* gave editorial support to the election of the Whitlam government in 1972. But within a few years Murdoch's relationship with Whitlam had soured, and he used his flagship paper to campaign savagely against the government until it was finally dismissed in November 1975. Murdoch's biographer Michael Wolff described the entire Whitlam period as "his first clear act of using his papers to gain influence – to project and to seize power."[76] Campaigning journalism would become a staple of *The Australian*, not least on neoliberal economics, industrial relations, Indigenous affairs and climate change, where its views were closely aligned with the advocacy groups of the right. The exception was its strong support for an Australian republic in the 1990s, an issue on which it was at odds with the Samuel Griffith Society.

The Fraser years saw *The Australian* adopt an increasingly strident economic position under the editorship of Les Hollings. Leading Liberal Party dries were promoted and, according to David McKnight, "the national daily took on an evangelical role in the wider public debate on behalf of ideas which until the late 1970s had been largely confined to neo-classically trained economists."[77] The paper did not let up following the election of the Hawke Labor government in 1983, when there was "a greater use of its news pages to support activities of the emerging think tanks and key ideologues, as well as the recruitment of a stable of columnists and journalists who projected the neo-liberal agenda."[78] The forceful tone on economics continued under the brief editorship of Frank Devine. In an echo of H.R. Nicholls' 1911 attack on H.B. Higgins, a column by Maxwell Newton in November 1989, titled 'Advance Australia fascist,' alleged a "corrupt alliance" between the government, unions and the "official Soviet-style Arbitration Commission" and its "labour judges." The Arbitration Commission brought legal action, which News Limited successfully defended all the way to the High Court on the grounds of free speech.[79]

In the 1990s *The Australian* provided extensive coverage of the emergence of the neo-assimilationists in the arena of Indigenous affairs. This was especially so in 1996, when Geoffrey Partington's book *Hasluck versus Coombs* was published, and in 1999–2000, when *Quadrant*'s seminars were crystallising right-wing opinion on Indigenous issues. The campaign against the *Bringing Them Home* report received extensive coverage, as did Keith Windschuttle's historical revisionism on frontier violence. These campaigns also spread to the News Limited tabloids, where Piers Akerman and Michael Duffy in Sydney's *Daily Telegraph* and Andrew Bolt in Melbourne's *Herald Sun* took to the cultural battlefield with glee. In the 2000s, with Chris Mitchell in the editor's chair, *The Australian* continued to be a key outlet for the neo-assimilationists, including Peter Howson, Gary Johns, Wesley Aird, Christopher Pearson and Frank Devine. When Keith Windschuttle published the first volume of *The Fabrication of Aboriginal History* in 2002, *The Australian*'s blanket coverage turned it into a "major national event."[80] In 2008 the Bennelong Society's website carried an acknowledgement of *The Australian*'s assistance with that year's annual conference.

Under Mitchell *The Australian* also enthusiastically backed the climate deniers associated with the Lavoisier Group and various other organisations. In what Robert Manne described as a "truly frightful hotchpotch of ideological prejudice and intellectual muddle,"[81] the non-scientific opinions of culture warriors such as Christopher Pearson, Frank Devine, Gary Johns, Alan Moran and Greg Sheridan were reinforced with the views of contrarian scientists such as Ian Plimer, William Kininmonth, Bob Carter, Garth Paltridge and Jennifer Marohasy. "The paper has opposed the Kyoto Protocol, emissions trading, renewable energy mandates, and a host of other measures that might reduce emissions in Australia," wrote Guy Pearse.[82] In 2011 the government's outgoing climate change adviser, Ross Garnaut, singled out *The Australian*'s climate coverage as among "the crudest and most distorted discussion of a major public policy issue" he had seen.[83]

The weekly *Bulletin* magazine was another enthusiastic publicist for the New Right in the 1980s. Founded in 1880, *The Bulletin* was predominantly literary (and overtly racist) until Frank Packer's Australian Consolidated Press took it over in 1960, after which it changed format into a news magazine. In 1984 and 1985 *The Bulletin* ran three major cover stories on the New Right, which brought considerable attention to the burgeoning phenomenon. All were written by sympathetic journalist Tim Duncan, who also contributed to the *IPA Review* and later worked as an adviser to Victorian Liberal Opposition leader Alan Brown. However, even in the 1980s *The Bulletin*'s circulation was in decline, and it relied on Kerry Packer's largesse to survive throughout the 1990s and 2000s. When Packer died in December 2005 the writing was on the wall, and the final edition was published in January 2008.[84]

In the 1980s *Quadrant* became a frequent publisher of many of the New Right activists who went on to play central roles in the establishment of the H.R. Nicholls Society. Those who were published regularly included Ray Evans, Hugh Morgan, John Stone, Peter Costello, Lauchlan Chipman and Gerard Henderson. Evans later joined *Quadrant*'s board, and when the Australia Council for the Arts reduced its taxpayer-funded grant to the magazine in the early 1990s, Western Mining chipped in to help keep it afloat.[85]

A blip in the *Quadrant*–New Right relationship occurred when a number of New Right figures fell out with editor Robert Manne in 1992. Under Manne the magazine no longer acted as a vessel for their ideas. However, Paddy McGuinness replaced Manne in 1998 and dramatically changed *Quadrant*'s editorial direction. His manifesto for the future of *Quadrant* unequivocally set the tone: "the aim will be to encourage free debate of a kind which has become unfashionable in Australia at present."[86] First and foremost among his priorities was the magazine's line on Indigenous affairs, which gave great prominence to the work of Ron Brunton, Peter Howson, Gary Johns, Keith Windschuttle and Geoffrey Partington. *Quadrant* also organised the seminars in 1999 and 2000 that led to the formation of the Bennelong Society. Manne wrote in 2001 that under McGuinness, "*Quadrant* became devoted to ever wilder and more extreme attacks on every cause and belief of the contemporary Aboriginal political leadership and its support base."[87] The attacks on Indigenous people continued under Windschuttle, who took over the editorship in 2008. Windschuttle was also eager to debate the science and politics of climate change in the magazine's pages. Ray Evans returned as a regular contributor, and other climate deniers were welcomed into the *Quadrant* family.

Long before he brought a hardline approach to Indigenous issues to *Quadrant*, Paddy McGuinness was preaching neoliberal economics at the *Australian Financial Review*, where he was economics editor (1974–1980), editor (1980–1982) and editor-in-chief (1982–1987). David Kemp described his output there as "especially influential on the policy debate" on both sides of politics.[88] The *Financial Review* also provided one of the few mainstream outlets for the Samuel Griffith Society's constitutional conservatism when it carried a regular column by John Stone from 1990 to 1998. After leaving politics in 1993, Peter Walsh also wrote a weekly column, in which he frequently sounded off about the threat posed by the environmental movement.

Fairfax's broadsheets, *The Age* and *The Sydney Morning Herald*, were not as consistent publishers of right-wing activists (though McGuinness and Henderson both had regular columns in the latter for long periods), but space was occasionally found on their opinion pages for the likes of Ray Evans and Peter Howson. Evans' view was that Fairfax (and the ABC) were "run by the left, for the left", although he was heartened by the continued presence of the "opposition press," by which he meant *The Australian* and other News Limited publications. "As long as you've got an opportunity to get different points of view out, different arguments up, it's a healthy situation," he said. "If there were no News Limited we would be in real strife."[89]

Another important outlet in the 1980s was the *IPA Review*, which published "most of those who were identified in one way or another with the New Right."[90] Regular economic commentators included John Stone, Peter Costello, Michael Porter and Des Moore. Later, it published Colin Howard and Greg Craven on the Constitution; Hugh Morgan, Ron Brunton and Gary Johns on Aboriginal affairs; and Ian Plimer, Bob Carter and Jennifer Marohasy on climate change. A number of these writers were also published in the CIS's *Policy* magazine, albeit less frequently. In 2012 *Policy* released a special issue on the state of Australian federalism, which featured the views of Craven and other committed federalists. Both the

IPA Review and *Policy* have very small readerships, but they remain important publications within the intellectual right.

In 2005 Connor Court Publishing was founded in the small Victorian town of Ballan. Its founder, Anthony Cappello, a product of B.A. Santamaria's National Civic Council, had worked mainly in Catholic publishing, but was looking to expand beyond religious titles. He used contacts such as John Roskam of the IPA to develop relationships with conservatives and before long became the "house publisher" of the Australian right.[91] Notable Connor Court titles include Ian Plimer's *Heaven and Earth*; Gary Johns' *Aboriginal Self-Determination*; Hal Colebatch's biography of Bert Kelly, *The Modest Member*; and the collection *Turning Left or Right*, which included contributions from Plimer, Johns, Evans, Bob Day and Julian Leeser. Prior to his death Evans was working on a book about the overthrow of Malcolm Turnbull, which Connor Court intended to publish. Evans left the incomplete manuscript with Cappello, who hoped to find someone to fill in the gaps, but it remains unpublished.[92]

Reactionary conservatism

Political scientist Hugh Collins argued in 1985 that in its utilitarianism, legalism and positivism, Australian society draws its distinctive character from the political philosophy of Jeremy Bentham. That is, those who created Australia's political institutions were concerned with the greatest good for the greatest number, with legal protections that work to ensure this, and with practical considerations over moral or philosophical abstractions. He pointed out that these strong traditions of state reliance were anathema to the prevailing opinion among the New Right, in which the state should be made as small and non-interventionist as possible. "Australia is a large grievance to latter-day disciples of laissez-faire economics and inhospitable to radical conservatives," wrote Collins. "For so long has its economy been a mixed system, so intricately interdependent are state socialism and private capitalism in its affairs, that the free-marketeers have to take their stand outside the nation's historical experience and on the margin of its political decision."[93] The radical right challenged this state of affairs, sig-nifying a new form of reactionary conservatism that was distinct from existing liberal-conservative traditions.

The single-issue advocacy groups of the hard right reflect the distinc-tive character of Australian conservatism in different ways. The H.R. Nicholls Society emerged from the neoliberal and libertarian movements of the 1970s. These movements represented a major threat to commonly held assumptions about Australia. In the words of Lindy Edwards:

> The rise of neo-liberalism was perhaps the most revolutionary of the political movements in Australia's history. It ran against the grain of our national identity and political culture, and demanded that Australia utterly remake itself. A country that had defined itself by its democratic egalitarian roots was asked to step away from government. It was asked to put its faith in free markets and competition.[94]

Australia's distinctive industrial relations system was an important aspect of this self-definition. But the H.R. Nicholls Society decided enough was enough and adopted a radical confrontational approach, both to trade unions and the industrial relations system as a whole. This was a dramatic shift from Australian conservatives' traditional approach to industrial relations, which had been to accept centralised wage fixation and the con-ciliation and arbitration system – including the central role of trade unions in the process – as set in stone.

Some business leaders reacted with horror to the radicalism of the H.R. Nicholls Society. But even so, the group still aligns with the general antipa-thy towards the trade union movement that political historian Norman Abjorensen has identified as one of the key characteristics of the Australian liberal-conservative tradition.[95] To younger observers, the aims of the group might seem relatively benign; what they were advocating was, in essence, standard pro-business industrial relations reform: labour market deregulation and restrictions on the power of trade unions. But in the con-text of a ruling Labor Party that had created an Accord with the trade union movement, and a much longer tradition of worker- and union-friendly industrial relations laws in Australia more broadly, the H.R. Nicholls Society was seen as an utterly radical challenge to the industrial relations status quo. With hindsight it looks less like a fundamental shift, but rather the same old battle between capital and labour, with added emphasis on taking the fight up to the union movement and the ALP – a shift in tactics rather than objectives. The H.R. Nicholls Society's approach was a radical response to Australia's distinctive industrial environment, but its politics can still accurately be described as conservative.

As Abjorensen has also noted, opposition to constitutional change is another key characteristic of the liberal-conservative tradition in Australia. Members of the Samuel Griffith Society saw the Constitution as "the greatest public work of Australian conservatives," but by the 1980s were alarmed at the fact that it was not appreciated as such by politicians, academics and the public at large.[96] The group always maintained a deep distrust of any attempts to reshape Australian political institutions to meet modern demands, especially when these attempts came from the left. In this sense, the Samuel Griffith Society is, without doubt, the most traditionally conservative of the four groups.

The Samuel Griffith Society is also highly suspicious of the tendency of governments of all persuasions to gradually acquire more power and move away from the federalist intentions of the drafters of the Constitution. While the Labor Party is seen as the most untrustworthy in this regard, the Society was also very critical of the Howard government's centralisation and dismissal of states' rights. Defenders of states' rights – in Australia and the United States – have often been criticised as having ulterior motives, usually involving the right to discriminate against non-white minorities, but they are undoubtedly an important element of the conservative tradition in both nations.

The Samuel Griffith Society recognises that from time to time it may be necessary to make changes to the Constitution but sees its primary role as ensuring that such proposals are intensely scrutinised. There is considerable variation in the extent to which individual members are willing to countenance even mild reform of the Constitution, but for Greg Craven, the point remains that the organisation exists to be a constructive voice in constitutional debates:

> It has been constructive in a number of ways, so that it does actually present
> I think, not always and not on every issue, but it does tend to promote

> a deeper conservative understanding and contribution to quite complicated issues. So, for example, it's very interesting that a person like Julian Leeser can understand very clearly that the conservative position on Indigenous recognition is not trying to defeat Indigenous recognition across the board. And I think to that extent there's part of Samuel Griffith, that you would never say about Bennelong or H.R. Nicholls, that it's Burkean.[97]

The Samuel Griffith Society takes seriously Edmund Burke's emphasis on slow and gradual reform and wariness of those who would try to artificially construct an ideal society, rather than let things naturally evolve.

The stated aims of the Bennelong Society gave the impression that the group was merely concerned with improving the welfare of Indigenous Australians, and that it held no particular ideological position as to how this could best be achieved. This was of course nonsense, as a brief perusal of the group's literature showed: the Society was heavily invested in a policy of neo-assimilation. Another characteristic of the Australian liberal-conservative tradition identified by Abjorensen is the belief in "individual freedom and self-reliance." Australian conservatives reject "collectivism in any form" and "any idealised view of social justice as a redistributive force in society."[98] These principles are reflected in the Bennelong Society's approach to Indigenous affairs, in which the solutions to the problems faced by Indigenous people are simply to be found in their assimilation with the mainstream economy and society.

Hal Wootten was alert to this approach in 2004, when he described the "narrative of the triumph of capitalist individualism" over self-determination that helped to bring about the demise of ATSIC. This narrative, he wrote, "posits that Aboriginals must simply forget about culture and identity, which are irrelevant in the modern globalised world, and become individual market-driven consumers and entrepreneurs, like all other sensible people."[99] In its sugar-coating of the assimilation era, the Bennelong Society was also nostalgic for an imagined golden age, which revealed its paternalist attitudes towards Indigenous Australians. Though it was not an exclusively white organisation, the overwhelming majority of its contributors were non-Indigenous. This gave an overriding impression of a white organisation insisting it knew what was best for Aboriginal people, again exhibiting conservatives' discomfort with the concept of Indigenous self-determination.

Waleed Aly offers some illuminating comments on the difficulty conservatives have in dealing with group identities and rights, especially with regard to the unique place of Australia's First Peoples: "ATSIC, native title, any kind of treaty and indeed almost the entire politics of symbolic reconciliation are very difficult to accommodate in a liberal-conservative worldview. Each requires the recognition of Aborigines as a distinct group within the citizenry. How, for instance, can a nation have a treaty with its own citizens? How can it recognise a form of title that, as a matter of law, is open only to some citizens and not all?"[100] The Bennelong Society could not accommodate such a worldview. The 1970s revolution in Indigenous affairs was a challenge to fundamental liberal-conservative principles, such as individual freedom and equality before the law.

With its radically oppositional approach to mainstream climate science, the Lavoisier Group is undoubtedly the least conservative of the four groups. While traditional Australian conservatism has long been suspicious of environmentalism and its association with the political left, the Lavoisier Group and its allies in the climate denial movement went beyond suspicion into outright conspiracy theories and nightmare fantasies. Their publications are not the works of calm, considered conservatives, but the extreme rantings of obsessive ideologues. Despite this, the Lavoisier Group and its allies were very successful in convincing ostensibly conservative politicians that climate change is a hoax or scam perpetrated by sinister elements within the bureaucracy and academia. An example: in 2014 the Abbott government discussed investigating the Bureau of Meteorology, amid claims published in *The Australian* that it was manipulating data in order to exaggerate the threat of global warming.[101]

Central to the Lavoisier Group's extreme, reactionary approach was its connection to the global network of climate denial. It formed links with like-minded think tanks, websites and blogs, where conspiratorial thinking was no barrier to social and political acceptance. It was happy to associate with such characters as Christopher Monckton, an eccentric Englishman who falsely claims to be a member of the House of Lords, and who in 2011 caused a furore after likening Australian economist and climate advocate Ross Garnaut to a Nazi.[102] Ray Evans abandoned the principles of conservative common sense when he described what he perceived as the intentions of the 2009 Copenhagen conference: "this new world order, Imperium Viridian, would supplant the nation-state as the basis of the world's polity."[103] This was not serious debate but a retreat into fantasy. In a 2012 paper on such fantasies Elaine McKewon identified a number of themes employed by climate deniers: climate scientists as rent-seeking frauds; climate scientists as dissent-stifling elite; climate science/environmentalism as religion; climate science as left-wing conspiracy; and climate change mitigation as money-spinning scam.[104] All were common in Lavoisier Group literature.

In recent years there have been attempts by American and British political figures to reclaim concern for the planet as a conservative ideal, invoking some of the great heroes of conservatism in support of their positions. For example, in 2014 the University of Chicago hosted a forum titled 'What Would Milton Friedman Do About Climate Change?' at which former Republican congressman Bob Inglis kicked things off by playing a 1979 clip of Friedman endorsing the idea of a tax on pollution in order to limit its negative effects. What, then, was the obvious answer to the forum's central question? Put a tax on carbon.[105] John Gummer, a minister in the Thatcher government and now chairman of the UK Committee on Climate Change, argues that "conservatives cannot properly be climate deniers. At the heart of their political stance is a desire to hand on something better to the future than they have received from the past."[106] Faced with the election of climate denier Donald Trump to the US presidency, Republican elder statesmen George Shultz and James Baker recalled Ronald Reagan's role in negotiating the Montreal Protocol as they encouraged climate action "based on a sound economic analysis that embodies the conservative principles of free markets and limited government."[107] Inglis and Gummer have both visited Australia to attempt to convince conservatives here that climate action is not only urgent, but the responsible thing to do. The message is yet to resonate within the Liberal–National Coalition.

While all four single-issue advocacy groups contained elements of the Australian liberal and conservative traditions to greater and lesser degrees, their combined philosophy is more accurately described as reactionary conservatism. In each case, the groups are defined by their opposition to what they perceive as left-wing or progressive causes. The H.R. Nicholls fought the "industrial relations club" and trade unions. The Samuel Griffith Society fought political centralists, activist judges and republicans. The Bennelong Society fought the "Aboriginal industry" and proponents of Indigenous self-determination. The Lavoisier Group fought environmentalists and advocates of climate action. They all share a perception that the left is in control, even during periods of conservative rule. This perception is commonly held by conservatives around the globe. "The conservative not only opposes the left," wrote American journalist Corey Robin, "he also believes that the left has been in the driver's seat since, depending on who's counting, the French Revolution or the Reformation."[108]

Australia's distinctive histories with regard to industrial relations, the Constitution and Indigenous affairs brought about the distinctive reactions of the H.R. Nicholls, Samuel Griffith and Bennelong societies. These groups saw little need to look abroad for inspiration and guidance, because they saw Australia's experiences as unique. The Lavoisier Group, on the other hand, dealt with the global issue of climate change by drawing on its connections to like-minded groups in the United States and the United Kingdom. This took it down an even more radical path, one that rejected respectful approaches to political conflict in favour of the demonisation of opponents and the promulgation of conspiracy theories. While this approach was successful in delegitimising the scientific consensus on climate change, it looks increasingly detached from mainstream conservatism.

The groups also brought to Australia a kind of relentless advocacy, one that accepted no compromises and warned of social and economic apocalypse if their demands were not met. They presented an Australia under siege: from trade unions, republicans, activist judges, Indigenous politicians and native title claimants, environmentalists, scientists and international bureaucrats.

In this, as in so many other respects, Australians were mimicking their American cousins. In 2012 – four years before Donald Trump mounted a hostile takeover of the Republican Party and transformed American politics – political scientist Mark Lilla wrote of the "mainstreaming of political apocalypticism" among right-wing intellectuals, publications and institutions, beginning in the 1980s:

This is the voice of highbrow reaction, and it was present on the right a good decade before Glenn Beck and his fellow prophets of populist doom began ringing alarm bells about educated elites in media, government, and the universities leading a velvet socialist revolution that only "ordinary Americans" could forestall. Apocalypticism trickled down, not up, and is now what binds Republican Party elites to their hard-core base. They all agree that the country must be "taken back" from the usurpers by any means necessary, and are willing to support any candidate, no matter how unworldly or unqualified or fanatical, who shares their picture of the crisis of our time.[109]

We have witnessed a similar process in Australia. The single-issue advocacy groups were Australia's voices of highbrow reaction. Their once radical views are now de rigueur on the right, and have spread into the wider culture. From the highest levels of government to the Liberal Party rank and file, from *The Australian*'s opinion page to the letters to its editor and anonymous online comments, reactionary conservatism reigns.

CONCLUSION

F OLLOWING THE POLITICAL, ECONOMIC and cultural upheav-
als of the 1970s, Australian conservatives went through a process
of radicalisation. Drawing on the influences of their British and
American counterparts, New Right organisations such as the Centre for
Independent Studies, the Centre of Policy Studies, the Australian Institute of Public Policy and a number of smaller groups emerged, while
older, established institutions such as the Institute of Public Affairs and
Quadrant magazine were compelled to reinvigorate their ideas and personnel in order to remain relevant. In doing so they helped to inspire
something of a renaissance for conservative politics in Australia.

From this fertile environment sprung the H.R. Nicholls Society, the
first of the four single-issue advocacy groups. The success of this group
saw the same collection of right-wing activists create other organisations
using the H.R. Nicholls Society template. With the single-issue advocacy
group of the right, Ray Evans and his associates pioneered a new type of
organisational form in Australian politics.

Lacking the resources and research capabilities of the likes of the IPA
or CIS, these groups could not be accurately classified as think tanks.
Neither were they interest groups in the same sense as, for example, their
allies at the Australian Mining Industry Council and National Farmers'
Federation, or their enemies at the ACTU, Friends of the Earth and other
such left-leaning organisations. The single-issue advocacy groups did
both less and more than these other groups that represent the particular
interests of an industry, community or social movement. Less in so far as
their interest was always specifically and tightly focused on a single area
of policy; more in so far as they were able to effect meaningful, demonstrable change in these areas. They provided networks for like-minded

ideologues to share passionate views about specific issues, and worked assiduously to transform these views into substantive political action. They often flew under the general public's radar, but the work of these groups was not a secretive right-wing conspiracy. Their opinions and objectives were plain for all to see.

Though strikingly similar in structure and personnel, each of these four groups had its own distinctive attributes and modes of operation. The H.R. Nicholls Society exploited business and political contacts to pressure Liberal Party MPs into adopting ever more hardline industrial relations policies, both in opposition and in government. Despite this privileged access to the corridors of power, H.R. Nicholls members delighted in their public image as political troublemakers, operating on the fringes of polite society. When High Court Justice Michael Kirby referred to them as "industrial ayatollahs" in 2004, Evans responded with gleeful mockery. "I presume that with these words virtually every member of the H.R. Nicholls Society stands condemned by his honour," he joked to fellow members.[1] Des Moore's next conference paper was titled 'Why the Ayatollahs are coming,' and featured a caricature of himself dressed as a sword-wielding ayatollah, drawn by *Herald Sun* cartoonist Mark Knight.[2]

The Samuel Griffith Society was the most stolid and traditional of the four groups. With its distinguished membership, organisational formality and impeccably presented published proceedings, it resembled a cross between a learned debating society and a national academy. But it is important not to let this impression mask the occasionally radical nature of its content, especially with regard to native title law and what was perceived as the pernicious influence of activist judges. The Bennelong Society's radicalism, on the other hand, was not hidden in any way. The forthright views of its members about every aspect of Aboriginal politics and culture were transparently on display on its website and in countless articles published in the popular press. Like all of the groups, the Bennelong Society was contemptuous of political correctness, and saw no reason to make its contributions less offensive to Indigenous people or anyone else.

The Lavoisier Group was the only one of the four to truly embrace the possibilities of the internet. While the other three organisations used their websites merely as archives for their articles and papers, the Lavoisier Group linked up with like-minded think tanks, advocacy groups, websites and blogs all over the globe. In doing this they were not only able to circulate their work to the rest of the world, but also to gather information and strategies from the global echo chamber of climate denial. The concentrated international networking of the Lavoisier Group and other Australian climate deniers has helped Australia to achieve the dubious distinction of having the highest rate of climate scepticism in the world, according to a University of Tasmania study.[3]

While all of the groups were widely described as conservative, and though they all exhibited attributes of traditional Australian conservatism, such a classification is insufficient. Their objectives and philosophical approaches were simply too radical for the term "conservative" to accurately encompass their ideological praxis. Their contrarian nature – the fact that they were largely defined by what they opposed – leads me to characterise their collective ideological position as reactionary conservatism.

I would also describe them as potent, effective players in public policy debates, and as we have seen, there are a number of examples where these single-issue advocacy groups of the hard right were able to intervene in politics and demonstrate significant clout, especially during the Howard years. Members of the H.R. Nicholls Society were central players in the 1998 waterfront dispute, and the organisation was a prominent voice as the Howard government orchestrated radical industrial relations reform with its Work Choices legislation. The establishment of the Samuel Griffith Society coincided with the High Court's Mabo judgement and a serious push for an Australian republic, and naturally the organisation made significant contributions to these two important and divisive constitutional debates, by attacking and undermining those in favour of progressive change at every turn. The Bennelong Society's neo-assimilationist approach to Indigenous affairs found particular favour with members of the Howard government, and the Society backed its controversial decisions to dissolve ATSIC and intervene in remote Indigenous communities. Partnered with a variety of organisations and individuals, the Lavoisier Group's "deny and delay" lobbying efforts have helped to shape the climate policies of the Liberal–National Coalition for the past two decades.

More broadly, these groups have powerfully contributed to a general rightward shift in Australian politics, evident even following Howard's defeat in 2007. What were once viewed as the crazed rantings of an extreme right-wing fringe – "political troglodytes and economic lunatics," in Bob Hawke's memorable phrase – are now very much part of mainstream Australian politics. Gradually yet unmistakably, our political culture has shifted to the right, and four very small, very cheap organisations run by a handful of passionate hard right activists have been central to that shift.

ACKNOWLEDGEMENTS

F IRST AND FOREMOST, I WANT TO OFFER my heartfelt gratitude
to Robert Manne, who played a fundamental role in making this
book a reality. Since I took his undergraduate classes at La Trobe
University in the early 2000s, Rob has been my teacher, research supervi-
sor, employer, mentor and friend, and has remained inspirational, wise
and supportive throughout. He helped devise the topic for this book (in its
initial form as a PhD thesis), and was always available during the research
and writing process to offer sound advice and engrossing memories of his
time dealing with many of the people that grace its pages. When the time
finally came to seek its publication, he was a passionate advocate on my
behalf. Rob, I cannot thank you enough.

To the other members of the La Trobe University Press editorial
board – Chris Feik and Morry Schwartz at Black Inc. and Elizabeth Finkel
of La Trobe University – thank you for taking a chance on a first-time
author. Also at Black Inc., sincere thanks to my brilliant editor Dion Kagan
for his patience, encouragement and sterling editorial judgement.

Thanks to my doctoral supervisors at La Trobe, Judith Brett and Gwenda
Tavan, who provided invaluable support throughout the book's long gesta-
tion period. And cheers to various friends and colleagues at La Trobe: Gavin
McLean, Liz Chapman, Jim Vale, Gijs Verbossen, Nick Barry, Jasmine-Kim
Westendorf, Aidan Craney, John Doyle, Nick Bisley, Bec Strating, Tim
Andrews, Michael O'Keefe, Ben Habib, Mark Ryan and Lawrie Zion. I also
want to thank my first ever politics lecturer, Andrew Scott, formerly at
RMIT but now at Deakin, who set me on the path of studying politics as a
vocation. Andrew, I'm sorry I transferred to La Trobe without telling you.

I'd like to thank those who gave up their time to be interviewed as part
of my research for this book: the late Ray Evans, Gary Johns, Wesley Aird,

ACKNOWLEDGEMENTS

John Herron, Des Moore, Andrew Norton, Anthony Cappello, Greg Craven and John Stone. Ray Evans was especially generous despite the great physical adversity he was experiencing.

Over the course of writing this book I've been fortunate to meet and/or converse with an array of talented writers and thinkers who, probably without knowing it, assisted me by simply sharing their thoughts and expertise. So thanks to Martin McKenzie-Murray, Russell Marks, Richard Cooke, David Marr, Jason Wilson, Elle Hardy, Russell Jackson, Gideon Haigh, Guy Rundle, Misha Ketchell, Megan Davis, Tim Boyle, Nick Feik, Myriam Robin and Guy Pearse.

To my oldest friend, Simon Liston, thanks for the pizza, wine and conversation. Let's never talk of my four weeks on the pizza oven again.

To Jeannine and Eric Hendy, thank you for opening up your beautiful country home and providing delicious home-cooked meals whenever Sarah and I needed a break.

My parents, Gabrielle and Don, instilled in me an interest in politics and the world around me without ever prescribing what form that interest should take. For that, and so much more, I will always be grateful. Thanks also to my brothers Luke and Xavier, and their respective partners Ezgi and Jess, and my niece Zoe. Our family seems to have a unique talent for staying out of each other's hair, but the week or so we spent together in Budapest celebrating Luke and Ezgi's wedding will remain a cherished memory for the rest of my life.

Finally, and most importantly, to Sarah Hendy, the one person without whose selfless support and encouragement, and above all incredible reserves of patience, this book simply would not have been completed. Sarah, I'm not sure I can ever adequately demonstrate how grateful I am for all that you've done for me over the past seven years; I am forever in your debt. From the bottom of my heart, thank you so much.

NOTES

Introduction

1   Malcolm Turnbull, quoted in Andrew Tillett, 'PM floats postal vote on republic,' *Australian Financial Review*, 2 January 2018.

2   Jonathan Hamberger, quoted in Matt O'Sullivan and Lisa Visentin, 'Reprieve as rail union ordered to abandon strike,' *The Sydney Morning Herald*, 26 January 2018.

3   Lucy McNally, 'Sydney train strike ruling by Fair Work Commission denies human rights: ACTU,' *ABC News*, 25 January 2018.

4   Scott Morrison and Matt Canavan, quoted in Ben Packham, 'Fossil fuel blueprint for power,' *The Australian*, 28 August 2018.

5   Jackie Huggins, quoted in Dana McCauley, 'Indigenous leaders blast envoy offer,' *The Age*, 28 August 2018.

6   Andrew Norton, 'Naming the right: from the New Right to economic rationalism to neoliberalism,' *Quadrant*, December 2001, pp. 62–65.

7   See for example Clive Hamilton, *Scorcher: The Dirty Politics of Climate Change*, Melbourne: Black Inc., 2007, pp. 132–44.

8   Mark Davis, *The Land of Plenty: Australia in the 2000s*, Melbourne: Melbourne University Press, 2008, p. 40.

9   Peter Coleman, 'Where the conservatives went wrong,' *The Weekend Australian*, 12 December 2009.

1   Ideas and Institutions of the Australian Right

1   Judith Brett, *Australian Liberals and the Moral Middle Class: From Alfred Deakin to John Howard*, Cambridge: Cambridge University Press, 2003, p. 2.

2   Robert Menzies, *Afternoon Light: Some Memories of Men and Events*, Melbourne: Cassell Australia, 1967, p. 286.

3   Edmund Burke, *Reflections on the Revolution in France*, Oxford: Oxford University Press, [1790] 1993, p. 21.

4   Russell Kirk, *The Conservative Mind: From Burke to Eliot* (5th edn), Chicago: Henry Regnery Company, 1972, pp. 7–8.

5   George H. Nash, *The Conservative Intellectual Movement in America since 1945*, New York: Basic Books, 1976, p. 69.

6 Rick Perlstein, *The Invisible Bridge: The Fall of Nixon and the Rise of Reagan*, New York: Simon & Schuster, 2014, pp. 453–54.

7 Irving Kristol, quoted in Andrew Hartman, *A War for the Soul of America: A History of the Culture Wars*, Chicago: University of Chicago Press, 2015, p. 64.

8 Jane Mayer, *Dark Money: How a Secretive Group of Billionaires is Trying to Buy Political Control in the US*, Melbourne: Scribe, 2016, p. 79.

9 David Harvey, *A Brief History of Neoliberalism*, Oxford: Oxford University Press, 2005, p. 2.

10 Friedrich Hayek, quoted in Philip Mirowski, *Never Let a Serious Crisis Go to Waste: How Neoliberalism Survived the Financial Meltdown*, London: Verso, 2013, p. 43.

11 Charles L. Heatherly (ed.), *Mandate for Leadership: Policy Management in a Conservative Administration*, Washington DC: Heritage Foundation, 1981, p. ix.

12 Jason Stahl, *Right Moves: The Conservative Think Tank in American Culture since 1945*, Chapel Hill: University of North Carolina Press, 2016, pp. 109–10.

13 Edwin J. Feulner, 'Ideas, think-tanks and governments,' *Quadrant*, November 1985, p. 22.

14 Antony Fisher, quoted in Richard Cockett, *Thinking the Unthinkable: Think-Tanks and the Economic Counter-Revolution, 1931–1983*, London: Fontana Press, 1995, p. 124.

15 Atlas Network, 'Global directory,' www.atlasnetwork.org/partners/global-directory

16 Harvey, *A Brief History of Neoliberalism*, p. 2.

17 Madsen Pirie, quoted in Alan Rusbridger, 'Adam Smith Institute's sense and nonsense,' *The Guardian*, 22 December 1987.

18 Cockett, *Thinking the Unthinkable*, p. 5.

19 Paul Kelly, *The End of Certainty: The Story of the 1980s*, Sydney: Allen & Unwin, 1992, pp. 1–16.

20 Judith Brett, 'Ideology,' in Judith Brett, James Gillespie and Murray Goot (eds), *Developments in Australian Politics*, Melbourne: Macmillan Education, 1994, p. 7.

21 Brett, *Australian Liberals and the Moral Middle Class*, p. 117.

22 David Kemp, 'Liberalism and conservatism in Australia since 1944', in Brian Head and James Walter (eds), *Intellectual Movements and Australian Society*, Melbourne: Oxford University Press, 1988, p. 342.

23 Kelly, *The End of Certainty*, p. 105.

24 John Howard, *Lazarus Rising: A Personal and Political Autobiography*, Sydney: HarperCollins, 2010, p. 654.

25 Robert Manne, 'The Howard years: a political interpretation', in Robert Manne (ed.), *The Howard Years*, Melbourne: Black Inc., 2004 pp. 3–4.

26 James Walter, 'Intellectuals and the political culture,' in Head and Walter, *Intellectual Movements and Australian Society*, p. 248.

27 IPA, 'About us,' ipa.org.au/about

28 George Coles, quoted in IPA, 'About the IPA,' *IPA Review*, April–June 1968, p. 35.

29 Kelly, *The End of Certainty*, p. 47.

30   Robert Menzies, quoted in IPA, 'About the IPA,' p. 36.

31   IPA, 'Milton Friedman's visit,' *IPA Review*, April–June 1975, p. 29.

32   IPA, 'Professor F.A. Hayek's Australian visit,' *IPA Review*, October–December 1976, p. 79.

33   Damien Cahill, quoted in Mike Seccombe, 'Former IPA head: radicals "hijacked" think tank,' *The Saturday Paper*, 27 August 2016.

34   Kemp, 'Liberalism and conservatism in Australia,' p. 329.

35   Rod Kemp, 'To our readers,' *IPA Review*, Summer 1982–83, p. 88.

36   Tim Duncan, 'New Right crusaders challenge the Labor line,' *The Bulletin*, 2 October 1984, p. 31.

37   Gerard Henderson, quoted in Brad Norington, 'The idea factories,' *The Sydney Morning Herald*, 11 August 2003.

38   Des Moore, interview with author, Melbourne, 10 August 2012.

39   David Walker, 'Last of the old guard quits think tank,' *The Age*, 17 February 1996.

40   Tom Duggan, 'Dry launch,' *The Age*, 19 December 1985.

41   John Nurick (ed.), *Mandate to Govern: A Handbook for the Next Australian Government*, Perth: Australian Institute for Public Policy, 1987, p. xv.

42   Alan Kohler, 'The radical right wing speeds the Kennett revolution,' *The Age*, 14 February 1997.

43   John Roskam, quoted in Ewin Hannan and Shaun Carney, 'Thinkers of influence,' *The Age*, 10 December 2005.

44   Ian Marsh, *Globalisation and Australian Think Tanks: An Evaluation of Their Role and Contribution to Governance*, Sydney: Committee for Economic Development of Australia, 1991, p. 29.

45   IPA, *IPA Annual Report 2016*, p. 1.

46   Mike Nahan, quoted in Wilson da Silva, 'The new social focus,' *Australian Financial Review Magazine*, June 1996, p. 24.

47   James McAuley, 'By way of prologue,' *Quadrant*, Summer 1956–57, p. 4.

48   *Quadrant*, 'About us,' quadrant.org.au/about-us/

49   Cassandra Pybus, *The Devil and James McAuley* (rev. edn), Brisbane: University of Queensland Press, 2001, p. 149.

50   Kemp, 'Liberalism and conservatism in Australia,' p. 333.

51   Pybus, *The Devil and James McAuley*, p. 220.

52   Duncan, 'New Right crusaders challenge the Labor line,' p. 29.

53   Robert Manne, quoted in Peter Ellingsen, 'Rapture in the right,' *The Age*, 22 July 1992.

54   Ray Evans, quoted in Gideon Haigh, 'Manne overboard,' *Independent Monthly*, April 1993, p. 7.

55   Ray Evans, quoted in Damien Murphy, 'Loose cannon of the Right,' *The Bulletin*, 2 November 1993, p. 43.

56   Robert Manne, *Left, Right, Left: Political Essays 1977–2005*, Melbourne, Black Inc., 2005, p. 10.

57   P.P. McGuinness, 'The future for *Quadrant*,' *Quadrant*, January–February 1998, p. 12.

58   Martin Krygier, 'The usual suspects: *Quadrant* at 50,' *The Monthly*, December 2006–January 2007, p. 28.

59   John Howard, 'A tribute to *Quadrant*,' *Quadrant*, November 2006, p. 22.

60   Greg Sheridan, 'No grounds for racial paranoia,' *The Australian*, 20 December 2001.

61   Greg Sheridan, 'Era of the unhinged,' *The Weekend Australian*, 19 January 2008.

62   Frank Devine, '*Quadrant* in search of can-do person with an eye for cant,' *The Australian*, 12 October 2007.

63   Keith Windschuttle, quoted in Andrew Stevenson, 'A voice from the frontier,' *The Sydney Morning Herald*, 22 September 2001.

64   Keith Windschuttle, quoted in Virginia Marsh, 'Lunch with the FT: the history wars,' *Financial Times*, 27 August 2005.

65   CIS, 'Mission & history,' www.cis.org.au/about/mission

66   Greg Lindsay, 'Why think tanks are here to stay,' *The Age*, 20 October 2000.

67   P.P. McGuinness, 'Where Friedman is a pinko,' *Australian Financial Review*, 4 April 1978.

68   Greg Lindsay and Andrew Norton, 'The CIS at twenty,' *Policy*, Winter 1996, p. 18.

69   Diana Bagnall, 'How this man controls your future,' *The Bulletin*, 28 September 2004, p. 24.

70   ibid., p. 23.

71   James G. McGann, *The Global "Go-To Think Tanks"* (rev. edn), Think Tanks and Civil Societies Program, University of Pennsylvania, 2010, p. 31.

72   Ian Marsh, quoted in da Silva, 'The new social focus,' p. 21.

73   Lindsay and Norton, 'The CIS at twenty,' p. 21.

74   Wilson da Silva, 'Signal drivers,' *Australian Financial Review Magazine*, July 2002, p. 26.

75   Ben Potter, 'Think tank a real agent of change,' *Weekend Australian Financial Review*, 29 April 2006.

76   Andrew Clark, 'Reframing the big picture,' *Australian Financial Review Magazine*, December 2012, pp. 29–30.

77   Bob Carr, quoted in da Silva, 'Signal drivers,' p. 28.

78   Bagnall, 'How this man controls your future,' p. 25.

79   Andrew Norton, interview with author, Melbourne, 14 August 2012.

80   da Silva, 'Signal drivers,' p. 26.

81   Marcus Smith and Peter Marden, 'Conservative think tanks and public politics,' *Australian Journal of Political Science*, vol. 43, no. 4 (December 2008), p. 713.

82   Greg Lindsay, quoted in Hannan and Carney, 'Thinkers of influence'.

83   Damien Cahill, *The Radical Neo-Liberal Movement as a Hegemonic Force in Australia, 1976–1996*, PhD thesis, University of Wollongong, 2004, p. 118.

84   Tim Duncan, 'Mark of Cain in attack on New Right academics,' *The Bulletin*, 14 October 1986, p. 26.

85   ibid., p. 28.

86   Michael Porter, quoted in David Elias and Simon Clarke, 'Academic outcry forces Coghill to withdraw FoI requests,' *The Age*, 9 October 1986.

87   Mark Davis, 'Private sector supports trans-Tasman uni project,' *Australian*

Financial Review, 27 November 1987.

88   Steve Lewis, 'Lack of funds puts paid to private Tasman University,' *Australian Financial Review,* 17 January 1990.

89   Michael Porter, quoted in Cahill, *The Radical Neo-Liberal Movement,* p. 121.

90   Alan Stockdale, 'The politics of privatisation in Victoria,' *Privatisation International,* November 1999, p. 4.

91   Michael Porter, 'Project's aim is to create jobs' (letter to the editor), *The Age,* 1 October 1992.

92   Brett Foley, 'Consultants ACIL and Tasman join forces,' *Australian Financial Review,* 18 November 2002.

93   Greg Sheridan, 'Just who are the New Right?' *Weekend Australian,* 6 September 1986.

94   John Hyde, quoted in Kelly, *The End of Certainty,* p. 41.

95   Kelly, *The End of Certainty,* pp. 41–42.

96   W.K. Hancock, *Australia,* Brisbane: Jacaranda Press, [1930] 1961, p. 71.

97   Hal G.P. Colebatch, *The Modest Member: The Life and Times of Bert Kelly,* Ballan: Connor Court, 2012, p. 2.

98   Gough Whitlam, in CIS, 'A tribute to the modest member: Bert Kelly,' *CIS Occasional Papers,* no. 60, 1997, p. 8.

99   Kemp, 'Liberalism and conservatism in Australia,' p. 346.

100   Peter McGauran, quoted in Marion Maddox, *God Under Howard: The Rise of the Religious Right in Australian Politics,* Sydney: Allen & Unwin, 2005, p. 215.

101   Michelle Grattan, 'Libs move to keep Abbott on track,' *The Age,* 6 July 2011.

102   Christopher Jay, 'New Right policy moves out of the politicians' hands,' *Australian Financial Review,* 11 February 1986.

103   Cahill, *The Radical Neo-Liberal Movement,* p. 119.

104   Australian Adam Smith Club, '20th anniversary dinner programme,' 18 November 2003, adamsmithclub.org/Menu.pdf

105   Alan Tate, 'Conservatives grab tax issue and run,' *The Sydney Morning Herald,* 2 July 1985.

106   Gerard Henderson, *Santamaria: A Most Unusual Man,* Melbourne: Miegunyah Press, 2015, p. 299.

107   Council for the National Interest, 'About us,' www.cniwa.com.au.

108   *National Observer,* 'Our mission,' www.nationalobserver.net/mission.htm

109   Cahill, *The Radical Neo-Liberal Movement,* p. 109.

110   Kemp, 'Liberalism and conservatism in Australia,' p. 340.

2   THE TROIKA

1   Patricia Howard, 'A blue-blooded company chief bobs back after bucketing,' *The Canberra Times,* 4 September 1993.

2   Gerard Henderson, *Australian Answers,* Sydney: Random House, 1990, p. 239.

3   ibid., p. 240.

4   Anne Davies, 'High-fliers fund Libs with blue-chip shares,' *The Sydney*

Morning Herald, 23 December 1997.

5   Sarah Burnside, 'Mineral booms, taxation and the national interest: the impact of the 1974 Fitzgerald Report on *The Contribution of the Mineral Industry to Australian Welfare*,' *History Australia*, vol. 10, no. 3 (December 2013), p. 172.

6   Thomas Fitzgerald, quoted in Burnside, 'Mineral booms,' p. 180.

7   AMIC, quoted in Burnside, 'Mineral booms', p. 184.

8   Hugh Morgan, quoted in Henderson, *Australian Answers*, p. 241.

9   Ronald T. Libby, *Hawke's Law: The Politics of Mining and Aboriginal Land Rights in Australia*, Perth: University of Western Australia Press, 1989, p. 57.

10 Hugh Morgan, 'The threat to Australia's private enterprise sector,' *The Bulletin*, 10 July 1984, p. 148.

11 Hugh Morgan, quoted in Paul Sheehan, 'The Right strikes back,' *The Sydney Morning Herald*, 2 March 1985.

12 Sheehan, 'The Right strikes back'.

13 David Kemp, 'Liberalism and conservatism in Australia since 1944,' in Brian Head and James Walter (eds), *Intellectual Movements and Australian Society*, Oxford: Oxford University Press, 1988, p. 351.

14 Paul Kelly, *The End of Certainty: The Story of the 1980s*, Sydney: Allen & Unwin, 1992, p. 42.

15 Wilson da Silva, 'The new social focus,' *Australian Financial Review Magazine*, June 1996, p. 24.

16 Tim Duncan, 'Western Mining's messiahs of the New Right,' *The Bulletin*, 2 July 1985, p. 66.

17 Henderson, *Australian Answers*, p. 242.

18 Peter Costello, 'The importance of ideas,' Address to the H.R. Nicholls Society, Melbourne, 8 February 2017.

19 Hugh Morgan, 'Ray's career as an advocate,' Eulogy at the funeral of Ray Evans, Melbourne, 27 June 2014.

20 Hugh Morgan, quoted in Andrew Cornell, 'Why Ray Evans is always right,' *Weekend Australian Financial Review*, 8 January 2005.

21 Greg Sheridan, 'Just who are the New Right?' *The Weekend Australian*, 6 September 1986.

22 Ray Evans, quoted in Michael Bachelard, 'Exit, stage Right,' *The Weekend Australian*, 10 August 2002.

23 Patrick Morgan, 'The life and career of Ray Evans,' *Quadrant*, September 2014, p. 78.

24 Andrew Knopfelmacher, 'The nine lives of Frank Knopfelmacher,' Address at the Retreat Hotel, Melbourne, 21 March 2002.

25 James Franklin, *Corrupting the Youth: A History of Philosophy in Australia*, Sydney: Macleay Press, 2003, p. 283.

26 Knopfelmacher, 'The nine lives of Frank Knopfelmacher'.

27 Cornell, 'Why Ray Evans is always right'.

28 Arthur Koestler, *The Invisible Writing: The Second Volume of an Autobiography*,

1932–40, London: Vintage, [1954] 2005, p. 382.

29 Robert Manne, email to author, 15 October 2018.

30 'Long-haired,' *Farrago*, 15 June 1962.

31 Ray Evans, interview with author, Melbourne, 5 June 2012.

32 Ray Evans, quoted in Cassandra Pybus, *The Devil and James McAuley* (rev. edn), Brisbane: University of Queensland Press, 2001, p. 241.

33 Gerard Henderson, *Santamaria: A Most Unusual Man*, Melbourne: Miegunyah Press, 2015, pp. 409–11.

34 Patrick Morgan, 'A remembrance of Ray Evans,' H.R. Nicholls Society Annual Conference, Melbourne, 28 November 2015.

35 Ray Evans, 'On joining the Gaullists,' letter to B.A. Santamaria, 19 September 1971, Papers of Bartholomew Augustine Santamaria, 1915–1998, State Library of Victoria, MS 13492, box 10.

36 Pybus, *The Devil and James McAuley*, p. 249.

37 Morgan, 'The life and career of Ray Evans,' p. 78.

38 ibid., p. 79.

39 Ray Evans, in CIS, 'A tribute to the Modest Member: Bert Kelly,' *CIS Occasional Papers*, no. 60, 1997, p. 25.

40 Ray Evans, 'Reflections on the Modest Member,' *Quadrant*, December 2012, p. 16.

41 Bob Day, 'Ray's career as an advocate,' Eulogy at the funeral of Ray Evans, Melbourne, 27 June 2014.

42 J.D. Heydon, 'The public life of John and Nancy Stone,' in *Upholding the Australian Constitution*, vol. 22, Proceedings of the Twenty-Second Conference of the Samuel Griffith Society, Perth, August 2010, p. 220.

43 John Stone, quoted in Craig McGregor, 'The heart of Stone,' *The Sydney Morning Herald*, 10 October 1987

44 Bob Hawke, *The Hawke Memoirs*, Melbourne: William Heinemann Australia, 1994, p. 8.

45 John Stone, quoted in John Howard, *Lazarus Rising: A Personal and Political Autobiography*, Sydney: HarperCollins, 2010, p. 103.

46 John Stone, 'The dismal beginning to the Fraser years,' *Quadrant*, July–August 2007, p. 19.

47 Heydon, 'The public life of John and Nancy Stone,' pp. 230–31.

48 John Stone, 'A last trumpet for Bert – Mr Valiant-for-Truth,' *Australian Financial Review*, 30 January 1997.

49 John Stone, 'Why I am working for Sir Joh,' *IPA Review*, May–July 1987, p. 42.

50 John Stone, 'Governor-General's speech – address-in-reply,' *Commonwealth Parliamentary Debates*, Senate, 16 September 1987, p. 169.

51 Kelly, *The End of Certainty*, p. 428.

52 John Stone, 'Our greatest prime minister?' in Keith Windshuttle, David Martin Jones and Ray Evans (eds.) *The Howard Era*, Sydney: Quadrant Books, 2009, p. 11.

53 Henderson, *Australian Answers*, p. 310.

54 Heydon, 'The public life of John and Nancy Stone,' p. 238.

55 McGregor, 'The heart of Stone'.

56 John Stone, 'The Liberals' Rudd,' *Spectator Australia*, 5 December 2015.

57 John Stone, letter to the editor, *The Australian*, 28 August 2018.

3 **RIGHT-WING REVIVAL**

1 Paul Kelly, *The End of Certainty: The Story of the 1980s*, Sydney: Allen & Unwin, 1992, p. 9.

2 Stuart Macintyre, *Winners and Losers: The Pursuit of Social Justice in Australian History*, Sydney: Allen & Unwin, 1985, p. 51.

3 ibid., p. 52.

4 Commonwealth of Australia, *Australia's Constitution*, Canberra: Australian Government Publishing Service, [1901] 1995, p. 19.

5 Kelly, *The End of Certainty*, pp. 8–9.

6 John Rickard, *H.B. Higgins: The Rebel as Judge*, Sydney: Allen & Unwin, 1984, p. 171.

7 H.B. Higgins, quoted in Rickard, *H.B. Higgins*, p. 172.

8 ibid. pp. 172–73.

9 Rickard, *H.B. Higgins*, p. 174.

10 H.B. Higgins, 'A new province for law and order: industrial peace through minimum wage and arbitration,' *Harvard Law Review*, vol. 29, no. 1 (November 1915), pp. 13–39.

11 Macintyre, *Winners and Losers*, p. 56.

12 Kelly, *The End of Certainty*, p. 111.

13 John Howard, quoted in Kelly, *The End of Certainty*, p. 111.

14 Gerard Henderson, 'The Industrial Relations Club,' *Quadrant*, September 1983, p. 23.

15 Tim Duncan, quoted in John Lyons, 'Bunfight among knights of the Right,' *The Sydney Morning Herald*, 11 February 1989.

16 Ray Evans, quoted in John Stone, 'Dinner address,' in *Fair is Foul and Foul is Fair*, Proceedings of the Twenty-Ninth Conference of the H.R. Nicholls Society, Melbourne, March 2009.

17 John Stone, '1929 and all that,' *Quadrant*, October 1984, p. 15.

18 ibid., p. 19.

19 Ray Evans, 'Justice Higgins: architect and builder of an Australian folly,' in John Hyde and John Nurick (eds), *Wages Wasteland: A Radical Examination of the Australian Wage Fixing System*, Sydney: Hale & Iremonger, 1985, p. 30.

20 Ralph Willis, quoted in Owen Covick, 'The Hancock Report on Australia's Industrial Relations System,' *Australian Economic Papers*, vol. 24, no. 45 (December 1985), p. 243.

21 P.P. McGuinness, 'The case against the arbitration commission,' *CIS Occasional Papers*, no. 11, 1985, p. 1.

22 Keith Hancock, quoted in Stuart Macintyre, 'Arbitration in action,' in Joe Isaac and Stuart Macintyre (eds), *The New Province for Law and Order: 100 Years of Australian Industrial Conciliation and Arbitration*, Cambridge: Cambridge

University Press, 2004, p. 93.

23 Shaun Carney, *Australia in Accord: Politics and Industrial Relations Under the Hawke Government*, Melbourne: Sun Books, 1998, p. 156.

24 John Howard, quoted in Kelly, *The End of Certainty*, p. 278.

25 Carney, *Australia in Accord*, p. 125.

26 Peter Costello with Peter Coleman, *The Costello Memoirs: The Age of Prosperity*, Melbourne: Melbourne University Press, 2008, p. 36.

27 Ray Evans, 'Particular principles and magic words,' *Quadrant*, January–February 2011, p. 36.

28 Evans, 'Justice Higgins,' p. 31.

29 ibid., p. 32.

30 'A modest judge,' *The Mercury*, 7 April 1911.

31 Rickard, *H.B. Higgins*, p. 187.

32 Ray Evans, quoted in Kelly, *The End of Certainty*, p. 260.

33 Andrew Cornell, 'Why Ray Evans is always right,' *Weekend Australian Financial Review*, 8 January 2005.

34 John Stone, 'Introduction,' in *Arbitration in Contempt*, Proceedings of the Inaugural Seminar of the H.R. Nicholls Society, Melbourne, February 1986, p. 13.

35 John Hyde, 'The political barriers to changing centralised industrial relations,' in *Arbitration in Contempt*, p. 156.

36 Braham Dabscheck, 'New Right or old wrong? Ideology and industrial relations,' *Journal of Industrial Relations*, vol. 29, no. 4 (December 1987), p. 429.

37 Kevin Tuffin, 'The privatization of history: Henry Richard Nicholls and the H.R. Nicholls Society,' *Parliamentary Library Legislative Research Service*, Canberra: Department of the Parliamentary Library, 1987, p. 7.

38 John Stone, Ray Evans, Barrie Purvis and Peter Costello, 'The invitation letter, 16 January 1986,' in *Arbitration in Contempt*, p. 317.

39 Stone, Evans, Purvis and Costello, 'The invitation letter,' p. 317.

40 Kelly, *The End of Certainty*, p. 261.

41 John Stone, quoted in Glenn Mitchell, 'Sir John brought in from the cold,' *The Australian*, 3 March 1986.

42 Carney, *Australia in Accord*, p. 89.

43 Ray Evans, interview with author, Melbourne, 5 June 2012.

44 Charles Copeman, 'The Robe River affair,' in *The Light on the Hill*, Proceedings of the Third Conference of the H.R. Nicholls Society, Mooloolaba, June 1987, p. 65.

45 Pamela Williams, 'Union busters: their tactics and targets,' *Business Review Weekly*, 22 August 1986, p. 49.

46 John Stone, 'The origins and influence of the H.R. Nicholls Society' in *Let's Start All Over Again*, Proceedings of the Twenty-Seventh Conference of the H.R. Nicholls Society, Sydney, March 2006.

47 Greg Sheridan, 'Just who are the New Right?' *The Weekend Australian*, 6 September 1986; David McKnight, 'The New Right: a consumer's guide,' *The Sydney Morning Herald*, 6 September 1986.

48 Bob Hawke, quoted in Michelle Grattan, 'Hawke hits "lunacy" of New Right,'

The Age, 29 August 1986.

49   Evans, interview with author.

50   John Halfpenny, quoted in Brendan Donohoe, 'Halfpenny likens Right's tactics to Klan's,' *The Age*, 9 September 1986.

51   Evans, interview with author.

52   Brian Powell, quoted in Sonya Voumard, 'New Right shows fascism: Powell,' *The Age*, 2 October 1986.

53   Sonya Voumard and Brendan Donohoe, 'Extreme or acceptable? Business at odds over the New Right,' *The Age*, 3 October 1986.

54   Geoffrey Blainey, 'Padded arguments from padded trade unions,' Address launching *Arbitration in Contempt*, Southern Cross Hotel, Melbourne, 30 September 1986.

55   Matthew Moore, 'Not quite top set at Nicholls gathering,' *The Sydney Morning Herald*, 1 October 1986.

56   Peter Costello, quoted in Wayne Errington and Peter van Onselen, *John Winston Howard: The Biography*, Melbourne: Melbourne University Press, 2007, pp. 134–35.

57   Evans, interview with author.

58   Andrew Clark, 'In their own image,' *Australian Financial Review Magazine*, March 2001, p. 36.

59   Pamela Williams, 'Liberals' secret plan to crack union power,' *Business Review Weekly*, 5 December 1986, p. 25.

60   Stone, Evans, Purvis and Costello, 'The invitation letter,' p. 317.

61   ibid., p. 314.

62   Hugh Morgan, quoted in 'The professionals form private club to swing Liberals to the right,' *The Sydney Morning Herald*, 28 August 1986.

63   H.R. Nicholls Society, 'Advertisement,' *The Weekend Australian*, 4 April 1987.

64   Evans, 'Justice Higgins,' pp. 31–32.

65   Unnamed source, quoted in 'The professionals form private club'.

66   Ray Evans, 'Are workers just another commodity?' in Tim Wilson, Carlo Carli and Paul Collits (eds), *Turning Left or Right: Values in Modern Politics*, Ballarat: Connor Court, 2013, p. 153.

67   Gerard Henderson, 'The fridge dwellers: dreamtime in industrial relations,' in *Arbitration in Contempt*, p. 287.

68   Des Moore, interview with author, Melbourne, 10 August 2012.

69   Costello with Coleman, *The Costello Memoirs*, p. 41.

70   Peter Hartley, 'The effects of minimum wage laws on the labour markets,' in *A New Province for Law and Order*, Proceedings of the Thirteenth Conference of the H.R. Nicholls Society, Adelaide, November 1992, p. 7.

71   G.O. Gutman, 'The Hancock Report: a last hurrah for the system,' in *Arbitration in Contempt*, p. 302.

72   Evans, 'Particular principles and magic words,' p. 36.

73   Gutman, 'The Hancock Report,' p. 302.

74   Hugh Morgan, 'The nature of trade union power,' in *Arbitration in Contempt*, p. 18.

75   ibid., p. 28.

76   Commonwealth of Australia, *Conciliation and Arbitration Act 1904*, s. 59.

77   Gutman, 'The Hancock Report,' p. 309.

78   Ray Evans, 'Is trade unionism dying?' in *Trade Union Reform*, Proceedings of the Second Conference of the H.R. Nicholls Society, Melbourne, December 1986, p. 12.

79   Stone, 'The origins and influence of the H.R. Nicholls Society'.

80   Peter Costello, quoted in Tim Duncan, 'Waving a mischievous Kerr flag,' *The Bulletin*, 18 March 1986, p. 27.

81   Evans, interview with author.

82   ibid.

83   Ray Evans, 'Introduction,' in *The Light on the Hill*, p. 5.

84   John Howard, 'Guest of honour's address,' in *Public Interest or Vested Interest?*, Proceedings of the Eighth Conference of the H.R. Nicholls Society, Sydney, March 1990.

85   Peter Costello, quoted in Williams, 'Liberals' secret plan to crack union power,' p. 25.

86   Evans, interview with author.

87   Moore, interview with author.

88   Brad Norington, 'Reith backs anti-union hardliners,' *The Sydney Morning Herald*, 25 March 1996.

89   Peter Reith, quoted in Braham Dabscheck, 'The waterfront dispute: of vendetta and the Australian way,' *Economic and Labour Relations Review*, vol. 9, no. 2 (December 1998), p. 156.

90   Ray Evans, quoted in Michelle Grattan, 'New Right denounces workplace reforms,' *Australian Financial Review*, 3 March 1997.

91   Peter Reith, *The Reith Papers*, Melbourne: Melbourne University Press, 2015, p. 127.

92   Braham Dabscheck, 'The waterfront dispute,' pp. 161–62.

93   Ray Evans, 'Introduction,' in *The Legacy of the Hungry Mile*, Proceedings of the Seventh Conference of the H.R. Nicholls Society, Melbourne, August 1989, p. vii.

94   David Trebeck, 'Achieving institutional change in shipping and the waterfront,' in *In Search of the Magic Pudding*, Proceedings of the Fifth Conference of the H.R. Nicholls Society, Lorne, August 1988, p. 72.

95   Paul Houlihan, 'Some vignettes from the waterfront,' in *The Legacy of the Hungry Mile*, p. 24.

96   Helen Trinca and Anne Davies, *Waterfront: The Battle that Changed Australia*, Sydney: Doubleday, 2000, p. 29.

97   Pamela Williams, 'Coalition's secret plan to break the docks union,' *Australian Financial Review*, 15 August 1997.

98   Bill Kelty, quoted in Ewin Hannan, 'Unions threaten wharf blockade,' *The Age*, 4 September 1997.

99   Trinca and Davies, *Waterfront*, p. 11.

100 Mark Davis and Stephen Long, 'Patrick feels the pinch in dock war,' *Australian Financial Review*, 26 March 1998.

101 Paul Houlihan, 'The 1998 waterfront dispute,' in *MUA–Here to Stay ... Today!*

Proceedings of the Nineteenth Conference of the H.R. Nicholls Society, Melbourne, August 1998.

102 Paul Kelly, *The March of Patriots: The Struggle for Modern Australia*, Melbourne: Melbourne University Press, 2009, p. 303.

103 Ray Evans, 'The bills we need,' in *Lining Up the Bills: Preparing for a Double Dissolution*, Proceedings of the Twenty-Fourth Conference of the H.R. Nicholls Society, Melbourne, May 2003.

104 Ray Evans, quoted in Cornell, 'Why Ray Evans is always right'.

105 Ray Evans, 'Workplaces left in shackles,' *Australian Financial Review*, 19 December 2005.

106 Ray Evans, quoted in Meaghan Shaw, 'Old ally blasts Howard's "Soviet style" work laws,' *The Age*, 27 March 2006.

107 John Howard, *Lazarus Rising: A Personal and Political Autobiography*, Sydney: HarperCollins, 2010, p. 578.

108 Nick Minchin, quoted in Adrian Rollins with Mark Skulley, 'PM cleans up Minchin IR slip,' *Australian Financial Review*, 9 March 2006.

109 Howard, *Lazarus Rising*, p. 579.

110 Michael Costa and Mark Duffy, 'We must change, even if it conflicts with ACTU,' *The Weekend Australian*, 2 December 1989.

111 Ray Evans, 'A retrospective,' in *Tenth Anniversary Conference*, Proceedings of the Seventeenth Conference of the H.R. Nicholls Society, Melbourne, May 1996.

112 Peter Costello, quoted in Roy Eccleston, 'The accidental treasurer,' *The Weekend Australian*, 16 November 1996.

113 Paul Robinson, 'Contempt of court,' *The Age*, 12 June 2000.

114 Marcus Priest, 'Remember HR Nicholls? A new industrial agenda is born,' *Weekend Australian Financial Review*, 20 November 2004.

115 Shaun Carney, 'Howard's big IR gamble,' *The Age*, 1 April 2006.

116 Michael Bachelard, 'Right-wing warriors who changed the workplace,' *The Age*, 15 December 2007.

117 Katharine Murphy, 'Lib MPs called to crusade,' *The Age*, 8 June 2011.

118 Adam Creighton, 'A shock to the Senate,' *The Weekend Australian*, 28 September 2013.

119 Adam Bisits, 'President's report,' H.R. Nicholls Society, December 2013.

120 Evans, 'Particular principles and magic words,' p. 37.

4   BACK TO FIRST PRINCIPLES

1   Geoffrey Sawer, *The Australian Constitution*, Canberra: Australian Government Publishing Service, 1975, p. 23.

2   Brian Galligan, *A Federal Republic: Australia's Constitutional System of Government*, Cambridge: Cambridge University Press, 1995, p. 38.

3   Commonwealth of Australia, *Australia's Constitution*, Canberra: Australian Government Publishing Service, [1901] 1995, p. 5.

4   Elaine Thompson, 'The "Washminster" mutation,' *Politics*, vol. 15, no. 2 (1980), pp. 32–40.

5   Galligan, *A Federal Republic*, p. 32.

6   Andrew Parkin and John Summers, 'The constitutional framework,' in
     Dennis Woodward, Andrew Parkin and John Summers (eds), *Government,
     Politics, Power and Policy in Australia* (9th edn), Sydney: Pearson Australia,
     2010, pp. 57–58.

7   Michael Coper and George Williams (eds), *How Many Cheers for Engineers?*
     Sydney: Federation Press, 1997, p. xiii.

8   Greg Craven, 'A Constitution that deserves better mates,' *IPA Review*,
     March 2005, p. 25.

9   John Roskam, 'Federalism and the Liberal Party,' in *Upholding the Australian
     Constitution*, vol. 18, Proceedings of the Eighteenth Conference of the Samuel
     Griffith Society, Canberra, May 2006, p. 371.

10   Robert Menzies, *Central Power in the Australian Commonwealth: An
     Examination of the Growth of Commonwealth Power in the Australian
     Federation*, London: Cassell, 1967, p. 24.

11   Liberal Party of Australia, *Federal Platform*, April 2002, p. 5.

12   E.G. Whitlam, *On Australia's Constitution*, Melbourne: Widescope, 1977, p. 16.

13   Malcolm Fraser, 'National objectives: social, economic and political goals,'
     Australian Quarterly, vol. 47, no. 1 (March 1975), p. 25.

14   Galligan, *A Federal Republic*, p. 49.

15   R.J.L. Hawke, *The Resolution of Conflict: 1979 Boyer Lectures*, Sydney:
     Australian Broadcasting Commission, 1979, p. 15.

16   ibid., pp. 18–19.

17   Whitlam, *On Australia's Constitution*, pp. 40–1.

18   Paul Kelly, *The End of Certainty: The Story of the 1980s*, Sydney: Allen &
     Unwin, 1992, p. 528.

19   Constitutional Commission, quoted in Galligan, *A Federal Republic*, p. 125.

20   John Stone, 'Governor-General's speech – address-in-reply,' *Commonwealth
     Parliamentary Debates*, Senate, 16 September 1987, p. 170.

21   Galligan, *A Federal Republic*, p. 126.

22   John Stone, 'Keeping power in the people's hands,' *Australian Financial
     Review*, 23 July 1992.

23   Cheryl Saunders, 'Chair of the Constitutional Centenary Foundation,' in
     Tim McCormack and Cheryl Saunders (eds), *Sir Ninian Stephen: A Tribute*,
     Melbourne: Melbourne University Press, 2007, p. 57.

24   ibid., p. 65.

25   Constitutional Centenary Foundation, 'Concluding statement: a constitutional
     review process,' quoted in John Stone, 'White-anting the Constitution: the
     Constitutional Centenary Foundation,' in *Upholding the Australian
     Constitution*, vol. 4, Proceedings of the Fourth Conference of the Samuel
     Griffith Society, Brisbane, July 1994, pp. 243–47.

26   John Stone, 'Constitution criticism lacks foundation,' *Australian Financial
     Review*, 11 April 1991.

27   Stone, 'White-anting the Constitution,' p. 214.

28 Saunders, 'Chair of the Constitutional Centenary Foundation,' p. 77.

29 Penelope Debelle, 'The Craven controversy,' *The Age*, 15 May 1995.

30 Greg Craven, 'Constitutional and other constraints on state governments seeking labour market reform,' in *No Vacancies*, Proceedings of the Tenth Conference of the H.R. Nicholls Society, Melbourne, April 1991, p. 12.

31 Greg Craven, phone interview with author, 27 October 2015.

32 ibid.

33 John Stone, quoted in Peter Costello and Phil Gude, 'Discussion,' in *No Vacancies*, p. 39.

34 Craven, interview with author.

35 ibid.

36 John Stone, email to author, 23 December 2015.

37 Samuel Griffith Society, 'Statement of purposes,' in *Upholding the Australian Constitution*, vol. 1, Proceedings of the Inaugural Conference of the Samuel Griffith Society, Melbourne, July 1992, p. 272.

38 Roger B. Joyce, *Samuel Walker Griffith*, Brisbane: University of Queensland Press, 1984, p. 123.

39 Samuel Griffith, quoted in Joyce, *Samuel Walker Griffith*, p. 147.

40 Joyce, *Samuel Walker Griffith*, p. 168.

41 ibid., p. 360.

42 Joan Priest, *Sir Harry Gibbs: Without Fear or Favour*, Mudgeeraba: Scribblers Publishing, 1995, p. 73.

43 ibid., p. 86.

44 ibid., p. 88.

45 Harry Gibbs, 'The threat to federalism,' in *Upholding the Australian Constitution*, vol. 2, Proceedings of the Second Conference of the Samuel Griffith Society, Melbourne, July 1993, p. 187.

46 Harry Gibbs, 'Re-writing the Constitution,' in *Upholding the Australian Constitution*, vol. 1, p. xiv.

47 J.D. Heydon, 'The public life of John and Nancy Stone,' in *Upholding the Australian Constitution*, vol. 22, Proceedings of the Twenty-Second Conference of the Samuel Griffith Society, Perth, August 2010, pp. 236–38.

48 David Flint, 'Presentation to Sir Harry Gibbs,' in *Upholding the Australian Constitution*, vol. 15, Proceedings of the Fifteenth Conference of the Samuel Griffith Society, Adelaide, May 2003, p. 128.

49 Stone, email to author, 2 January 2016.

50 John Stone, 'Invitation letter of 5 May 1992,' in *Upholding the Australian Constitution*, vol. 1, pp. 268–71.

51 Stone, email to author, 27 March 2016.

52 Priest, *Sir Harry Gibbs*, p. 133.

53 Gibbs, 'Re-writing the Constitution,' p. xx.

54 Bill Hayden, quoted in Michael Gordon, 'Hayden warns of new "radical" conservative body,' *The Sunday Age*, 16 August 1992.

55 John Stone, quoted in Megan Backhouse, 'Canberra's powers rising, warns

Stone,' *The Age*, 17 August 1992.

56   John Stone, quoted in Jenny Hutchison, 'Samuel Griffith Society enters the debate on constitutional reform', *Parliament Program*, 4 September 1992.

57   Geoffrey Barker, 'Why fear a new society focusing on federalism,' *The Age*, 18 August 1992.

58   Tony Stephens, 'The republican debate: wigs v tea-cosies,' *The Sydney Morning Herald*, 20 November 1992.

59   Roderick Meagher, 'Address launching *Upholding the Australian Constitution*, Volume 1,' in *Upholding the Australian Constitution*, vol. 3, Proceedings of the Third Conference of the Samuel Griffith Society, Fremantle, November 1993, pp. 145–53.

60   Samuel Griffith Society, 'Statement of purposes,' p. 272.

61   ibid., pp. 273–74.

62   John Stone, 'Foreword,' in *Upholding the Australian Constitution*, vol. 1, pp. vii–viii.

63   Samuel Griffith Society, 'Statement of purposes,' p. 275.

64   Paul Kelly, 'How Howard governs,' in Nick Cater (ed.), *The Howard Factor: A Decade that Changed the Nation*, Melbourne: Melbourne University Press, 2006, p. 4.

65   Gibbs, 'Re-writing the Constitution,' p. x.

66   Samuel Griffith Society, 'Statement of purposes,' p. 275.

67   Geoffrey de Q. Walker, 'Ten advantages of a federal constitution,' in *Upholding the Australian Constitution*, vol. 10, Proceedings of the Tenth Conference of the Samuel Griffith Society, Brisbane, August 1998, p. 283.

68   Craven, 'A Constitution that deserves better mates,' p. 25.

69   John Stone, 'Introductory remarks,' in *Upholding the Australian Constitution*, vol. 17, Proceedings of the Seventeenth Conference of the Samuel Griffith Society, Coolangatta, April 2005, pp. xxxi–xxxii.

70   John Howard, 'Reflections on Australian federalism,' Address to the Menzies Research Centre, Melbourne, 11 April 2005.

71   Ray Evans, quoted in Stephen Long, 'IR changes bring unlikely alliances,' *Inside Business*, ABC TV, 26 March 2006.

72   Ray Evans, 'Particular principles and magic words,' *Quadrant*, January– February 2011, p. 38.

73   Tanya Josev, 'The late arrival of the judicial activism debate in Australian public discourse,' *Public Law Review*, vol. 24, no. 1 (March 2013), pp. 17–36.

74   Ian Callinan, 'An over-mighty court?' in *Upholding the Australian Constitution*, vol. 4, pp. 81–118.

75   Greg Craven, 'Reflections on judicial activism: more in sorrow than in anger,' in *Upholding the Australian Constitution*, vol. 9, Proceedings of the Ninth Conference of the Samuel Griffith Society, Perth, October 1997, pp. 205–6.

76   Samuel Griffith Society, 'Statement of purposes,' p. 275.

77   Garfield Barwick, 'Parliamentary democracy in Australia,' in *Upholding the Australian Constitution*, vol. 5, Proceedings of the Fifth Conference of the

Samuel Griffith Society, Sydney, March 1995, p. 211.

78 John Stone, 'PM's Constitution threat,' *Australian Financial Review*, 10 December 1992.

79 Samuel Griffith Society, 'Statement of purposes,' p. 275.

80 ibid., p. 276.

81 John Stone, 'Not paranoid, just public spirited' (letter to the editor), *The Age*, 2 September 1992.

82 Ian Callinan, 'President's report,' Samuel Griffith Society, November 2013.

83 John Stone, quoted in Backhouse, 'Canberra's powers rising, warns Stone'.

84 Stone, email to author, 27 March 2016.

85 Paul Houlihan, 'A constitutional fairy tale,' in *Upholding the Australian Constitution*, vol. 19, Proceedings of the Nineteenth Conference of the Samuel Griffith Society, Melbourne, August 2007, p. 207.

86 Craven, interview with author.

87 Andrew Norton, interview with author, Melbourne, 14 August 2012.

88 John Stone, 'Early days, but signs of trouble,' *Australian Financial Review*, 20 June 1996.

89 John Stone, 'Foreword,' in *Upholding the Australian Constitution*, vol. 7, Proceedings of the Seventh Conference of the Samuel Griffith Society, Adelaide, June 1996, p. viii.

90 Stone, email to author, 27 March 2016.

91 Craven, interview with author.

92 Stone, 'Invitation letter of 5 May 1992,' p. 270.

93 Paul Kelly, *The March of Patriots: The Struggle for Modern Australia*, Melbourne: Melbourne University Press, 2009, p. 180.

94 Jeff Kennett, 'The Crown and the states,' in *Upholding the Australian Constitution*, vol. 2, pp. ix–xxx.

95 Harry Gibbs, 'A republic: the issues,' in *Upholding the Australian Constitution*, vol. 8, Proceedings of the Eighth Conference of the Samuel Griffith Society, Canberra, March 1997, pp. 4–5.

96 John Stone, 'Foreword,' in *Upholding the Australian Constitution*, vol. 10, p. vii.

97 David Flint, 'The republic referendum: mere symbolism or substantial change?' in *Upholding the Australian Constitution*, vol. 11, Proceedings of the Eleventh Conference of the Samuel Griffith Society, Melbourne, July 1999, p. xiii.

98 Stone, email to author, 14 April 2016.

99 Greg Craven, 'The republican debate and the true course of constitutional conservatism,' in *Upholding the Australian Constitution*, vol. 11, p. 1.

100 David Smith, 'What a nice referendum – pity about the debate,' in *Upholding the Australian Constitution*, vol. 11, p. 59.

101 Craven, interview with author.

102 David Smith, 'The referendum: a post-mortem' in *Upholding the Australian Constitution*, vol. 12, Proceedings of the Twelfth Conference of the Samuel Griffith Society, Sydney, November 2000, pp. 141–80.

103 *Mabo v. Queensland [No. 2]* (1992) 175 CLR 1.

104 ibid.

105 David Solomon, *The Political High Court: How the High Court Shapes Politics*, Sydney: Allen & Unwin, 1999, p. 27.

106 John Stone, 'Strains of the third world,' *Australian Financial Review*, 5 August 1993.

107 Hugh Morgan, 'The Australian Constitution: a living document,' in *Upholding the Australian Constitution*, vol. 1, pp. 18–19.

108 Paul Keating, quoted in Margaret Easterbrook, 'Morgan a bigot over land rights, says PM,' *The Age*, 14 October 1992.

109 Hugh Morgan, quoted in Bain Attwood, 'Mabo, Australia and the end of history,' in Bain Attwood (ed.), *In the Age of Mabo: History, Aborigines and Australia*, Sydney: Allen & Unwin, 1996, p. 104.

110 Peter Gill, 'Morgan splits miners after Mabo outburst,' *Australian Financial Review*, 1 July 1993.

111 Bill Hassell, 'Mabo and federalism: the prospect of an Indigenous peoples' treaty,' in *Upholding the Australian Constitution*, vol. 2, p. 53.

112 ibid., pp. 72–73.

113 Peter Connolly, 'Should the courts determine social policy?' in *Upholding the Australian Constitution*, vol. 2, p. 88.

114 S.E.K. Hulme, 'The High Court in Mabo,' in *Upholding the Australian Constitution*, vol. 2, p. 154.

115 Colin Howard, 'The High Court,' in *Upholding the Australian Constitution*, vol. 4, p. 78.

116 Geoffrey Partington, 'The aetiology of Mabo,' in *Upholding the Australian Constitution*, vol. 4, pp. 1–30.

117 Samuel Griffith Society, 'Contributors,' in *Upholding the Australian Constitution*, vol. 8, p. 297.

118 Published as John Stone, 'Fifty years of unremitting failure: Aboriginal policy since the 1967 referendum,' *Quadrant*, November 2017, p. 64.

119 Andrew Markus, 'Between Mabo and a hard place: race and the contradictions of conservatism,' in Attwood, *In the Age of Mabo*, pp. 89–93.

120 Attwood, 'Mabo, Australia and the end of history,' p. 100.

121 Liam Mannix, 'Inside Adelaide's conservative HQ,' *InDaily*, 4 September 2013.

122 Commonwealth of Australia, *Australia's Constitution*, p. 16.

123 Sarah Martin, 'Day "sold" office but benefit remained,' *The Australian*, 3 November 2016.

124 John Stone, 'Another divisive referendum out of tune with national thinking,' *The Australian*, 22 November 2010.

125 Damien Freeman and Julian Leeser, *The Australian Declaration of Recognition: Capturing the Nation's Aspirations by Recognising Indigenous Australians*, April 2014.

126 Stone, email to author, 14 April 2016.

127 Craven, interview with author.

128 Stone, email to author, 14 April 2016.

129 Julian Leeser, 'Introduction,' in *Upholding the Australian Constitution*, vol. 23,

Proceedings of the Twenty-Third Conference of the Samuel Griffith Society, Hobart, August 2011, p. x.

130 John Stone, 'Some words of thanks,' in *Upholding the Australian Constitution*, vol. 22, pp. 271–72.

131 Craven, interview with author.

132 Greg Craven, 'The law, substance and morality of recognition,' in Damien Freeman and Shireen Morris (eds), *The Forgotten People: Liberal and Conservative Approaches to Recognising Indigenous Peoples*, Melbourne: Melbourne University Press, 2016, p. 36.

5 ASSIMILATION REDUX

1 John Stone, 'Fifty years of unremitting failure: Aboriginal policy since the 1967 referendum,' *Quadrant*, November 2017, p. 62.

2 Instructions to Arthur Phillip, quoted in W.E.H. Stanner, *The Dreaming and Other Essays*, Melbourne: Black Inc, 2010, p. 93.

3 C.D. Rowley, *The Destruction of Aboriginal Society*, Melbourne: Penguin, 1970.

4 Stanner, *The Dreaming and Other Essays*, p. 189.

5 Paul Hasluck, *Shades of Darkness: Aboriginal Affairs, 1925–1965*, Melbourne: Melbourne University Press, 1988, p. 70.

6 Paul Hasluck, *Native Welfare in Australia*, Perth: Paterson Brokensha, 1953, pp. 56–57.

7 Geoffrey Bolton, *Paul Hasluck: A Life*, Perth: UWA Publishing, 2014, p. 75.

8 Tim Rowse, 'Introduction,' in Tim Rowse (ed.), *Contesting Assimilation*, Perth: API Network, 2005, p. 2.

9 Commonwealth of Australia, *Australia's Constitution*, Canberra: Australian Government Publishing Service, [1901] 1995, p. 19.

10 ibid., p. 44.

11 Bain Attwood and Andrew Markus, *The 1967 Referendum: Race, Power and the Australian Constitution*, Canberra: Aboriginal Studies Press, 2007, p. 67.

12 Rowse, 'Introduction,' p. 19.

13 Peter Sutton, *The Politics of Suffering: Indigenous Australia and the End of the Liberal Consensus* (rev. edn), Melbourne: Melbourne University Press, 2011.

14 Published as Hugh Morgan, 'Aboriginal land rights: a view,' in Australian Mining Industry Council, *Minerals Outlook Seminar 1984: Proceedings*, Canberra: AMIC, May 1984, pp. 80–92.

15 Andrew Markus, *Race: John Howard and the Remaking of Australia*, Sydney: Allen & Unwin, 2001, p. 61.

16 Gerard Henderson, *Australian Answers*, Sydney: Random House, 1990, p. 243.

17 Margot O'Neill and Jill Baker, 'The wrath of God and man descends on Hugh Morgan,' *The Age*, 4 May 1984.

18 Hugh Morgan, quoted in Henderson, *Australian Answers*, p. 243.

19 Peter Walsh, quoted in Amanda Buckley, 'Land rights criticism splits govt,' *The Sydney Morning Herald*, 4 May 1984.

20 Ronald T. Libby, *Hawke's Law: The Politics of Mining and Aboriginal Land*

Rights in Australia, Perth: University of Western Australia Press, 1989, p. 59.

21 Ray Evans, 'Memories of Peter and Kitty Howson,' *Quadrant*, April 2009, p. 53.

22 ibid., p. 54.

23 Tim Rowse, *Obliged to be Difficult: Nugget Coombs' Legacy in Indigenous Affairs*, Cambridge: Cambridge University Press, 2000, p. 63.

24 Peter Howson, 'Dedication,' in Gary Johns, *Aboriginal Self-Determination: The Whiteman's Dream*, Ballan: Connor Court, 2011, p. 11.

25 Evans, 'Memories of Peter and Kitty Howson,' p. 53.

26 Christopher Pearson, 'Vivid memories of 1973,' *The Weekend Australian*, 21 June 2008.

27 Christopher Pearson, 'Separatism's tireless foe,' *The Weekend Australian*, 7 February 2009.

28 Paul Hasluck, 'Howson's role on the political fringe,' *The Age*, 9 June 1984.

29 Rowse, *Obliged to be Difficult*, p. 59.

30 Max Champion, 'Foreword,' in *The Churches: Native to Australia or Alien Intruders?* Proceedings of the Inaugural Conference of the Galatians Group, Melbourne, 1994, p. v.

31 Uniting Church of Australia, 'Covenanting statement,' 10 July 1994.

32 Max Champion, quoted in Geraldine O'Brien and James Woodford, 'Church divided over apology to Aborigines,' *The Sydney Morning Herald*, 15 August 1994.

33 Frank Devine, 'Guilt-edged views threaten stability,' *The Australian*, 22 August 1994.

34 Evans, 'Memories of Peter and Kitty Howson,' p. 54.

35 Patrick Morgan, 'The life and career of Ray Evans,' *Quadrant*, September 2014, p. 80.

36 Howson, 'Dedication,' pp. 11–12.

37 Geoffrey Partington, *Hasluck versus Coombs: White Politics and Australia's Aborigines*, Sydney: Quakers Hill Press, 1996, pp. 152–53.

38 Paul Hasluck, review of C.D. Rowley, *A Matter of Justice* and H.C. Coombs *Kulinma: Listening to Aboriginal Australians*, in *Aboriginal History*, vol. 4, no. 2 (1980), p. 201.

39 H.C. Coombs, quoted in Dennis Shanahan, 'Herron promotes 50s black policy call,' *The Australian*, 17 June 1996.

40 John Herron and Noel Pearson, quoted in Lisa McLean, 'Assimilation policies still have relevance: Herron,' *The Australian*, 18 June 1996.

41 Suvendrini Perera et al., 'Chilling return to support for assimilation' (letter to the editor), *The Australian*, 26 June 1996.

42 Gerard Henderson, 'Time to lift your game, Minister,' *The Sydney Morning Herald*, 2 July 1996.

43 Dennis Shanahan, 'Howard greets assimilation policy supporter,' *The Weekend Australian*, 29 June 1996.

44 Tim Rowse, '"Past has merit": minister,' *Meanjin Quarterly*, vol. 55, no. 4 (1996), p. 628.

45 Megan Saunders, 'Stolen children "rescued", by rights,' *The Australian*, 16 June 1999.

46   Peter Howson, 'Academia's sorry obsession,' *The Age*, 3 April 2001.

47   John Howard, 'A tribute to *Quadrant*,' *Quadrant*, November 2006, p. 23.

48   Andrew Stevenson, 'A voice from the frontier,' *The Sydney Morning Herald*, 22 September 2001.

49   Geoffrey Partington, 'The origins of the Bennelong Society,' Bennelong Society, May 2001, p. 24.

50   Ray Evans, quoted in Pearson, 'Separatism's tireless foe'.

51   Keith Vincent Smith, 'Bennelong among his people,' *Aboriginal History*, vol. 33 (2009), p. 7.

52   Dirk van Dissel, 'Woollarawarre Bennelong, the bush politician,' Bennelong Society, 2004.

53   Smith, 'Bennelong among his people,' p. 22.

54   Marcia Langton, 'Rum, seduction and death: "Aboriginality" and alcohol,' *Oceania*, vol. 63, no. 3 (March 1993), p. 200.

55   ibid., p. 198.

56   John Herron, interview with author, Brisbane, 20 July 2012.

57   Evans, 'Memories of Peter and Kitty Howson,' p. 54.

58   Gary Johns, 'Steering Aboriginal policy onto a better path,' in Keith Windschuttle, David Martin Jones and Ray Evans (eds), *The Howard Era*, Sydney: Quadrant Books, 2009, p. 392.

59   Peter Howson, 'No more sit-down money,' *Quadrant*, November 2004, p. 23.

60   Evans, 'Memories of Peter and Kitty Howson,' p. 55.

61   Tony Koch, 'Too decent for politics,' *The Courier-Mail*, 20 December 2000.

62   John Howard, *Lazarus Rising: A Personal and Political Autobiography*, Sydney: HarperCollins, 2010, pp. 270–74.

63   Rowse, *Obliged to be Difficult*, p. 220.

64   John Herron, 'Realistic reconciliation,' *The Courier-Mail*, 16 May 2001.

65   Gary Johns, interview with author, Brisbane, 19 July 2012.

66   ibid.

67   Gary Johns (ed.), *Waking Up To Dreamtime: The Illusion of Aboriginal Self-Determination*, Sydney: Quadrant eBook, 2012, p. iv.

68   Bob Hawke, quoted in Damien Murphy, 'The Right, and prejudice, brought me down: Hawke,' *The Age*, 1 January 2016.

69   Johns, *Waking Up To Dreamtime*, p. iv.

70   Joe Ross, quoted in Michael Madigan, 'Thanks but no think-tanks – appointee,' *The Courier-Mail*, 15 May 2001.

71   Misha Schubert and Stuart Rintoul, 'Face of alternative vision for blacks,' *The Australian*, 20 April 2004.

72   Wesley Aird, interview with author, Brisbane, 19 July 2012.

73   P.P. McGuinness, 'Change of tone in Aboriginal debate,' *The Sydney Morning Herald*, 26 August 1999.

74   Paul Sheehan, 'Stolen Generation report a "disgrace",' *The Sydney Morning Herald*, 19 August 2000.

75   Christopher Pearson, 'Culture wars,' in Nick Cater (ed.), *The Howard Factor:*

A Decade that Changed the Nation, Melbourne: Melbourne University Press, 2006, pp. 23–24.

76 Tony Koch, 'New deal gives voice to Aborigines,' *The Courier-Mail*, 20 May 2000.

77 Christopher Pearson, 'Indigenous affairs seen in a new light,' *Australian Financial Review*, 23 April 2001.

78 Robert Manne, 'Aboriginal debate makes a sharp right,' *The Sydney Morning Herald*, 4 June 2001.

79 Roger Sandall, *The Culture Cult: Designer Tribalism and Other Essays*, Boulder: Westview Press, 2001, pp. ix–x.

80 Bennelong Society, 'Home,' www.bennelong.com.au/pages/ben-home.html (website now defunct; author accessed via web.archive.org)

81 Eve Vincent, 'Who is Bennelong?' *Arena Magazine*, June–July 2007, p. 47.

82 Johns, interview with author.

83 Ray Evans, 'Aboriginal land rights in Australia,' in *Aboriginal Policy: Failure, Reappraisal and Reform*, Proceedings of the Formative Workshop of the Bennelong Society, Melbourne, December 2000.

84 Ray Evans, 'Reflections on the Aboriginal crisis,' in *Upholding the Australian Constitution*, vol. 7, Proceedings of the Seventh Conference of the Samuel Griffith Society, Adelaide, June 1996, p. 190.

85 Rosemary Neill, *White Out: How Politics is Killing Black Australia*, Sydney: Allen & Unwin, 2002, pp. 42–43.

86 Peter Howson, *The Howson Diaries: The Life of Politics* (edited by Don Aitkin), Melbourne: Viking Press, 1984, p. 861.

87 Ray Evans, 'Gnosticism and the High Court of Australia,' in *Surrendered Values: The Challenge for Church and Society*, Proceedings of the Fifth Conference of the Galatians Group, Melbourne, August 1998, p. 27.

88 Peter Howson, 'Land rights: the next battleground,' *Quadrant*, June 2005, p. 29.

89 Peter Howson, 'Back to Coombs, or forward?' *Quadrant*, January–February 2009, p. 61.

90 Gary Johns, 'The land rights initiative has failed,' *The Australian*, 7 February 2006.

91 Johns, interview with author.

92 Aird, interview with author.

93 Gary Johns, 'Can we ever reconcile our past?' in Tim Wilson, Carlo Carli and Paul Collits (eds), *Turning Left or Right: Values in Modern Politics*, Ballarat: Connor Court, 2013, p. 412.

94 Neill, *White Out*, p. 123.

95 Howson, 'Back to Coombs, or forward?' p. 59.

96 Johns, *Aboriginal Self-Determination*, p. 23.

97 Noel Pearson, 'Don't listen to those who despise us,' *The Age*, 26 June 2006; 'A peculiar path that leads astray,' *The Weekend Australian*, 21 October 2006.

98 Gary Johns, 'The bad old ways' (letter to the editor), *The Age*, 29 June 2006; Christopher Pearson, 'Beware of a relapse, Noel,' *The Weekend Australian*, 1 July 2006.

99 Database of Indigenous Violence, indigenousviolence.org/dnn

100 Johns, interview with author.

101 Des Moore, 'Aboriginal reconciliation – a solution or an unhelpful diversion?' *Institute for Private Enterprise Newsletter*, April 2000.

102 Des Moore, 'The stolen generationists take one step backward,' *Institute for Private Enterprise Newsletter*, March–April 2001.

103 Johns, interview with author.

104 *Aboriginal and Torres Strait Islander Commission Act*, quoted in Angela Pratt and Scott Bennett, 'The end of ATSIC and the future administration of Indigenous affairs,' *Parliamentary Library Current Issues Brief No. 4, 2004–05*, Canberra: Department of Parliamentary Services, 2004, p. 7.

105 John Howard, 'Administration of Aboriginal affairs,' *Commonwealth Parliamentary Debates*, House of Representatives, 11 April 1989, p. 1332.

106 John Herron, quoted in Lisa McLean and Michael Gordon, 'Herron clashes with ATSIC chief,' *The Weekend Australian*, 22 June 1996.

107 Raimond Gaita, 'Not right,' *Quadrant*, January–February 1997, p. 46.

108 John Howard, 'Interview with Alan Jones,' *Radio 2UE*, 2 May 1997.

109 Peter Howson, 'The doctor's stiff potion is needed,' *Herald Sun*, 15 May 1998.

110 Gary Johns, 'Look for strength in mainstream,' *The Australian*, 22 November 2001.

111 Wesley Aird, 'Exploring the meaning of integration,' in *Celebrating Integration*, Proceedings of the Second Conference of the Bennelong Society, Brisbane, August 2002.

112 Mark Metherell, 'Latham gazumps PM's black policy,' *The Sydney Morning Herald*, 31 March 2004.

113 John Howard, quoted in Pratt and Bennett, 'The end of ATSIC,' pp. 10–11.

114 Jane Robbins, 'The Howard government and Indigenous rights: an imposed national unity,' *Australian Journal of Political Science*, vol. 42, no. 2 (June 2007), p. 323.

115 Peter Howson, 'Pointing the bone: reflections on the passing of ATSIC,' *Quadrant*, June 2004, pp. 12–13.

116 Peter Howson, 'Submission to the inquiry into the progress towards national reconciliation,' Senate Legal and Constitutional References Committee, December 2002.

117 Amanda Vanstone, 'Opening address,' in *Pathways and Policies for Indigenous Futures*, Proceedings of the Fourth Conference of the Bennelong Society, Sydney, September 2004.

118 Howard, *Lazarus Rising*, p. 639.

119 Patricia Karvelas, 'How Macklin took on Left to transform Indigenous policy,' *The Weekend Australian*, 23 November 2013.

120 Gary Johns, 'I'm your pal, brother, can you spare a cafe-latte?' *The Australian*, 1 April 2010.

121 Johns, interview with author.

122 Keith Windschuttle, 'Bennelong medal presentation to Mal Brough,' in *The NT*

Emergency Response: Appraisal and Future, Proceedings of the Eighth
Conference of the Bennelong Society, Melbourne, June 2008.

123   John Howard, quoted in Judith Brett, *Relaxed and Comfortable: The Liberal
Party's Australia*, Quarterly Essay, no. 19 (2005), p. 30.

124   Des Moore, interview with author, Melbourne, 10 August 2012.

125   Bess Price, David Price and Gary Johns, 'Bess Nungarrayi Price on the NT
Intervention' *Big Ideas*, ABC TV, 15 February 2010.

126   Mal Brough, 'Address launching *Aboriginal Self-Determination*,' Brisbane,
April 2011.

127   Johns, interview with author.

128   Gary Johns, quoted in John Ferguson, 'Lack of interest kills Bennelong
Society,' *The Australian*, 22 November 2011.

129   Ray Evans, interview with author, Melbourne, 5 June 2012.

130   Aird, interview with author.

131   Johns, interview with author.

132   Gary Johns, quoted in Ferguson, 'Lack of interest kills Bennelong Society'.

133   Recognise What? 'About,' recognisewhat.org.au/about (website now defunct;
author accessed via web.archive.org)

134   Gary Johns, 'Welcome to the debate,' Recognise What?, 26 June 2014.

135   Gary Johns, 'A No case must be funded,' Recognise What?, 28 July 2014.

136   Gary Johns, 'Recognise this' (letter to the editor), *The Australian*, 21 December
2016.

6   JUNK SCIENCE AND ALARMISM

1   Rachel Carson, *Silent Spring*, London: Hamish Hamilton, 1962, p. 5.

2   Paul R. Ehrlich, *The Population Bomb*, New York: Ballantine Books, 1968, p. xi.

3   Garrett Hardin, 'The tragedy of the commons,' *Science*, 13 December 1968,
p. 1244.

4   William J. Lines, *Patriots: Defending Australia's Natural Heritage*, Brisbane:
University of Queensland Press, 2006, p. 106.

5   Drew Hutton and Libby Connors, *A History of the Australian Environment
Movement*, Cambridge: Cambridge University Press, 1999, p. 126.

6   James Hansen, *Storms of My Grandchildren: The Truth About the Coming
Climate Catastrophe and Our Last Chance to Save Humanity*, New York:
Bloomsbury, 2009, p. xv.

7   Margaret Thatcher, *The Downing Street Years*, London: HarperCollins, 1993, p. 641.

8   United Nations, 'Protection of global climate for present and future
generations of mankind,' General Assembly Resolution 43/53, 6 December
1988.

9   United Nations, *UN Framework Convention on Climate Change*, 1992.

10   John Stone (ed.), *The Environment in Perspective*, Melbourne: Institute of
Public Affairs, 1991, p. 3.

11   ibid., p. 21.

12 ibid., p. 40.

13 Fred Singer, 'Global warming: is there a problem?' in Stone, *The Environment in Perspective*, p. 22.

14 ibid., p. 25.

15 Chris Mooney, 'Some like it hot,' *Mother Jones*, May–June 2005, p. 41.

16 James Hoggan with Richard Littlemore, *Climate Cover-Up: The Crusade to Deny Global Warming*, Vancouver: Greystone Books, 2009, p. 140.

17 Naomi Oreskes and Erik M. Conway, *Merchants of Doubt: How a Handful of Scientists Obscured the Truth on Issues from Tobacco Smoke to Global Warming*, New York: Bloomsbury Press, 2010.

18 Hugh Morgan, 'Mining and political power,' *Quadrant*, July 1989, p. 18.

19 Ray Evans, quoted in Peter Vincent, 'The debate hots up,' *The Sydney Morning Herald*, 30 October 2003.

20 Ray Evans, 'Nine lies about global warming,' Lavoisier Group, February 2006, p. 1.

21 Ray Evans, interview with author, Melbourne, 5 June 2012.

22 Ray Evans, 'Russia backs Australia's stand on the Kyoto Protocol,' *Online Opinion*, 4 November 2003.

23 Evans, interview with author.

24 Clive Hamilton, *Running from the Storm: The Development of Climate Change Policy in Australia*, Sydney: UNSW Press, 2001, p. 53.

25 Aaron M. McCright and Riley E. Dunlap, 'Defeating Kyoto: the conservative movement's impact on U.S. climate change policy,' *Social Problems*, vol. 50, no. 3 (August 2003), pp. 348–73.

26 Clive Hamilton, *Scorcher: The Dirty Politics of Climate Change*, Melbourne: Black Inc, 2007, p. 137.

27 Hamilton, *Running from the Storm*, p. 79.

28 Evans, interview with author.

29 Ray Evans, 'The politics behind Kyoto,' *Australia and World Affairs*, no. 37 (Winter 1998), p. 26.

30 ibid., p. 29.

31 Ray Evans, 'The Kyoto Protocol: fast road to global governance,' in *Upholding the Australian Constitution*, vol. 12, Proceedings of the Twelfth Conference of the Samuel Griffith Society, Sydney, November 2000, pp. 71–72.

32 Peter Walsh, *Confessions of a Failed Finance Minister* (rev. edn), Sydney: Random House, 1996, pp. 3–5.

33 Gary Johns, interview with author, Brisbane, 19 July 2012.

34 Walsh, *Confessions of a Failed Finance Minister*, p. 21.

35 Graham Richardson, *Whatever It Takes*, Sydney: Bantam Books, 1994, p. 158.

36 Walsh, *Confessions of a Failed Finance Minister*, p. 208.

37 ibid., p. 212.

38 Peter Walsh, 'Truth about our climate,' *Australian Financial Review*, 16 September 1997.

39 Peter Walsh, 'H.R. Nicholls Society,' *Commonwealth Parliamentary Debates*, Senate, 26 March 1987, p. 1384.

40 Evans, interview with author.

41 W.R. Aykroyd, *Three Philosophers: Lavoisier, Priestley and Cavendish*, London: William Heinemann, 1935, *passim*.

42 Lavoisier Group, 'Antoine-Laurent Lavoisier,' www.lavoisier.com.au/lavoisier-biography.php

43 Galileo Movement, 'Who we are,' www.galileomovement.com.au/who_we_are.php

44 Josh Taylor, 'Malcolm Roberts: the One Nation climate denier too out there for Andrew Bolt,' *Crikey*, 4 August 2016.

45 David Archibald, 'Failure to Warm,' Occasional address to the Lavoisier Group, October 2007.

46 Australian Honours Database, www.pmc.gov.au/government/its-honour

47 Shane Rattenbury, Unpublished report on the Lavoisier Group conference, Melbourne, May 2000.

48 Peter Walsh, quoted in Rattenbury, Unpublished report on the Lavoisier Group conference.

49 Hugh Morgan, 'Opening address,' in *Kyoto and the National Interest*, Proceedings of the Inaugural Conference of the Lavoisier Group, Melbourne, May 2000.

50 Hugh Morgan, quoted in Rattenbury, Unpublished report on the Lavoisier Group conference.

51 Unnamed source, quoted in Guy Pearse, *High & Dry: John Howard, Climate Change and the Selling of Australia's Future*, Melbourne: Viking, 2007, p. 283.

52 Alan Oxley, 'The Kyoto chimera,' in *Kyoto and the National Interest*.

53 Peter Walsh, quoted in Rattenbury, Unpublished report on the Lavoisier Group conference.

54 Frank Devine, 'Greenhouse emission protocols a lot of hot air,' *The Australian*, 30 May 2000.

55 Evans, interview with author.

56 Gary Gray, quoted in Emma Alberici, 'Challenge for new resources minister,' *Lateline*, ABC TV, 25 March 2013.

57 Aaron M. McCright and Riley E. Dunlap, 'Organized climate change denial,' in John S. Dryzek, Richard B. Norgaard and David Schlosberg (eds), *The Oxford Handbook of Climate Change and Society*, Oxford: Oxford University Press, 2011, p. 151.

58 Hamilton, *Scorcher*, p. 20.

59 Ben Cubby, 'Scientist denies he is mouthpiece of US climate-sceptic think tank,' *The Sydney Morning Herald*, 16 February 2012.

60 Robert M. Carter, 'There IS a problem with global warming... it stopped in 1998,' *Sunday Telegraph* (UK), 9 April 2006.

61 Robert M. Carter, 'Human-caused global warming: McCarthyism, intimidation, press bias, censorship, policy-advice corruption and propaganda,' Testimony before the Committee on Environment and Public Works, United States Senate, 6 December 2006.

62 Bob Carter, quoted in Sarah Ferguson, 'Malcolm and the malcontents,' *Four*

Corners, ABC TV, 9 November 2009.

63　Robert M. Carter, *Climate: The Counter Consensus*, London: Stacey International, 2010, pp. 148–49.

64　Collated at Heartland Institute, 'Robert M. Carter (1942–2016),' www. heartland.org/robert-m-carter

65　Claude Allegre et al., 'No need to panic about global warming,' *The Wall Street Journal*, 27 January 2012.

66　Bureau of Meteorology statement, quoted in Graham Readfearn, 'Australian Meteorology Bureau corrects record on former research head William Kininmonth's actual climate change experience,' *DeSmogBlog*, 2 February 2012.

67　William Kininmonth, *Climate Change: A Natural Hazard*, Brentwood: Multi-Science Publishing, 2004, p. iii.

68　Lavoisier Group, 'Latest at Lavoisier,' www.lavoisier.com.au/papers/lav-papers.html

69　John Zillman, 'Address launching *Climate Change: A Natural Hazard*,' Melbourne, 22 November 2004.

70　John Zillman, quoted in Melissa Fyfe, 'Global warming: the sceptics,' *The Age*, 27 November 2004.

71　Leigh Dayton, 'Ark verdict spells ruin for geologist,' *New Scientist*, 7 June 1997.

72　Ian Plimer, *Heaven and Earth: Global Warming, the Missing Science*, Ballan: Connor Court, 2009, pp. 462–63.

73　Anthony Cappello, email to author, 24 July 2014.

74　Ray Evans, quoted in Lenore Taylor, 'Businessmen throw stones at greenhouse,' *Australian Financial Review*, 11 April 2000.

75　Lavoisier Group, 'Aims,' www.lavoisier.com.au/pages/lav-aims.html

76　Hamilton, *Running from the Storm*, p. 139.

77　Pearse, *High & Dry*, p. 286.

78　William R.L. Anderegg, James W. Prall, Jacob Harold and Stephen H. Schneider, 'Expert credibility in climate change,' *PNAS: Proceedings of the National Academy of Sciences of the United States of America*, vol. 107, no. 27 (6 July 2010), p. 12107.

79　Oreskes and Conway, *Merchants of Doubt*, pp. 6–7.

80　William Kininmonth, 'Climate change: a natural hazard,' Lavoisier Group, November 2002, p. 10.

81　Bob Foster, 'Climate change made easy: it's the sun,' Lavoisier Group, June 2003.

82　Ray Evans, 'Thank God for carbon,' Lavoisier Group, November 2008, p. 1.

83　Ray Evans, 'Nine facts about climate change,' Lavoisier Group, November 2006, p. 24.

84　Michael E. Mann, *The Hockey Stick and the Climate Wars: Dispatches from the Front Lines*, New York: Columbia University Press, 2012, p. 209.

85　Nick Hordern, 'Industry greets plan for carbon tax with horror,' *Australian Financial Review*, 15 September 1999.

86　Lavoisier Group, 'Submission to the inquiry into the Kyoto Protocol,' Joint Standing Committee on Treaties, August 2000.

87　Ray Evans, 'The chilling costs of climate catastrophism,' *Quadrant*, June 2008, p. 13.

88   Ray Evans, 'The social and political consequences of the CPRS (*sic*) Act 2009,'
     in *Back to the 19th Century: Australia Under the Carbon Pollution Reduction
     Scheme (sic) Act 2009*, Melbourne: Lavoisier Group, September 2009, p. 3.

89   Evans, interview with author.

90   Robert Manne, 'A dark victory: how vested interests defeated climate science,'
     The Monthly, August 2012, p. 27.

91   Peter Walsh, 'President's report,' Lavoisier Group, October 2007.

92   Graham Readfearn, 'Australia's place in the global web of climate denial,'
     ABC News, 29 June 2011.

93   Pearse, *High & Dry*, p. 217.

94   Lavoisier Group, 'Links to other sites,' www.lavoisier.com.au/pages/lav-links.html

95   Paul J. Georgia, 'News from Australia,' *Cooler Heads Digest*, 22 January 2002.

96   Myron Ebell, 'Cooler Heads Coalition welcomes two new members,' *Cooler
     Heads Digest*, 7 December 2004.

97   Australian Environment Foundation, 'About the AEF,' www.
     australianenvironment.org/about-us

98   Melissa Fyfe, 'New green group makes conservationists see red,' *The Age*, 8
     June 2005.

99   Jennifer Marohasy, 'Vale Ray Evans and how to win an argument,' *Jennifer
     Marohasy* (blog), 19 June 2014.

100 Australian Climate Science Coalition, 'About Us,' www.auscsc.org.au/
     about_us.html

101 John Roskam, quoted in Ben Cubby and Antony Lawes, 'The benefit of the
     doubt,' *The Sydney Morning Herald*, 8 May 2010.

102 Rattenbury, Unpublished report on the Lavoisier Group conference.

103 Sonja Boehmer-Christiansen, 'Witness testimony at the Inquiry into the Kyoto
     Protocol,' Joint Standing Committee on Treaties, Melbourne, 13 September
     2000, p. 60; Richard Lindzen, 'Witness testimony at the Inquiry into the Kyoto
     Protocol,' Joint Standing Committee on Treaties, Canberra, 3 November 2000,
     p. 283.

104 Mann, *The Hockey Stick and the Climate Wars*, p. 187

105 Ross Gelbspan, *The Heat is On: The Climate Crisis, the Cover-Up, the
     Prescription* (rev. edn), Reading, Massachusetts: Perseus Books, 1998, p. 49.

106 Unnamed source, quoted in Pearse, *High & Dry*, p. 267.

107 John Howard, *Lazarus Rising: A Personal and Political Autobiography*, Sydney:
     HarperCollins, 2010, pp. 553–54.

108 Unnamed source, quoted in Guy Pearse, *Quarry Vision: Coal, Climate Change
     and the End of the Resources Boom*, Quarterly Essay, no. 33 (2009), p. 49.

109 Ray Evans, Address launching 'Nine lies about global warming,' Canberra,
     11 May 2006.

110 Dennis Jensen, 'Maiden speech,' *Commonwealth Parliamentary Debates*,
     House of Representatives, 17 November 2004, p. 120.

111 Martin Ferguson, quoted in Sarah Smiles, 'Climate change sceptics get a warm
     reception,' *The Age*, 1 March 2007.

112 Cory Bernardi, 'Cool heads needed on global warming,' *The Advertiser*, 25 April 2007.

113 Ray Evans, Address launching 'Thank God for carbon,' Adelaide, 27 January 2009.

114 Ray Evans, Address launching 'Thank God for carbon,' Perth, 25 March 2009.

115 Nick Minchin, quoted in Ferguson, 'Malcolm and the malcontents'.

116 Hamilton, *Running from the Storm*, p. 138.

117 Pearse, *High & Dry*, p. 129.

118 Robert Hill, email to author, 14 July 2016.

119 Tony Walker, 'Government team reflects PM's social conservatism,' *Australian Financial Review*, 27 November 2001.

120 David Kemp, quoted in Sid Marris and Roy Eccleston, 'Stoush in the greenhouse,' *The Australian*, 8 March 2002.

121 Evans, 'Russia backs Australia's stand on the Kyoto Protocol'.

122 Pearse, *High & Dry*, p. 77.

123 Hugh Morgan, 'Carbon blackmail doesn't lead to greener future,' *The Australian*, 10 June 2002.

124 Howard, *Lazarus Rising*, p. 548.

125 Ray Evans, quoted in Katharine Murphy and Brendan Nicholson, 'Greenhouse sceptics to congregate,' *The Age*, 28 February 2007.

126 Howard, *Lazarus Rising*, p. 555.

127 Evans, interview with author.

128 Peter Walsh, 'An open letter to the Prime Minister,' Lavoisier Group, 28 May 2003.

129 Pearse, *High & Dry*, p. 86.

130 Ray Evans, 'Letter to Andrew Robb, AO MP,' Lavoisier Group, 3 December 2008.

131 Angus Grigg, 'The player,' *Australian Financial Review Magazine*, October 2006, p. 64.

132 Evans, 'Letter to Andrew Robb'.

133 Evans, interview with author.

134 Tony Abbott, *Battlelines* (rev. edn), Melbourne: Melbourne University Press, 2013, p. 184.

135 Malcolm Turnbull, quoted in Paddy Manning, *Born to Rule: The Unauthorised Biography of Malcolm Turnbull*, Melbourne: Melbourne University Press, 2015, p. 337.

136 Ferguson, 'Malcolm and the malcontents'.

137 Malcolm Turnbull, quoted in Lenore Taylor and David Uren, *Shitstorm: Inside Labor's Darkest Days*, Melbourne: Melbourne University Press, 2010, p. 189.

138 Tony Abbott, quoted in Philip Chubb, *Power Failure: The Inside Story of Climate Politics Under Rudd and Gillard*, Melbourne: Black Inc, 2014, p. 78.

139 Abbott, *Battlelines*, p. 184.

140 Ray Evans, 'Ray Evans reviews the denialist victory,' *Jo Nova* (blog), 8 August 2012.

141 Hugh Morgan, 'President's report,' Lavoisier Group, November 2010.

142 Cubby and Lawes, 'The benefit of the doubt'.

143 'Top 50/Politics: Ray Evans,' *The Australian*, 30 January 2012.

144   Andrew Norton, interview with author, Melbourne, 14 August 2012.

145   Ray Evans, quoted in David Alexander, 'Who's afraid of a war on carbon?' *The Canberra Times*, 13 December 2008.

146   Morgan, 'President's report'.

147   John Stone, email to author, 27 March 2016.

148   Viv Forbes, 'Summary statement on the formation of Clexit,' 1 August 2016.

149   Clexit, 'Clexit committee and founding members,' July 2016.

150   Pearse, *High & Dry*, pp. 149–50.

151   Des Moore, interview with author, Melbourne, 10 August 2012.

7 AN ANATOMY OF REACTIONARY CONSERVATISM

1   Ray Evans, interview with author, Melbourne, 5 June 2012.

2   John Warhurst, 'Interest groups and political lobbying,' in Dennis Woodward, Andrew Parkin and John Summers (eds), *Government, Politics, Power and Policy in Australia* (9th edn), Sydney: Pearson Australia, 2010, p. 335.

3   Josh Gordon, 'Coalition flirtation with right could go wrong,' *The Age*, 19 July 2014.

4   Scott Melzer, *Gun Crusaders: The NRA's Culture War*, New York: New York University Press, 2009, p. 16.

5   Americans for Tax Reform, 'About,' www.atr.org/about

6   'Signing away the right to govern,' *The New York Times*, 19 July 2011.

7   John Warhurst, 'Interest groups and political lobbying,' p. 349.

8   Ray Evans, quoted in Matthew Moore, 'Not quite top set at Nicholls gathering,' *The Sydney Morning Herald*, 1 October 1986.

9   Paul Pollard, quoted in Clive Hamilton, *Scorcher: The Dirty Politics of Climate Change*, Melbourne: Black Inc, 2007, p. 143.

10   Melissa Fyfe, 'Global warming: the sceptics,' *The Age*, 27 November 2004.

11   Aaron M. McCright and Riley E. Dunlap, 'Cool dudes: the denial of climate change among conservative white males in the United States,' *Global Environmental Change*, vol. 21, no. 4 (October 2011), pp. 1171.

12   Andrew Clark, 'In their own image,' *Australian Financial Review Magazine*, March 2001, p. 39.

13   John Stone, 'We only want those prepared to be like us,' *The Australian*, 26 November 2001.

14   John Stone, 'Another divisive referendum out of tune with national thinking,' *The Australian*, 22 November 2010.

15   Geoffrey Partington, 'The origins of the Bennelong Society,' Bennelong Society, May 2001, p. 6.

16   Peter Howson, 'Pointing the bone: reflections on the passing of ATSIC,' *Quadrant*, June 2004, p. 11.

17   Gary Johns, *Aboriginal Self-Determination: The Whiteman's Dream*, Ballan: Connor Court, 2011, p. 23.

18   Stephen Gray, 'A culture condemned,' *The Weekend Australian*, 30 April 2011.

19   Gary Johns, 'No contraception, no dole,' *The Australian*, 30 December 2014.

20   Gary Johns, quoted in Andrew Bolt, *The Bolt Report*, Channel Ten, 12 July 2015.

21   Calla Wahlquist, 'Minister urged to investigate charities commissioner Gary Johns' "offensive" views,' *The Guardian*, 26 October 2018.

22   Ray Evans, quoted in Hugh Morgan, 'Ray's career as an advocate,' Eulogy at the funeral of Ray Evans, Melbourne, 27 June 2014.

23   Hugh Morgan, 'Remarks at the dinner marking Ray Evans's retirement from the H.R. Nicholls Society,' Melbourne, 7 October 2010.

24   Ray Evans, quoted in Michael Bachelard, 'Exit, stage Right,' *The Weekend Australian*, 10 August 2002.

25   Peter Costello, quoted in Bob Day, 'Ray's career as an advocate,' Eulogy at the funeral of Ray Evans, Melbourne, 27 June 2014.

26   Patrick Morgan, 'The life and career of Ray Evans,' *Quadrant*, September 2014, p. 79.

27   Hugh Morgan, quoted in Tim Duncan, 'Western Mining's messiahs of the New Right,' *The Bulletin*, 2 July 1985, p. 69.

28   Duncan, 'Western Mining's messiahs of the New Right,' p. 67.

29   ibid., p. 68.

30   Robert Manne, quoted in Gideon Haigh, 'Prophet of gloom,' *The Weekend Australian*, 31 July 1993. Manne has confirmed to me that he was Haigh's source.

31   Hal Wootten, quoted in Haigh, 'Prophet of gloom'.

32   Hugh Morgan, quoted in Paul Sheehan, 'The Right strikes back,' *The Sydney Morning Herald*, 2 March 1985.

33   Duncan, 'Western Mining's messiahs of the New Right,' p. 70.

34   Morgan, 'Ray's career as an advocate'.

35   Unnamed mining analyst, quoted in Patricia Howard, 'A blue-blooded company chief bobs back after bucketing,' *The Canberra Times*, 4 September 1993.

36   'Morgan must go from WMC,' *Australian Financial Review*, 21 January 1994.

37   John Garnaut and Jane Counsel, 'Different shades of Hugh,' *The Sydney Morning Herald*, 17 August 2002.

38   Elizabeth Knight, 'Morgan: why I shouldn't be sacked,' *The Sydney Morning Herald*, 5 February 1994.

39   Robert Manne, *In Denial: The Stolen Generations and the Right*, Quarterly Essay, no. 1 (2001), p. 52.

40   Ray Evans, quoted in Morgan, 'Ray's career as an advocate'.

41   Ray Evans, quoted in Richard Gluyas, Michael Bachelard and Sid Marris, 'BCA goes into battle with a great Hugh and cry,' *The Australian*, 9 December 2003.

42   John Stone, 'A tribute to Ray Evans,' H.R. Nicholls Society, 18 June 2014.

43   Andrew Bolt, 'Ray Evans, pilgrim,' *Herald Sun*, 18 June 2014.

44   Roger Franklin, 'Vale Ray Evans, gentleman and sceptic,' *Quadrant*, 18 June 2014.

45   James Paterson, 'Vale Ray Evans,' Institute of Public Affairs, 19 June 2014.

46   John Roskam, 'A quiet shaper of the right's ideas,' *Australian Financial Review*, 20 June 2014.

47   Gerard Henderson, 'Ray Evans – R.I.P.' *Media Watch Dog*, 20 June 2014.

48 Scott Ryan, 'Mr Ray Evans,' *Commonwealth Parliamentary Debates*, Senate, 23 June 2014, p. 3660.

49 Day, 'Ray's career as an advocate'.

50 Morgan, 'Ray's career as an advocate'.

51 John Warhurst, 'Interest groups and political lobbying,' pp. 341–42.

52 David Kemp, 'Occasional address,' in *Tenth Anniversary Conference*, Proceedings of the Seventeenth Conference of the H.R. Nicholls Society, Melbourne, May 1996.

53 Paul Kelly, *The End of Certainty: The Story of the 1980s*, Sydney: Allen & Unwin, 1992, p. 253.

54 Australian Electoral Commission, 'Annual returns locator service,' periodicdisclosures.aec.gov.au

55 Morgan, 'Remarks at the dinner marking Ray Evans's retirement'.

56 Garnaut and Counsel, 'Different shades of Hugh'; Guy Pearse, *High & Dry: John Howard, Climate Change and the Selling of Australia's Future*, Melbourne: Viking, 2007, p. 268.

57 Australian Honours Database, www.pmc.gov.au/government/its-honour. The remarkable number of climate deniers awarded honours by the Howard government was first noted in Pearse, *High & Dry*, p. 227.

58 Judith Brett, *Australian Liberals and the Moral Middle Class: From Alfred Deakin to John Howard*, Cambridge: Cambridge University Press, 2003, p. 187.

59 John Howard, 'Address to the Australian Liberal Students Federation,' Sydney, 8 July 1996.

60 John Howard, 'A sense of balance: the Australian achievement in 2006,' Address to the National Press Club, Canberra, 25 January 2006.

61 John Howard, *Lazarus Rising: A Personal and Political Autobiography*, Sydney: HarperCollins, 2010, p. 565.

62 John Stone, 'Our greatest prime minister?' in Keith Windschuttle, David Martin Jones and Ray Evans (eds), *The Howard Era*, Sydney: Quadrant Books, 2009, p. 26.

63 Judith Brett, *Exit Right: The Unravelling of John Howard*, Quarterly Essay, no. 28 (2007), p. 76.

64 Ray Evans, 'The rulers and guardians of industrial relations,' *Quadrant*, September 2010, p. 29.

65 Howard, *Lazarus Rising*, p. 102.

66 John Stone, 'Howard's great betrayal,' *The Australian*, 18 April 2005.

67 Stone, 'Our greatest prime minister?' p. 7.

68 Howard, *Lazarus Rising*, p. 271.

69 Mick Dodson, 'Indigenous Australians,' in Robert Manne (ed.), *The Howard Years*, Melbourne: Black Inc, 2004, p. 120.

70 Howard, *Lazarus Rising*, p. 277.

71 John Herron, quoted in Gary Johns, 'Steering Aboriginal policy onto a better path,' in Windschuttle, Jones and Evans, *The Howard Era*, p. 375.

72 Dodson, 'Indigenous Australians,' p. 121.

73   Ian Lowe, 'The environment,' in Manne, *The Howard Years*, p. 263.

74   Ray Evans, 'John Howard and the environmentalists,' in Windschuttle, Jones and Evans, *The Howard Era*, p. 498.

75   ibid., p. 515.

76   Michael Wolff, *The Man Who Owns the News: Inside the Secret World of Rupert Murdoch*, Sydney: Vintage Books, 2008, p. 266.

77   David McKnight, '"A world hungry for a new philosophy": Rupert Murdoch and the rise of neo-liberalism,' *Journalism Studies*, vol. 4, no. 3 (2003), p. 352.

78   ibid., p. 355.

79   Denis Cryle, *Murdoch's Flagship: The First Twenty-Five Years of the* Australian Newspaper, Melbourne: Melbourne University Press, 2008, pp. 52–54.

80   Robert Manne, *Bad News: Murdoch's Australian and the Shaping of the Nation*, Quarterly Essay, no. 43 (2011), p. 9.

81   Manne, *Bad News*, p. 40.

82   Pearse, *High & Dry*, p. 284.

83   Ross Garnaut, quoted in Sally Neighbour, 'The united states of Chris Mitchell: the power of a Murdoch man,' *The Monthly*, August 2011, p. 27.

84   Gideon Haigh, 'Packed it in: the demise of *The Bulletin*,' *The Monthly*, March 2008, p. 32.

85   Damien Murphy, 'Loose cannon of the Right,' *The Bulletin*, 2 November 1993, p. 43.

86   P.P. McGuinness, 'The future for *Quadrant*,' *Quadrant*, January–February 1998, p. 11.

87   Manne, *In Denial*, p. 58.

88   David Kemp, 'Liberalism and conservatism in Australia since 1944,' in Brian Head and James Walter (eds), *Intellectual Movements and Australian Society*, Melbourne: Oxford University Press, 1988, p. 351.

89   Evans, interview with author.

90   Kemp, 'Liberalism and conservatism in Australia,' p. 348.

91   Dominic Kelly, 'Publishing rights,' *The Saturday Paper*, 23 August 2014.

92   Anthony Cappello, email to author, 25 July 2014.

93   Hugh Collins, 'Political ideology in Australia: the distinctiveness of a Benthamite society,' *Daedalus*, vol. 114, no. 1 (Winter 1985), p. 158.

94   Lindy Edwards, *The Passion of Politics: The Role of Ideology and Political Theory in Australia*, Sydney: Allen & Unwin, 2013, p. 158.

95   Norman Abjorensen, *John Howard and the Conservative Tradition*, Melbourne: Australian Scholarly Publishing, 2008, p. 31.

96   Greg Craven, 'The new centralism and the collapse of the conservative Constitution,' Department of the Senate Occasional Lecture, Canberra, 14 October 2005.

97   Greg Craven, phone interview with author, 27 October 2015.

98   Abjorensen, *John Howard and the Conservative Tradition*, p. 31.

99   Hal Wootten, 'Self-determination after ATSIC,' *Dialogue*, vol. 23, no. 2 (2004), pp. 18–19.

100   Waleed Aly, *What's Right? The Future of Conservatism in Australia*, Quarterly Essay, no. 37 (2010), p. 23.

101   Jake Sturmer, 'Tony Abbott's department discussed investigation into Bureau of Meteorology over global warming exaggeration claims, FOI documents reveal,' *ABC News*, 24 September 2015.

102   Tom Arup, 'Sceptic Lord under fire, but speech to go ahead,' *The Age*, 24 June 2011.

103   Ray Evans, 'Copenhagen: end game for green imperialism,' *Quadrant*, March 2010, p. 57.

104   Elaine McKewon, 'Talking points ammo: the use of neoliberal think tank fantasy themes to delegitimise scientific knowledge of climate change in Australian newspapers,' *Journalism Studies*, vol. 13, no. 2 (2012), pp. 284–85.

105   Jeff McMahon, 'What would Milton Friedman do about climate change? Tax carbon,' *Forbes*, 12 October 2014.

106   John Gummer, 'As Thatcher understood, true Tories cannot be climate change deniers,' *The Guardian*, 19 January 2017.

107   George P. Shultz and James A. Baker, 'A conservative answer to climate change,' *The Wall Street Journal*, 8 February 2017.

108   Corey Robin, *The Reactionary Mind: Conservatism from Edmund Burke to Sarah Palin*, Oxford: Oxford University Press, 2011, p. 25.

109   Mark Lilla, 'Republicans for revolution,' *The New York Review of Books*, 12 January 2012, p. 16.

Conclusion

1   Ray Evans, quoted in Andrew Cornell, 'Why Ray Evans is always right,' *Weekend Australian Financial Review*, 8 January 2005.

2   Des Moore, 'Why the Ayatollahs are coming,' in *Carpe Diem*, Proceedings of the Twenty-Sixth Conference of the H.R. Nicholls Society, Melbourne, March 2005.

3   Bruce Tranter and Kate Booth, 'Scepticism in a changing climate: a cross-national study,' *Global Environmental Change*, vol. 33 (July 2015), pp. 154–64.

INDEX

INDEX